FREUD AND THE DORA CASE
A Promise Betrayed

Cesare Romano

Taylor & Francis Group

LONDON AND NEW YORK

First published in Italian in 2012 by Alpes Editore, Roma, as *Freud e il caso Dora. Una promessa tradita*.

Translation from the Italian by Wissia Fiorucci, based on a revised version of the original text.

First published 2015 by
Karnac Books Ltd.

Published 2018 by Routledge
2 Park Square, Milton Park, Abingdon, Oxon OX14 4RN
711 Third Avenue, New York, NY 10017, USA

Routledge is an imprint of the Taylor & Francis Group, an informa business

Copyright © 2015 by Cesare Romano

The right of Cesare Romano to be identified as the author of this work have been asserted in accordance with §§ 77 and 78 of the Copyright Design and Patents Act 1988.

All rights reserved. No part of this book may be reprinted or reproduced or utilised in any form or by any electronic, mechanical, or other means, now known or hereafter invented, including photocopying and recording, or in any information storage or retrieval system, without permission in writing from the publishers.

Notice:
Product or corporate names may be trademarks or registered trademarks, and are used only for identification and explanation without intent to infringe.

British Library Cataloguing in Publication Data

A C.I.P. for this book is available from the British Library

ISBN-13: 9781782200963 (pbk)

Typeset by V Publishing Solutions Pvt Ltd., Chennai, India

CONTENTS

ACKNOWLEDGEMENTS   vii

ABOUT THE AUTHOR   ix

SERIES EDITOR'S FOREWORD   xi

AUTHOR AND TRANSLATOR'S NOTE   xvii

FOREWORD   xix

PART I: THE CASE HISTORY

CHAPTER ONE
The first encounter with Dora   3

CHAPTER TWO
The second encounter with Dora and the beginning of the analysis   7

CHAPTER THREE
The first trauma: a disgusting kiss   19

CHAPTER FOUR
From archaeologist to burglar   45

CHAPTER FIVE
The dream of the burning house   53

CHAPTER SIX
The second dream   79

CHAPTER SEVEN
Confusion of tongues and the traumatolytic
    function of the dream   93

CHAPTER EIGHT
Conclusions   103

PART II: THE COUNTERTRANSFERENCE

CHAPTER NINE
Dora's analysis and her analyst's vicissitudes: a frame
    for Freud's countertransference   109

CHAPTER TEN
Spinach, cocaine, and countertransference in a dream of Freud's   133

CHAPTER ELEVEN
Conclusions   175

NOTES   181

REFERENCES   203

FURTHER READING   213

INDEX   217

ACKNOWLEDGEMENTS

I would like to express my gratitude towards Professor Peter L. Rudnytsky, for taking the time and effort to read the book in Italian, and proposing to translate it into English. I am sincerely grateful to him also for patiently reading the first English version and therefore suggesting many revisions to improve the comprehension of the text.

My thanks and appreciations also go to Rod Tweedy, Editor, who has followed me during the first phases of the project and Oliver Rathbone, Publisher and Managing Director, together with Constance Govindin, Publicity and Digital Content Manager, both in charge of the editorial contract.

I also express my warm thanks to Kate Pearce, Project Manager, and to Cecily Blench, Publishing Assistant, who have followed me with patience during the revision of the text.

ABOUT THE AUTHOR

Cesare Romano is a psychiatrist and psychotherapist. He has worked for the Veneto Region National Health Service, in the Department of Mental Health, and as an honorary judge in the Tribunal of Minors in Venice. He has published several articles on the history of psychiatry and of psychoanalysis in Italian journals (*Quaderni Italiani di Psichiatria, Psicoterapia e Scienze Umane, Quaderni di Psicoterapia Infantile, Il Vaso di Pandora, Medicina delle Tossicodipendenze*). He currently lives in Piove di Sacco (Padua), where he holds his own private practice as a psychotherapist.

SERIES EDITOR'S FOREWORD

Although it may not be the most consequential text in the history of psychoanalysis, Freud's case history of the young woman he called Dora is surely the most controversial, serving as it has as a flashpoint for feminist critiques. Now, in a comprehensively researched and impressively original study, the Italian psychiatrist and psychotherapist, Cesare Romano, enters the lists.

By his subtitle, *A Promise Betrayed*, Romano alludes to Freud's declaration in the opening paragraph of his "Prefatory Remarks" that the ensuing narrative will "substantiate those views" set forth in his writings of 1895 and 1896 that are commonly known as the "seduction theory." As Romano points out, this statement of Freud's intention has attracted surprisingly little scrutiny from the legion of scholars who have commented on the case, the most notable exception being Karin Ahbel-Rappe, who properly cautions that the pair of scenes with Herr K., when Dora was already in her teens, "would not qualify as seductions in terms of the seduction theory," which refers to sexual assaults perpetrated on children before the age of eight. Ahbel-Rappe, however, limits her consideration to the way the seduction theory haunts what she calls the "theoretical unconscious" of the Dora case or, in Romano's paraphrase, to "Freud's anxiety over the abandonment of the seduction theory," and she does not entertain the possibility that there may indeed have been "real episodes of seduction in Dora's early childhood."

This is the first of two decisive steps forward taken by Romano in this book. In his reconstruction, the panoply of oral symptoms exhibited by Dora, as well as her enuresis, can most satisfactorily be understood if "the trauma experienced with Herr K.," when he kissed her on the mouth at age fourteen, activated by means of deferred action "an analogous sexual episode with the father which had occurred during Dora's early childhood." Freud's harping on Dora's having masturbated in childhood, the cessation of which purportedly led to the onset of her hysterical symptoms, therefore, according to Romano, turns a blind eye to his earlier recognition, as he wrote in "Further Remarks on the Neuro-Psychoses of Defence" of 1896, that precocious "masturbation itself is a much more frequent consequence of abuse or seduction" than had been generally supposed. Thus, in addition to his signal lack of empathy for his vulnerable patient, Freud's therapeutic calamity with Dora "derived from the fact that he had not gone far enough back in time to reconstruct the infantile scenes" at the root of her traumas, and the "betrayed promise" in the case is not simply his failure to vindicate his previously articulated views but also, at a more profound level, Freud's abandonment of the seduction theory itself, which was fundamentally on the right track in its focus on the shattering effects of abuse and neglect by their caretakers on the emotional lives of children.

The second outstanding contribution made by Romano is the unprecedented depth of his exploration of Freud's countertransference to Dora in light of what we now know about his private life at the time, especially his relationship with his sister-in-law, Minna Bernays. Although he proffers the disclaimer that "it is not essential to establish whether or not Freud had an affair with Minna," it is clear that Romano sides with the growing number of scholars who are convinced that the pair indeed consummated their romance during their travels together in the summer of 1900, and he argues that this circumstance must have decisively impacted Freud's treatment of Dora and is everywhere hidden in plain sight in his case history, which—like *On Dreams* and *The Psychopathology of Everyday Life*—was composed by Freud in a feverish burst of productivity in the five months following his return in September to Vienna.

By an uncanny coincidence, the health resort of Merano where Freud left Minna after their holiday, ostensibly for a lung condition but very possibly also to procure an abortion, was likewise where Dora's father had taken his family to live for a decade for the sake of his health and the site of the kiss that was the first of Herr K.'s two attempted seductions of Dora, while Lake Garda, where Freud had just spent five glorious days with Minna, was the site of the second scene, a verbal proposition, which ensued two years later when she was sixteen. Freud's comparison of Dora to a governess when she informed him that she had decided to break off the treatment two weeks before coming to see him for the last time, as well as his explanation in the *Psychopathology* that he had chosen the pseudonym Dora after a governess in the household of his sister Rosa who could not keep her own name because it was the same as his sister's, furthermore, both point to Minna, who assumed the role of nursemaid or governess to Sigmund and Martha Freud's six children after she took up permanent residence at Berggasse 19 in 1896. Most crucially, as Romano discerns, "if Freud had just partaken in an intimate liaison with his sister-in-law, he could not have listened to the reiterated accusations Dora addressed towards her father" concerning his adulterous relationship with Frau K. "without himself feeling guilty" for his analogous relationship with Minna, and Freud's notorious suggestion to Dora that, had she only yielded to Herr K., an arrangement whereby her father would exchange his daughter for his friend's wife "'would have been the only possible solution for all the parties concerned'" no longer seems out of character once we see Freud as a man willing to swap his wife for his sister-in-law when it suited his purposes.

Eminently sound though I believe these cornerstones of Romano's book to be, I must question one component of his scaffolding. Despite Freud's statement in his letter to Fliess of October 14, 1900 that his practice has "brought a new patient, an eighteen-year-old girl, a case that has opened smoothly to the existing collection of picklocks," Romano is convinced that Freud would not have used the metaphor of picklocks "if he were referring to a therapy that had only just begun," and thus "Dora could have been a patient of Freud's since his return to Vienna, that is to say a month before he reported the case to Fliess," notwithstanding the fact that there is no mention of her either in Freud's detailed letter of September 14 or in his shorter letter of September 24, and he explicitly terms her "a new patient" on October 14.

Establishing the precise date when Dora's analysis began might seem of little moment, but Romano's initial speculation is the underpinning for a further leap concerning Freud's countertransference to Dora, which he believes is exhibited in the *"table d'hôte"* dream that forms the centerpiece of *On Dreams*. Again contrary to Freud's declaration to Fliess on October 14 that he is "writing the dream" pamphlet, which almost certainly means that he must have had the *"table d'hôte"* dream that is integral to its conception and design before that date, Romano contends that Freud "could have begun drafting the essay by writing an introduction, waiting for a suitable dream to analyse and present to the reader's attention," and thus could have had the dream "after 14 October 1900." By these two strokes, the inception of Dora's analysis is pushed back to mid-September and the *"table d'hôte"* dream is pushed forward to "the period of 18 to 26 October," and he arrives at the conclusion that Freud must have been dreaming about Dora.

Although Romano's departures from established chronology may not persuade most readers, they do not affect the larger contours of his argument. Even if Dora does not figure in the *"table d'hôte"* dream, it remains true that Freud's encounter with Ida Bauer took place in the aftermath of the most crucial interlude in his life, when he broke irrevocably with Fliess and then violated the incest taboo with Minna Bernays, and that the aftershocks of this upheaval are registered in *Fragment of an Analysis of a Case of Hysteria*, just as they are in *On Dreams* and the *Psychopathology*. There are many instances when Romano's intuitions strike pay dirt. His reading of the *"table d'hôte"* dream as a reprise of the cocaine episode is illuminating, as are his reflections on the case to which Freud adverted in both "Psychoanalysis and Telepathy" and the chapter "Dreams and Occultism" in the *New Introductory Lectures*, about a patient who "had a sexual relationship with his sister-in-law but then decided to marry her daughter instead, that is, his own niece," a story that seems to condense Freud's love affair with Minna and Ferenczi's triangle with Gizella and Elma Pálos, and must have had an uncanny resonance for Freud.

Above all, Romano delivers on his promise to reread the Dora case in light of Freud's seduction theory. Even though it can never be proven that Ida was initiated into masturbation by her brother Otto, who also suffered from enuresis, and that the latter's "habit of masturbating was most probably aroused by paternal seduction," while the mother's obsessive rituals and blocking access to her son's bedroom at night were "actually meant to protect her children from being infected by a syphilitic and tubercular father" who may have abused not one but both of his children, Romano's archeological spadework yields results at least as plausible as any derived from Freud's exercises in lock-picking, and he shows how the clinical data can be used to arrive at very different conclusions from the ones Freud himself reached from the same material. Contrary to the widespread belief that only with the abandonment of the seduction theory did Freud begin to recognize the importance of the inner world, and in the process begat psychoanalysis, Romano rejoins that "the seduction theory embraces both realities, the internal and the external one, and does so thanks to the mechanism of *Nachträglichkeit*," as a result of which what was originally an event in external reality is reactivated as a memory that imbues subsequent experiences with psychically laden meaning.

The question ultimately posed by Cesare Romano's return to this most contested of Freud's texts, therefore, is not *whether* we are committed to psychoanalysis, but *what sort* of psychoanalysis do we want to espouse, and the answer he gives us—as encapsulated by his chapter title "Confusion of tongues and the traumatolytic function of the dream"—is that sort whose paramount source of inspiration has been Sándor Ferenczi.

Professor Peter L. Rudnytsky
Series Co-editor
Gainesville, Florida

AUTHOR AND TRANSLATOR'S NOTE

Male pronouns (he, his, etc.) are used in this text when gender is unspecified. This is solely a linguistic convention, as we believe that the use of he/she (and so on) would affect the readability of the text.

When quoting from *Fragment of an Analysis of a Case of Hysteria* (Volume 7 of the *Standard Edition*) only the page number is provided; for all other quotations, the year of publication, the *Standard Edition* volume number, and the page number are given.

Quotations from Freud are taken from *The Standard Edition of the Complete Psychological Works of Sigmund Freud*, translated by Alix and James Strachey in collaboration with Anna Freud (Vintage, 2001).

When quoting from a text originally written in a language other than English and for which no official English translation is available, it is to be assumed that the translation is our own.

Italicised words in citations are indicated with "italics added" if the author has done this. This clarification is omitted if italics were present in the original text.

FOREWORD

Freud's exposition of Dora's case history opens with a promise on his part that will transpire to be groundless, not only because in no part of the text does Freud maintain this promise but also because, as the case unfolds through the text, the reader realises that he could never have fulfilled it. In *Fragment of an Analysis of a Case of Hysteria* (1905e [1901]), he sets out his intention to substantiate the theoretical standpoints previously assumed in 1895 and 1896, while he was by now far away from those theories. The following excerpt shows how Freud attempts to deceive his readers:

> In 1895 and 1896 I put forward certain views upon the pathogenesis of hysterical symptoms and upon the mental processes occurring in hysteria. Since that time several years have passed. In now proposing, therefore, to substantiate those views by giving a detailed report of the history of a case and its treatment, I cannot avoid making a few introductory remarks [...] [p. 7]

He is referring here to *Studies on Hysteria* (1895d) and to a series of works that he published in 1896, wherein he advances the thesis that hysteria originates in an infantile trauma. This thesis is then brought to completion in *The Aetiology of Hysteria* (1896c), and is today considered as the theory of infantile sexual seduction. The other essays from this period in which Freud proposes his theory of the infantile sexual trauma are *Heredity and the Aetiology of the Neuroses* (1896a) and *Further Remarks on the Neuro-Psychoses of Defence* (1896b). It seems that, as he was about to write up Dora's case history, Freud was rethinking his claim in *Heredity and the Aetiology of the Neuroses* (1896a), in which he had maintained that one can ascertain the reality of infantile memories through analytical work, as long as "one can follow in detail the report of a psychoanalysis of a case of hysteria" (S. E., 3, p. 153).

Freud thus has these writings in mind when he refers to his views from 1895 and 1896. We must nonetheless not neglect other important publications that pre-date his writing-up of Dora's case history, namely *Screen Memories* (1899a), as well as, of course, *The Interpretation of Dreams* (1900a) and the short essay *On Dreams* (1901a). Yet in addition to these official publications, we must take into account the considerations, hypotheses, and drafts that Freud had formulated privately and submitted to the attention of his friend Fliess, with whom he remained in correspondence during the period of Dora's treatment, even though their friendship was about to come to an end.

In his introduction to *Fragment of an Analysis of a Case of Hysteria* (1905e), Freud continues by declaring that:

> No doubt it was awkward that I was obliged to publish the results of my enquiries without there being any possibility of other workers in the field testing and checking them, particularly as those results were of a surprising and by no means gratifying character. [p. 7]

Here, he is not only referring to the sexual aetiology of hysteria, but also to the seduction theory, that is, to the discovery that hysterical symptoms were to be ascribed to sexual abuses suffered at an early age, the blame for which he would later ascribe mostly to patients' fathers. He then continues to develop his argument with even more surprising claims:

> But it will be scarcely less awkward now that I am beginning to bring forward some of the material upon which my conclusions were based and make it accessible to the judgment of the world. [p. 7]

Freud intends to persuade his reader that his account of Dora's case history is in accordance and in continuity with his studies and the ensuing results he had achieved in 1896, as if Dora's were one of the eighteen cases of hysteria from which he drew his conclusions in *The Aetiology of Hysteria* (1896c). Thus, Freud addresses his readers as if that "long pause" of time that divides him from 1896 (five years from when he started writing the case, but nine at the moment of its publication) had not had the slightest effect on his theoretical viewpoints on hysteria. Yet, he nonetheless puts forward a case history that was in complete discordance with the positions he had intended "to substantiate".

Let us dwell now upon the development of Freud's aetiologic thinking on hysteria, from the seduction theory to the libido theory, drawing on Makari (1998), in order to ascertain the position that Dora's case history occupies within Freud's shift from seduction to masturbation as aetiological factors in hysteria.

As part of this transition from seduction to libido, Freud passed through "a heretofore-neglected intermediary phase in his theorizing that [...] situates his post-seduction hypothesis thinking in fin de siècle Viennese medicine [...] during this intermediary phase of theorizing, he was chiefly concerned with the causes and ramifications of childhood masturbation" (p. 640) as traumatic aetiologic agent. Freud began to rework his neuroses thesis, Makari explains, "under the continued influence of a disease model in which an earlier condition interacted with a later specific cause [...] he began to lay greater weight on another cause of early sexual over-stimulation" (p. 644), that is, masturbation.

Freud "rejuvenated an environmental theory of psychoneuroses by broadening his notion from paternal seduction as the specific cause, to some childhood 'sexual experiences'. Early nonspecific childhood sexual experience remained as a 'framing' etiology, without the specificity (and epidemiologic unlikelihood) of paternal seduction. Multiple sorts of sexual experience could account for an overly stimulated sexual foundation in this model [...]. But in the fall of 1897, he shifted the role of masturbation, from an etiologically irrelevant result of seduction to an etiologically later element. His new theory of hysteria preserved a foundational, though nonspecific, early sexual stimulation, while adding a later sexual etiology that was quite specific and in part determining: masturbation" (p. 649). As soon as child's masturbation was repressed, hysteria emerged.

Makari (1998) argues that Freud's new two-stage model "cohered with fin de siècle medical discourse in that, first, masturbation was a plausible etiology for hysteria, and second, childhood masturbation was seen by many to be caused by prior sexual experiences like seductions. But his new model also incorporated another element that was central to medical debates on masturbation: fantasy. Masturbatory fantasy was becoming, for some, the central pathogenic component of masturbation [...]. Hysteria developed only when such fantasies and the attendant masturbation were repressed" (pp. 649–650).

"So," continues Makari, "in the last months of 1897, Freud was entertaining competing models for the etiology of hysteria. His paternal seduction theory had lost much luster, but still had not been finally and completely rejected [...] then he began to articulate a hypothesis that unspecific early sexual experiences led to longing, fantasies, and later masturbation, which when repressed made for hysteria" (p. 651).

Finally, in "Freud's 1899 synthesis, hysteria resulted from both an undercurrent of autoerotic pathology and unspecified alloerotic pathology" (p. 656).

Makari (1998) asks himself if "stimulation emerges from experiences like seduction or masturbation, or had Freud by 1900 already come to the belief that the sexual constitution, libido, was responsible?" (p. 657) The author claims that the answer can be found in the case history of Dora, since Freud "did not rework his basic etiologic understanding of Dora's hysteria to tally with his 1905 libido theory, for its structure is based in trauma theory and the specific trauma of masturbation" (p. 657).

This was no longer the seduction theory, and Freud had returned to the sexological theories within the context of European thought at the end of the century. He therefore cannot call upon Dora's case history in order to "substantiate" his views from 1895 and 1896 in relation to the aetiology of hysteria, as he claims at the beginning of his *Fragment*.

Therefore, Jones (1953), comparing the first case histories included in *Studies on Hysteria* (1895d) with Dora's, claims: "The almost clumsy groping in the one and the confident penetration in the other, could let one well believe that they proceeded from two different men. And, indeed, they did. For the self-analysis separated the two not only in time, but in nature" (Vol. I, p. 399). However, self-analysis led Freud to the irrefutable conclusion presented in the letter to Fliess from 3 January 1899: "To the question 'What happened in earliest childhood?' the answer is, 'Nothing, but the germ of a sexual impulse existed'" (Masson, 1985, p. 338). Again, this belief was inconsistent with the seduction hypothesis that Freud would corroborate with Dora's history. Jones has therefore overlooked the incipit of Dora's case history, the initial proposition on Freud's part that he would later confirm his 1895 and 1896 theories. This omission is also noticeable in many other historians and critics of psychoanalysis after him: as Blass has claimed (1992, p. 160), subsequent studies set out to reaffirm Jones's position. With Dora's case history, "It was no longer Freud the novice of the outdated seduction theory that had to be contended with. It was now the Freud of fantasy, dream, wish, and transference, all centering around the newly self-discovered oedipal constellation with which the authors must take issue."

I shall not investigate the question as to why, when he began writing up the case history, Freud believed that it would be able to corroborate his seduction theory. Nor shall I question why he did not afterwards revise this part of the foreword, in which he commits himself to a task he does not in fact carry out, before submitting the book for publication. These questions would have no easy answer, especially in light of the lack of relevant information. Even in the private correspondence between Freud and Fliess in the period from 1887–1904, very few references may be found to Dora's case history, while Freud kept his friend regularly informed of other treatments. No further reference to it is contained in the few letters that he sent to Fliess after the one from 14 October (in which he announced the new case history), until he started writing his account of the case. On 1 January 1901, the day after Dora had left for good, he wrote to Fliess: "My few patients are doing well." Was this indifference or denial? Freud himself recognises, albeit indirectly, that he had shown very little interest in this patient when, once the exposition of the case was concluded, he indulged in a few observations about the treatment: "Might I perhaps have kept the girl under my treatment if I myself had acted a part, if I had exaggerated the importance to me of her staying on, and had shown a warm personal interest in her—a course which, even after allowing for my position as her physician, would have been tantamount to providing her with a substitute for the affection she longed for? I do not know" (p. 109). Freud leaves behind, here, the empathetic attitude he had recommended in *Studies on Hysteria* (1895d), more specifically relating to the case of Elisabeth von R., when he had found himself dealing with a patient who "is aware of the origin and the precipitating cause of her illness. [...] The interest shown in her by the physician, the understanding of her which he allows her to feel and the hopes of recovery he holds out to her—all these will decide the patient to yield up her secret" (S. E., 2, p. 138).[1]

That said, I must add that I have deliberately taken into account only a limited amount of literature on this case, about which much has already been written.[2] Most of the literature on Dora's case falls outside of my present field of enquiry, thus having no direct bearing on my research. Dealing with unrelated literature would have implied unnecessary detours, and space-related constraints would have prevented me from engaging with such texts appropriately. I only dwell on the most prominent works that deal with the case.

Jennings (1986) has provided an accurate and exhaustive literature review covering up to the 1980s, revealing that most criticism against Freud addresses the issue of technique. He also individuates two main currents: one tackling the debate on countertransference, and the other discussing Freud's insufficient understanding of adolescence-related subject matters. These critiques are in hindsight; they refer to knowledge and progress in psychoanalytical theory achieved subsequently.

Very few authors have dealt with Dora's case in light of the seduction theory. Slipp (1977) has highlighted interpersonal factors, and whilst keeping in mind the seduction theory, he has interpreted the concept of seduction in very broad terms as a familial relational pattern. Among the few scholars who have reinterpreted the case history with particular attention to Freud's seduction theory, Rachel Blass (1992) and Karin Ahbel-Rappe (2009) deserve a mention. I therefore dedicated specific attention to their works. The former, considering Freud's gradual abandonment of seduction theory, observes, "there is a complete and striking absence of studies examining the place of this hypothesis in Freud's analysis of Dora" (Blass, 1992, p. 162). Among the few exceptions, Blass (1992, p. 161) mentions the collected papers edited by Bernheimer and Kahane (1990) in which "Freud's understanding of Dora in terms of oedipal fantasy is viewed as the product of his mistaken abandonment of his early theories which ascribed to incest and actual seduction the most prominent pathogenic role. In a more general way, however, most reviews of the Dora case see in it a sharp break, in the main a positive one, from his earlier theory of seduction." These authors have failed to acknowledge that Freud's initial proposition stands in stark contrast with the conclusions he reaches in exposing the case. Moreover, they have not taken into account the fact that, with those explicit declarations, Freud was still attributing undisputed theoretical validity to his seduction theory. The main merit of Blass' article lies in its having demonstrated that, during Dora's analysis, Freud had not yet come to a complete formulation of the oedipal complex, an achievement that would continue to elude him a full five years later, when the case was published. Blass also points out, therefore, that the Oedipus complex cannot be used to examine the case history, even though the majority of critics have endeavoured to attribute oedipal interpretations to it.

Gladwell (1997, p. 200) claims to have dealt with the case by drawing on the seduction theory; he therefore goes as far as to maintain that: "I believe it is clear that Dora was sexually abused by a family friend with the willing connivance of her father." Only an unacceptably hyperbolic interpretation would lead us to claim that Herr K.'s maladroit attempts at seduction could be classified as episodes of sexual abuse. It is extremely misleading to identify the stolen kiss on the doorway in these terms, and even more so Herr K.'s verbal propositions to Dora during the walk along the lake. Critics claiming that Dora's case can be interpreted in light of the seduction theory, by considering Herr K.'s advances to be sexual abuses, should also, for the sake of coherence, interpret the symptoms that Dora developed when she was eight years old as the consequence of a sexual trauma. Instead, such critics follow Freud in maintaining the focus on the recent trauma. In so doing, they draw the reader's attention away from a piece of crucial information, namely, that Dora's father had had ample opportunity to abuse her while weaning her off enuresis. Since Dora's mother had refused to carry out the task, because of her neurosis in connection with the genitals, her father had been presented with many occasions to indulge in genital touching.

This incongruity discredits the aetiological value of the seduction theory, and leads the reader away from the multiple references to Dora's childhood that Freud was not coherent enough to develop according to the path he had himself indicated in the seduction theory. In this book, I intend to amend this inconsistency and interpret Dora's case following Freud's seduction theory. In so doing, I will reinstate its theoretical validity and take up again the archaeological work that Freud had interrupted. I will also identify all the clues that may lead us back to the "paternal aetiology" Freud had recognised between 1895 and 1897, substantiating those clues with the very declarations of "Freud the archaeologist" at his best. All the critics who have dealt with Dora's case beginning with the seduction theory have then either lost their way in the labyrinth of the oedipal complex, or been satisfied with stopping at infantile masturbation. Gladwell himself (1997, p. 201), who accuses Freud of "avoid[ing] the issue of confronting the sexual abuse directly" and who underlines in a note the connection between secondary enuresis and sexual abuse in Dora, then lets Freud misdirect him into the terrain of masturbation. Despite acknowledging that "without Freud we could not even begin to work with abused patients" (p. 208), Gladwell cannot resolve that contradiction between the traumatic aetiology of Dora's hysterical symptoms as an adolescent, and the autoerotic aetiology of infantile symptoms, nor does he manage to avoid the oedipal trap entirely.

Among the most recent and accurate scholars worth mentioning is Ahbel-Rappe (2009), who has discussed the *Fragment* in relation to the seduction theory. The author expresses the opinion that, although one can detect several allusions to the seduction theory in Freud's essay, most of which are implied, it is in Dora's case that Freud publicly abandons this theory. The author's main argument is that Freud is unconsciously in conflict with himself for not having applied the intuitions of the seduction theory to his understanding of Dora's case history. As regards the famous letter to Fliess of 21 September 1897, she claims that this was "mythologized as the site of Freud's 'abandonment' of the seduction theory" (p. 596). Ahbel-Rappe acknowledges that, after having communicated to Fliess that he no longer believed in his "neurotica": "for at least two more years in the letters, Freud carries along both the seduction theory *and* the new ideas centering on infantile sexuality that take center stage in Dora. It is close to a sort of split theoretical consciousness, with two ideas pursued side by side and in isolation from one another for the most part" (pp. 596–597). She is among the few scholars to have noticed the contradiction with Freud's initial declaration of intent, and asks: "what are we to make of Freud's claims in the foreword to *Fragment* that the Dora case will confirm these older theories? What is the place of these older theories relative to what is new in Dora?" (p. 597)

Ahbel-Rappe sees, in Dora's case history, a sort of "theoretical autobiography" of Freud, wherein the seduction theory is never explicitly mentioned, and only in a footnote does he mention *The Aetiology of Hysteria* (1896c), his "manifesto" of the seduction theory. Ahbel-Rappe claims, as previously mentioned, that "the scenes with K. would not qualify as seductions on the terms of the seduction theory […] Freud's discussion of the scenes with K. is not an application of the seduction theory" (p. 604).[3] She stresses that, according to the seduction theory, for the early sexual episode to be recognised as such it must have remained unconscious and then been recreated during the analysis; it must also have occurred before the age of eight, bearing the characteristics of a manifest sexual abuse. Dora retains the memory of the traumatic episodes she relates to Freud, but according to the seduction theory, "only unremembered, unconscious infantile sexual trauma is neurotogenic" (Ahbel-Rappe, 2006, p. 176). Freud does not venture to retrieve earlier sexual episodes that could be more suited to explaining her hysterical symptoms. "If the seduction theory were still etiologically relevant to Freud," Ahbel-Rappe explains, "these scenes with K. would alert him to the question whether Dora had experienced sexual abuse very early in life. We would find a Freud alert for reconstructive data pointing that way. There is no such Freud in the Dora paper. Instead [...] the scene at fourteen is etiologically relevant to Freud in that it triggers Dora's prior oral fixation. *That* is not the seduction theory" (pp. 604–605).

As regards the declaration in the 1905 foreword in which Freud committed himself to confirming his theories of 1895 and 1896, the author describes it as "a sort of parapraxis, a motivated misstatement expressing Freud's repressed, conflicted misgivings about leaving his seduction theory behind" (p. 619). Ahbel-Rappe maintains that the many references to Dora's eighth year of age in the description of her case (a key element in the seduction theory, which for Freud represents a boundary line for hysteria) are indicative of Freud's anxiety "over not wondering, as the seduction theory would lead him to wonder, what other sexually abusive experience might have befallen this young woman" (p. 621). This being said, Ahbel-Rappe immediately distances herself from this affirmation and warns the reader that she is not suggesting that Dora was herself subjected to any such a seduction. The author makes it clear that she is not advancing any hypothesis of real episodes of seduction in Dora's early childhood. What she intends to stress, rather, is only Freud's anxiety over his abandonment of the seduction theory. According to what she calls "theoretical unconscious", in his work on Dora, Freud has not abandoned the seduction theory; on the contrary: "the seduction theory haunts the theoretical unconscious of the Dora paper like a ghost. What were key theoretical signifiers in 1896 become spectral signifiers in 1905, reminders of the question Freud does not ask about Dora. In that sense, the Dora paper represents the first chapter in the history of what I call the disavowal of the seduction theory" (p. 627).

I do not agree, however, with Ahbel-Rappe (2009, p. 615) when she associates the long pause with the interval that separates the composition of the case history from its publication. She claims: "In the forward [...] Freud writes of having waited 'four years time' to publish the report on Dora, out of concern for his patient's confidentiality. This, presumably, is the long pause he has in mind." The "long pause" that Freud feels the need to justify to his readers certainly cannot be this one, because the reader could not know that Freud had withheld this writing for many years. Nor, indeed, could this have held the same interest for readers of the time as it does for historians of psychoanalysis today. The long pause which the reader of the time would have been aware of, and which Freud deemed in need of justification, was the one between the first formulation of the seduction theory—that is to say, *The Aetiology of Hysteria* of 1896—and the new hysteria case Freud was now presenting to the reader, which totalled an interval of nine years. This is therefore the temporal interval referred to by Freud, as is also demonstrated (as mentioned above) by his wish to confirm his theories of 1895 and 1896 through this case history.

Hengehold (1993) acknowledges the possibility that Dora was the victim of sexual abuse during childhood, grounding his opinion on physical signs such as leucorrhoea and the late enuresis, rather than on Dora's psychic symptoms. Unfortunately, he does not expand on this subject and relegates it to an endnote (p. 70, endnote 6).

I still consider Freud's formulation of the seduction theory to be a valid one. Furthermore, I believe this theory to have been amply confirmed by clinical evidence that proves the pathogenic relevance of early sexual traumas, in borderline pathology and in other personality disorders.[4] Many authors have criticised the seduction theory because of the excessive emphasis it places on external reality and real trauma to the detriment of internal reality, and have seen in its abandonment the birth of psychoanalysis with its focus on the patient's internal world. I believe that the seduction theory embraces both realities, the internal and the external one, and does so thanks to the mechanism of *Nachträglichkeit* and of its two times. In the first, external reality and real trauma occupy a foremost position. In the second time, internal reality is ascribed aetiological pre-eminence in the origins of hysteria, for the reactivation of the memory of sexual abuse and its recording *after*

(*Nach-Tragen*) as a sexual trauma. We can thus say that both realities, external and internal, play a part in the seduction theory. Therefore, claiming that it was only thanks to the abandonment of the seduction theory that it became possible to focus on the internal reality is a mistake. Internal reality was already conceived of as a traumatic reality, and the origin of the neurotical symptoms in light of the *Nachträglichkeit* biphasic action. Freud would never have needed to resort to hysterical fantasies in order to downgrade the traumatic potential of the external reality, because this was already implied in the dual mechanism of the seduction theory. The external trauma had not engendered any pathogenic effect at the moment of its occurrence, and all the traumatic potential had fallen on the repression of the event. Thus, the source of the trauma was no longer the event itself but rather the mnemonic reactivation of the repressed infantile trauma by another traumatic event; thereby the mnemonic reactivation became a psychic reality.

I intend to endorse my reading of this case history by referring only to Freud's writings and theories—both those he made public and those he exposed in private communications—up to the publication of Dora's case history. I will thereby demonstrate that he could have maintained his initial aim of confirming his seduction theory and the "paternal aetiology". Several scholars reassessing Dora's case, besides detecting a few technical inconsistencies on Freud's part, have aimed to find in it a confirmation of their own theoretical viewpoints, and have reassessed it in light of the object relations theory; the interpersonal theory (Maddi, 1974; Slipp, 1977; Kuriloff, 2005); familial roles (Langs, 1976; Holmes, 1983; Akavia, 2005);[5] oedipal and preoedipal dynamics (Krohn & Krohn, 1982; Van Den Berg, 1987; Simon, 1992; Blass, 1992), or the dynamics of transference and countertransference (Muslin & Gill, 1978; Begel, 1982; Glenn, 1986; Barale, 1993; Makari, 1997). Decker has even read in the case a testimony of the socio-cultural milieu of a *fin de siècle* Vienna (Decker, 1991). An anthropological reading has also been given, according to which the case history "holds significance for psychological anthropology because it evokes principles of the incest taboo, the exchange of women, and rules of kinship and marriage" (Banks, 1991).

I will reconsider Dora's case history by focusing on Freud's (in)consistencies within his own theories on the aetiology of hysteria. I will criticise Freud's work from within, that is by comparing and contrasting the case with his previous writings on hysteria, thus highlighting the fundamental contradiction that emerges from the first lines, and which most critics have nonetheless missed. Thus, I will make reference primarily to Freud's text (both in the original and the English translation) and to other writings from the "hysteria period". However, particular attention will also be paid to Mahony's book *Freud's Dora* (1996).

In the following pages, I will try to demonstrate how Freud could have kept his promise to the reader. In order to do so, I will reread Dora's case history in light of the theories of hysteria Freud had elaborated up to the year 1900, not only drawing on his published works, but also, and more importantly, on his correspondence with Fliess, from which the variable path of the traumatic theory of hysteria, and of Freud's ideas on infantile sexual seduction, emerge. Dora's case history will thus be presented in a completely new light, and an infantile history will surface, which had been neglected, or at least sidelined, in Freud's account. It is worth noting here that Freud, who in *Studies on Hysteria* (1895d) had written "that the case histories I write should read like short stories" (*S. E.*, 2, p. 160), warns doctors from Vienna, in the preface to this new case history, against reading it "as a *roman à clef* designed for their private delectation" (p. 9). Yet, this declaration seems to be a rhetorical expedient intended precisely to stir those doctors' morbid curiosity and gain a wider audience. After all, just like a novelist, Freud altered the text many times, "restor[ing] what is missing" (p. 12), deleting parts of it, and avoiding the reproduction of "the process of interpretation to which the patient's associations and communications had to be subjected", limiting himself to reporting "only the results of that process" (pp. 12–13). He also modified "in some places the order in which the explanations are given; and this has been done for the sake of presenting the case in a more connected form" (p. 10).

Lopez (1967) claims, moreover, that the book reads like a novel from start to end, and that one may even experience frustration at its lack of a conclusion, caused by the interruption of the analysis. This demonstrates the considerable value of the work from the point of view of its aesthetic realisation. Ellenberger (1970) has affirmed that the work is noteworthy for both its literary value and the author's ability to sustain the suspense throughout the narration: in his view, Freud's Dora may be compared to a novel by Schnitzler. Gay (1988, p. 247) also compares Freud to Schnitzler: "Perhaps only Arthur Schnitzler, whose disenchanted stories and plays sketched the intricate choreography of Vienna's erotic life, could have imagined such a scenario." More recently, Rodrigué

(1996) has hinted at a parallel with Schnitzler's *La Ronde* (1897) because of the Bauers' personalities, with Freud's clinical fragment opening an indiscreet door onto the erotic baroque life of the Viennese upper bourgeoisie. In a recent work, Kandel (2012) compares Dora's case history with Schnitzler's drama *Fräulein Else* (1925), underlining the latter's greater skills as a psychologist of women. Kandel (2012, p. 88) affirms: "Dora's is a sad case, a low point in Freud's career."

Marcus (1990) has said that "what Freud has written is in parts rather like a play by Ibsen, or more precisely like a series of Ibsen's plays" (p. 64) managing "to create a kind of Nabokovian frame" (p. 68), and that the case is built with "virtual Proustian complexity" (p. 73); "we know we are in a novel, probably by Proust" (p. 81). Other authors have suggested a parallel between Dora's story and two novels by Henry James, namely, *What Maisie Knew* (Hertz, 1983) and *Turn of the Screw* (Marantz Cohen, 1986).

Hélène Cixous (1990, p. 277), who has transformed this case history into a "theatrical piece" (Cixous, 1983), declares: "I read the text in a sort of dizziness, exploding over the situation presented, where at heart I found myself siding frenetically with the various characters. I immediately worked out a reading that was probably not centred in the way Freud had wanted it to be. I had to bring center stage obliterated characters, characters repressed in notes, at the bottom of the page, and who were for me in the absolute foreground. I read it like fiction." Hillman (1983, pp. 5–6), who defines Dora's case as "the Iliad of our field", asserts that this case history "draws our attention to its literary technique, even while it present itself as a medical technique". Hillman very clearly highlights the fact that scientific requirements are sacrificed to literary ones, because, "despite showing his awareness of the requirements of empiricism, our author begs off that method of writing in which he was thoroughly competent from his earlier work in brain pathology and cocaine experiments. A case history as empirical evidence as in science would have to offer some means for public verification. It could not be merely a record from memory, unless it was to be taken only as anecdotal reminiscence: and the whole therapeutic technique employed—Freud's main omission—would have to belong to the record. We expect to learn exactly what the doctor did. Freud tells us only darkly and in part." Lavagetto (2005) claims that, like a good narrator, Freud manipulates and deforms the chronology. He does not do so with an eye to finally revealing his role, however, and

Dora's story remains hidden in the shadows. Contrary to what happens to characters in most novels, Dora has no further destiny to be told (Giglioli, 2005). The curious thing is that Freud's novelisation of her case has in turn instigated the writing of many other psychoanalytical novels, in one of which Freud is a candidate presenting his *Fragment of an Analysis of a Case of Hysteria* to be admitted to the "American Psychoanalytic Association", and the author is a member of the committee in charge of considering his application (Bornstein, 2005). In another, the writer-narrator takes the role of the analyst to whom Dora turns for a second analysis, many years after the first one with Freud (Ornstein, 2005).

Let us now endeavour to briefly compare Freud's writing style with the hysteric's narration, in order to establish whether or not the modifications he introduced were really supposed to present "the case in a more connected form" (p. 10).[6] Freud claims that the hysteric's narration of her life and illness is often incoherent, as "the sequence of different events is uncertain" (p. 16). This is further complicated not only by her "*conscious* disingenuousness", but also by her "*unconscious* disingenuousness" (p. 17). Furthermore, her account is strewn with amnesias and paramnesias. But even when "the events themselves have been kept in mind" (p. 17), the sick person can achieve the same effect induced by amnesia "by destroying a connection, and a connection is most surely broken by altering the chronological order of events" (p. 17). Freud claims that, in his own narration, he has "altered ... in some places the order in which the explanations are given ... for the sake of presenting the case in a more connected form" (p. 10). Would it not be possible to allege that he thereby obtains the same result achieved by the hysteric "by altering the chronological order of events", that is to say "by destroying a connection", and thus concealing historical truth?

So proficient was Freud in elaborating this clinical narration that even careful readers were led to believe that Dora had worked through her history and infantile traumas with him, while Freud in fact did not unravel her past in this depth, and she did not give him enough time to do so.[7] Actually, "Dora is a victim of Freud's unconscious erotic feelings about her that affected his need to dominate and control her. Dora has no voice in Freud's text; we hear nothing of her direct dialog, and her historical and Jewish identities are both suppressed. He never understands her story at all and simply tries to bully her into accepting his version of events. His interpretations of her problem reflect his own obsessions with masturbation, adultery, and homosexuality. Thus, the 'hysterical narrative' reflects Freud's hysteria rather than Dora's. She never becomes a subject, only the object of Freud's narrative" (Showalter, 1993, p. 27). In the second part of this book, I deal with these themes in more depth.

Many of the authors I have mentioned seem to have been fascinated by this case history, and to have read it precisely as Freud suggested not to, like a *"roman à clef"*. Only Hillman (1983) stresses the inconsistencies of a case history, which does not provide the necessary means for public verification, anticipating what Spence (1994) later claims about Freud's five case histories. According to Spence (1994, p. 68), if one bases conclusions on one example only, the risk is that one will end up building a theory on contingencies that may not be repeated: "Because interpretations are always contingent and apply only to the specific situation, the clinician is almost always in error when he asserts a one-time observation as a general truth."

Hillman accuses Freud of having failed to reveal his therapeutic technique, which Spence (1994, p. 71) extends to Freud's reservations in dealing with his own experiences, and ultimately his countertransference. "In order to properly communicate the way in which the clinical facts hang together," he observes, "the reporting clinician must also be able to make public a good portion of his mental life at the moment when the clinical happening occurred. We need to know what he was thinking because it is through these thoughts that the clinical details acquire their specific meaning. If we are deprived of this particular context of consciousness, then we either take the details at their face value assuming there is one, or assimilate them to the conventional stereotype. Misunderstanding is the inevitable result."

I have tried to make up for this lacuna in the penultimate chapter of this book, by considering Dora's analysis within the context of Freud's personal life experiences, and of his mental life during the period of his analysis with the patient. I have thus attempted to reconstruct aspects of Freud's countertransference, which might have played a role during the analysis. Spence (1994) has repeatedly remarked upon the role of Freudian rhetoric, which appears to have been particularly effective in Dora's case, considering that many authors have focused on its literary qualities.

In his *The Aetiology of Hysteria* (1896c), Freud formulated a principle that he considered to be as important as the discovery of the *caput Nili*, namely "that at the bottom of every case of hysteria there are *one or more occurrences of premature sexual experience*, occurrences which belong to the earliest years of childhood but which can be reproduced through the work of psycho-analysis in spite of the intervening decades" (S. E., 3, p. 203).

Freud would have us believe that he had performed conscientious archaeological work with Dora, and brought "to the light of day after their long burial the priceless though mutilated relics of antiquity" (p. 12), to which he would then add certain elements in order to complete the original picture:

> I have restored what is missing, taking the best models known to me from other analyses; but, like a conscientious archaeologist, I have not omitted to mention in each case where the authentic parts end and my constructions begin. [p. 12]

Later on, he reiterates this concept so as to reassure the reader as to the validity of his claim:

> It is only because the analysis was prematurely broken off that we have been obliged in Dora's case to resort to framing conjectures and filling in deficiencies. Whatever I have brought forward for filling up the gaps is based upon other cases which have been more thoroughly analysed. [p. 85]

This archaeological work appears disputable to say the least. Also, the fact that Freud would fill up the gaps by drawing on other cases cannot but raise some perplexities: as he confesses in his private correspondence with Fliess, up until then he had not brought any treatment to successful completion.[8] To avoid the risk of my claim appearing to be no more than gratuitous slander, I will let Freud speak directly, quoting a few passages from his letters to Fliess:

> As long as no case has been clarified and seen through to the end, I do not feel sure and I cannot be content. [Masson, 1985, 17 December 1896, p. 218]
>
> At our next congress I hope there will be important things to talk about. I think by Easter at the latest, maybe in Prague. Perhaps

by then I shall have carried one case to completion. [Masson, 1985, 3 January 1897, pp. 219–220]

I have not yet finished a single case; am still struggling with the difficulties of treatment and of understanding, which depending on my mood appear to me larger or smaller. [Masson, 1985, 7 March 1897, p. 232]

I am still having the same difficulties and have not finished a single case. [Masson, 1985, 29 March 1897, p. 233]

My banker, who was furthest along in his analysis, took off at a critical point, just before he was to bring me the last scenes. This certainly also damaged me materially, and convinced me that I do not yet know everything after all about the mainspring of the matter. But refreshed as I was, I easily took it in stride and told myself, so I shall wait still longer for a treatment to be completed. It must be possible and must be done. [Masson, 1985, 16 May 1897, pp. 243–244]

I have been seeing the same people every day, and last week I even started a new case, which is still in the trial stage and perhaps once again will not go beyond it. [Masson, 1985, 11 March 1900, p. 402]

In any event, there has been a slight break: an evening patient has left me—my most difficult case, and the most certain as far as etiology is concerned. [...] I found the keys, that is to say, I could convince myself that the keys found elsewhere fitted her and, as far as the short time (December until now) permitted. I have deeply and fundamentally influenced her condition. She took leave of me today with the words, "What you have done for me is invaluable." [Masson, 1985, 16 May 1900, pp. 413–414]

Yesterday the fourth patient said good-bye on the most cordial terms, in excellent shape [...] This case gave me the greatest satisfaction and is perhaps complete. [Masson, 1985, 20 May 1900, p. 415]

So, what could these "best models" have been? After all, even if Freud were relying on treatments that had lasted longer than Dora's, they had still not been brought to completion, having been interrupted, in the majority of cases, because of the patient's departure, and therefore yielding nothing but fragments of analysis.[9] Thus, Freud the archaeologist had completed the fragments of Dora's analysis by supplementing them with other fragments, borrowed from other cases, because he did not yet have a complete model at his disposal. This, in my view, cannot be defined as "conscientious" work, not even for an archaeologist of the psyche.

The account of this case history was initially to be entitled *Dreams and Hysteria*, since it appeared to Freud "peculiarly well-adapted for showing how dream-interpretation is woven into the history of a treatment and how it can become the means of filling in amnesias and elucidating symptoms" (p. 10). He also stressed, "that a thorough investigation of the problems of dreams is an indispensable prerequisite for any comprehension of the mental processes in hysteria and the other psychoneuroses" (p. 11). These assertions may suggest that Freud was planning to publish Dora's story as early as during the course of her treatment, since he was at the time simultaneously working on the brief study *On Dreams* (1901a). This work, which was submitted to his editor before Dora's treatment was terminated, would turn out to be particularly useful for those colleagues of his who wished to tackle *Fragment of an Analysis of a Case of Hysteria* (1905e) without being forced to study *The Interpretation of Dreams* (1900a).[10] After all, Freud's clinical account is entirely based on the analysis of two of Dora's dreams, and he himself admits to having unveiled very little of his analytic technique, besides dream analysis:

> I have as a rule not reproduced the process of interpretation to which the patient's associations and communications had to be subjected, but only the results of that process. Apart from the dreams, therefore, the technique of the analytic work has been revealed in only a very few places. [pp. 12–13]

This way of proceeding deprives us of the possibility of knowing, on the one hand, Dora's real communications and associations, and on the other, the interpretative work through which Freud arrived at his conclusions. Therefore, these "mutilated relics" may have led Freud to unearth completely different findings in departure from the original, counting on the reader's ignorance, and thus determining the original model on which to base his work of reconstruction. In the clinical account, Dora's voice only emerges a few times; for the most part

Freud speaks for her, thus forcing us to rely on the trustworthiness of a reconstruction that Mahony (1996) has proven to be unreliable.

My rereading of this case history will likewise be centred on Dora's two dreams. I will draw on *On Dreams* (1901a), taking into consideration the passage where Freud elucidates one of his patient's dreams, in which the latter goes to the butcher's to buy some meat but is told that "that's not obtainable any longer". Freud remarks:

> A few days earlier I had explained to the patient in those very words that the earliest memories of childhood were '*not obtainable any longer* as such', but were replaced in analysis by 'transferences' and dreams. [S. E., 5, p. 668][11]

This sentence will be central to my interpretation of Dora's dreams, as I will attempt to reconstruct the pathogenesis of the hysterical symptoms following the theories elaborated by Freud in 1895 and 1896, which he had intended to corroborate in his account of this analysis. In so doing, I will assume the reader to be familiar with the case history. I will therefore not summarise the case history, and will refer to relevant quotations only when necessary. I will not attempt to engage in any consideration of a technical nature in my argument. I will limit myself to supplying those interpretations and identifying the shifts of meaning that allow us to connect Dora's dreams with Freud's initial declaration. By so doing, I will follow Freud's own declaration that "this case history presupposes a knowledge of the interpretation of dreams" (p. 11), and that "the technique of interpreting dreams may be easily learnt from the instructions and examples which I have given" (pp. 10–11).

PART I

THE CASE HISTORY

CHAPTER ONE

The first encounter with Dora

Freud saw Dora for the first time before 30 June 1898 (Mahony, 1996, p. 19). Back then she was not yet sixteen, she suffered from coughing and hoarseness, and Freud immediately judged her as being "unmistakably neurotic" (p. 19). During this first encounter, which had no follow-up, Freud only had the opportunity to gather a little information from her father, who accompanied her. He may have had the chance to carry out an accurate anamnesis of the patient, since he recommended that she undergo psychological treatment. Yet, because Dora's symptoms spontaneously receded, Freud's advice was not followed.

We can formulate the hypothesis that, during this first visit, Freud was informed by Dora's father that she had suffered from enuresis at the age of seven, since her father had himself been assigned by her mother the task of weaning her off the habit of bed-wetting. Let us examine Freud's ideas on infantile enuresis at the time. In September 1898, he was treating a young hysteric, a twenty-five year old patient who had suffered from enuresis at the age of seven. With regard to this symptom, Freud formulated the following hypothesis, which he communicated to his friend Fliess in a letter dated 27 September 1898:

> Now, a child who regularly wets his bed until his seventh year [without being epileptic or the like] must have experienced sexual excitation in his earlier childhood. Spontaneous or by seduction? [Masson, 1985, 27 September 1898, p. 329]

By "spontaneous excitation" we must not understand "masturbation", since if this were the case Freud would have made explicit reference to an auto-erotic activity on the child's part. We must, rather, think of the child's having witnessed a scene of a sexual nature (such as the primal scene) or experienced a self-induced sexual excitement, stimulated in any of the multiple ways whereby a child seeks to satisfy his own sexual curiosity. The other alternative is seduction at the hands of an adult, thus some kind of sexual activity initiated by an adult. We will see later how Dora's dream of the burning house provides motives for opting, in her case, for this second hypothesis.

Thus, at the time of his first encounter with Dora, Freud might already have suspected that the patient's hysterical symptomatology could be ascribed to an early sexual trauma. In fact, although he had confessed to Fliess that he no longer believed in his "neurotica", and notwithstanding his refutation of the seduction theory, he had not yet abandoned it completely, and he periodically continued not only to pursue its confirmation, but also to find it in his case histories.[1]

Dora's father had unashamedly lied about the nature of his relationship with Frau K. He described this erotic relationship as a sincere friendship between two poor creatures suffering from a nervous condition who would simply offer each other mutual sympathy. Not even this lie could alter Freud's positive judgement of Dora's father. Since Philip Bauer himself deemed his version to be not entirely convincing, he felt the need to add: "With my state of health I need scarcely assure you that there is nothing wrong in our relations" (p. 26). It is rather puzzling that Freud would have believed him, particularly since a few lines above he had criticised, in a footnote, those colleagues of his who, dealing with hysteric patients, would give up at the first disavowal of sexual factors. Lopez (1967, p. 230), moreover, cannot comprehend how Freud could sympathise with Herr K. who, "all things considered, does not seem very pleasant and certainly was not a worthy individual". In the same vein, Mahony (1999, p. 3) describes Philip Bauer as "crippled in both body and mind", as well as "given to hypocrisy and self-serving secrecy". Yet, for some undisclosed reason, Freud straight away formed a very positive opinion of Philip Bauer, Dora's father, judging him to be an extremely intelligent person and an individual full of admirable qualities—an opinion that he repeats on multiple occasions.[2] Nothing would subsequently affect Freud's judgement, not even that extreme mental confusion accompanied by slight psychic ailments which, had it not been treated in time by Freud with an antileutic therapy, could have resulted at the time in a paralytic dementia.

Thus, it was extremely unlikely that Freud could have held this man, whose "intelligence and his character" (p. 18) he esteemed, responsible for a sordid perversion such as the sexual abuse of his little daughter. Yet on 14 November 1897, thus only seven months prior to his first encounter with Dora, Freud had written a long letter to Fliess which, as we will see, seems to anticipate all the sexual themes that would later be tackled in Dora's case history. Yet, his solution in that case differed significantly from his earlier suggestions.

For these reasons, I believe, Freud initially refers to the *Studies on Hysteria* (1895d) in the theoretical reflections incorporated into Dora's case history. He distances himself from Breuer's theory of hypnoid states, and only later would he mention the traumatic theory (the seduction theory) and the *Aetiology of Hysteria* (1896c) in sufficiently convincing terms:

> *If, therefore, the trauma theory is not to be abandoned, we must go back to her childhood and look about there for any influences or impressions which might have had an effect analogous to that of a trauma.* Moreover, it deserves to be remarked that in the investigation even of cases in which the first symptoms had not already set in in childhood I have been driven to trace back the patient's life history to their earliest years. [p. 27; italics added]

We will see, nonetheless, that these influences and impressions no longer pertain to adult perversion and sexual seduction. They are represented, rather, by the primal scene, that is, by the child having witnessed or overheard the parents' coitus—a normal adult sexuality which is offered to the child's gaze and his, not always involuntary, indiscreet hearing of it.

As regards the figure of Dora's mother, whom Freud never met personally and whom he was not even interested in meeting, he is satisfied with the (probably tendentious) information provided by the father and daughter, who were allied against her. Freud describes Dora's mother as "an uncultivated woman and above all as a foolish one", affected by "housewife's psychosis" (p. 20). The contempt he showed towards her was as uncritical as the appreciation he had manifested for her father, from the outset. Mahony (1996, p. 3) observes that, "though telling, the particulars about Käthe are sparse. If she zealously scoured the house, Freud thoroughly wiped her out of his case history." Lewin (1973, pp. 519–520) affirms that Freud "accepted as accurate the description of the mother given by Dora and her father, a team of observers unreliable because of their personal biases, as Freud discovered later. He never re-examined Dora's relationship with her mother and the cause of their feud. In fact Freud never filled that gap in Dora's history, her early years with her mother." Akavia (2005, p. 200) has observed, "Freud's view of the mother's relation to Dora is ambivalent. On the one hand, he tried to marginalize her role in Dora's psychodynamics and to present their relationship as one based solely on rivalry and jealousy. On the other hand, he viewed the latent and repressed symptoms, uncovered during treatment, as indications of Dora's identification with her mother."

When Dora's father claimed that his daughter had inherited his stubbornness, Freud observed "on other occasions he tried to put the chief blame for Dora's impossible behaviour on her mother—whose peculiarities made the house unbearable for every one. But I had resolved from the first to suspend my judgement of the true state of affairs till I had heard the other side as well" (p. 26). Yet, Freud and Käthe, Dora's mother, would never meet.[3]

CHAPTER TWO

The second encounter with Dora and the beginning of the analysis

Two years after their first encounter, Freud took Dora into treatment—she "was by that time in the first bloom of youth— a girl of intelligent and engaging looks" (p. 23). She had already become the object of Herr K.'s attention—her father's friend.

We know with certainty the date when the treatment was interrupted, 31 December 1900, but the date of its beginning remains uncertain. Everyone who has commented on the case has taken it for granted that the treatment began around 14 October 1900, the day Freud communicated to Fliess that he had a new case, involving a young female patient. Jones strengthens the thesis that the treatment lasted under three months, and he declared with confidence, but rather superficially, that "the treatment lasted only eleven weeks" (Jones, 1953, vol. I, p. 397). This affirmation was uncritically repeated by the majority of historians of psychoanalysis and scholars dealing with Dora's case, an assertion that, if further examined, appears implausible for a number of reasons. I believe it is possible to prove that the treatment began at least a month before this time, and that it therefore lasted almost four months, rather than the canonically received three months determined on the basis of Freud's declarations, and of his confused memories of the therapy. Later, in his writings of 1914 and in a footnote added in

1923, he dated it between October and December 1899, that is a year before the actual date.

On 14 October 1900, Freud announces to Fliess that he is working on an essay about the dream, and also that he has a new patient. He says that the case "has smoothly opened to the existing collection of picklocks" (Masson, 1985, p. 427). Thus, it appears doubtful that Dora's treatment began around that date, 14 October, because—leaving aside for a moment the vulgarly erotic metaphor used by Freud—he would not have used this expression if he were referring to a therapy that had only just begun. As able a "cat burglar of the unconscious" as Freud was, we must nonetheless presume that he took a long time to overcome the resistances of this reluctant adolescent. Thus, 14 October had to mark a more advanced phase of the therapy. Freud had returned to Vienna after his summer holiday on 10 September, and, as he reported to Fliess on 14 September, "on the very same day was back in harness". Therefore, Dora could have been a patient of Freud's since his return to Vienna, that is to say a month before he reported the case to Fliess. After all, we should not assume that Freud was always so timely in giving news to his friend from Berlin; what is more, since he had come back from his holidays, Freud had only written three letters to Fliess. First, on 14 September, when he indulged in describing his summer travels and where his attention was far too focused on his holidays to mention the new patient; then, in a brief letter dated 24 September, containing just a few lines, in which he talks about the "psychology of everyday life"; and lastly, through the 14 October letter in which he refers to his scientific activity and the new case history. Thus, it appears plausible that Dora's treatment had begun soon after Freud's return to Vienna, that is, around mid-September, and that he had communicated this to his friend a month later. Freud claims that "the following autumn […] the family left the health-resort of B—for good and all. They first moved to the town where her father's factory was situated, and then, *scarcely a year later*, settled permanently in Vienna" (pp. 22–23; italics added). Thus, Dora's family had left Merano in the autumn of 1899,[1] and less than a year later, before the autumn of 1900, they had settled in Vienna, where they might already have been living at the beginning of September, before Freud's return from his summer holiday.

Furthermore, even if one were not entirely convinced by this evidence as to the reason Freud would write to Fliess about the case one month later, we must bear in mind that he was still under the effect of the recent

"Breuerization".[2] This had occurred at the end of May, and Freud had announced to his friend that such an event would have an impact on their relationship. Therefore, I find it reasonable to suppose that Dora's treatment had begun as early as at the start of the "Viennese autumn", hence around the middle of September 1900, soon after Freud's return from his summer vacation.

To support my thesis, I could also add that Anzieu (1986) believes that the *table d'hôte* dream, which he situates in October 1900, contains a reference to the erotic transference with which Dora solicited Freud. It would not be plausible to assume that Dora had developed an erotic transference for Freud at the beginning of the treatment, and that he had included his young patient in a dream after a few days of treatment. Rather, it seems more likely to suppose that this took place a month into the therapy. Anzieu (1986, p. 544) goes so far as to "assum[e] that the dream of 'Company at table d'hôte' preceded the letter to Fliess of October 14". Referring to Dora's story and the two traumatic scenes with Herr K.—that of the kiss and that by the lake—he maintains that the dream is contemporaneous with the investigation of these scenes and of the childhood memories connected to them. Yet, it would have happened before the production of the two dreams that form the backbone of the case study. The collocation of the dream with the investigation of the two traumatic scenes appears to be a rough guess on the author's part, and he deduces it from his interpretation of the dream: neither the correspondence with Fliess nor the text *On Dreams* (1901a) contain any clear indications that Freud's dream and the phase achieved in the Dora analysis are linked.

At any rate, the fact that Anzieu situates the dream prior to the letter in which Freud announced the new case history to Fliess confirms our hypothesis that Dora's treatment began in mid-September, soon after Freud's return to Vienna. Then, if it is true that Freud saw Dora six times a week for treatment, as Decker has claimed (1991, p. 94), when Freud wrote this to Fliess the treatment would probably have already been in its twentieth meeting. This would make the tone and burglar-metaphor with which Freud announced the new patient to his friend from Berlin more understandable, even if still not very orthodox.[3]

When Freud took Dora in for treatment, he was at a peculiar moment of his life that certainly will have affected his judgement of the familial events that emerged during the analysis. If it is true, as Swales (1982) has suggested, that in the summer of 1900 Freud had an affair with his sister-in-law Minna,[4] then when, back in Vienna, he began Dora's therapy and was informed of the erotic patterns involving the two families, he would not have been in a position to express his disapproval for Philip Bauer's and Herr K.'s conduct. Freud had spent the last two weeks of the summer vacation travelling around Trentino with Minna. His summer holidays lasted over six weeks, the first four of which had been spent with his wife Martha, and the last two, the most interesting ones according to Freud's account, with his sister-in-law Minna. He describes these two weeks to his friend Fliess as follows:

> Finally—we have now reached August 26—came the relief. I mean Minna, with whom I drove through the Puster Valley to Trentino, making several short stops along the way. Only when I was completely in the South did I begin to feel really comfortable; under ice and snow something was missing, though at the time I could not have defined it. The sun was very amiable in Trentino, in no way as intolerable as in Vienna. From Trentino we made an excursion to the extraordinarily beautiful Castel Toblino. That is where the choice *vino santo* grows, which is pressed only at Christmas. There I also saw my beloved olive tree again. Minna wanted a taste of a high-altitude sojourn; therefore, we went over a spectacular mountain road to Lavarone (1,200 meters), a high plateau on the side of the Valsugano, where we found the most magnificent forest of conifers and undreamed-of solitude. The nights began to be cool, however, so I headed directly for Lake Garda, as you must have known from the card from Torbole. We finally stopped for five days at Riva, divinely accommodated and fed, *luxuriating without regrets, and untroubled* [...] Two long boat trips took us one time to Salò and the other to Sirmione, where I climbed around in the ruins of what is purported to be Catullus' villa.
>
> On 8 September I took Minna to Merano, where she is supposed to stay for either a few weeks or a few months to cure her pulmonary apicitis [inflammation]. I believe I have told you that the recurrence of this affliction, for which she was sent to Sicily at the age of seventeen, casts a shadow on the immediate future. *I arrived feeling outrageously merry and well in Vienna*, found my family in good spirits, *and on the very same day was back in harness*. [Masson, 1985, 14 September 1900, pp. 423–424; italics added]

Given this mental disposition and that he had spent two weeks of intimacy with his sister-in-law, how could Freud show indignation for the erotic affairs of Dora's father and for Herr K.'s attempts to seduce Dora by the same location, Garda Lake,[5] where he had taken two long boat trips with Minna? Rather, is it not likely that Dora's accounts served to remind her analyst of his recent experiences with his sister-in-law, thus making him relive that "outrageously merry" affective state he had light-heartedly enjoyed while "luxuriating without regrets, and untroubled"? Decker (1991, p. 99) has drawn attention to Freud's "sympathies for Philipp's sexual situation" and stressed "Freud's tacit acceptance of the pernicious interfamilial relationship in which Dora was enmeshed", claiming that "Freud's silence on these matters is more easily understood if seen as a product of his identification with Dora's father" (Decker, 1982, p. 125).

Were it true that Freud had had a relationship of a sexual nature with Minna, this would also have had an impact on his countertransference towards Dora. This transpired, for instance, when he accused Dora of behaving like a governess, because in the Freud household, Minna had been a nursemaid—even if, as claimed by Gay (1990, p. 168), she had been more of "a manager, a privileged nurse". Moreover, a trace, albeit a feeble one, of this illicit relationship of Freud's may be found in the attitude that led him to re-direct onto Dora all of the accusations she had herself addressed against her father. Undeniably, if Freud had just partaken in an intimate liaison with his sister-in-law, he could not have listened to the reiterated accusations Dora addressed towards her father in relation to the latter's illicit relationship with Frau K., without himself feeling guilty for his recent, equally illicit, relationship with his sister-in-law. Thus if we apply to Freud the same explanation he himself made of Dora's accusations towards her father, we must assume that the accusations he repeatedly addressed towards Dora were a defence from his self-accusation over his relationship with his sister-in-law. Freud says:

> A string of reproaches against other people leads one to suspect the existence of a string of self-reproaches with the same content. All that needs be done is to turn back each particular reproach on to the speaker himself. There is something undeniably automatic about this method of defending oneself against a self-reproach by making the same reproach against same one else. [p. 35]

Freud reprimands Dora for having long ignored her father's relationship with Frau K., and for having made herself an accomplice in the affair. He fails, up to a point—that is, until the adventure by the lake—to open her eyes to the true nature of that relationship despite the many warnings of her old governess, the same person who had initiated her to erotic readings. Freud affirms that Dora "had made herself an accomplice in the affair, and had dismissed from her mind every sign which tended to show its true character […] and would hear of nothing that might make her think ill of her relations with her father" (p. 36), although a few pages before he had said of Dora that: "In her mind there was no doubt that what bound her father to this young and beautiful woman was a common love-affair. Nothing that could help to confirm this view had escaped her perception, which in this connection was pitilessly sharp …" (p. 32) This awareness, after all, had not manifested itself in Dora after the episode by the lake, but had been present, rather, since the beginning: the fact that she would not go to Frau K.'s when she knew the children had been sent away confirms that she was at some level aware of the nature of her father's visits to Frau K. Patently, Dora knew, but preferred to say nothing. The governess was herself in love with Dora's father, and when he was around "she was once more ready with every sort of service and assistance" (p. 37) for Dora, while in his absence she showed a lack of interest towards her. Freud comments on these facts claiming that:

> What the governess had from time to time been to Dora, Dora had been to Herr K.'s children. She had been a mother to them, she had taught them, she had gone for walks with them, she had offered them a complete substitute for the slight interest which their own mother showed in them. [p. 37]

Freud supposes that by looking after Herr K.'s children and displaying affection for them, Dora—like the governess—was in truth expressing an interest in their father. Freud does not consider, even briefly, that Dora's attentions for the children might have been genuine, and that she might in fact have wanted to give them what she had herself been denied during her own childhood because of her mother's indifference. Dora's behaviour might have been completely sincere. She might have identified with these children, in light of the affective deprivations to which they were subjected: they were sent away from home, so that their mother could pursue her sexual relationship with her lover.

I am not surprised by Freud's failure to grasp the natural, genuine aspect of Dora's interest in Herr K. and Frau K.'s children, an interest that was without sexual implications. I think Freud was blinded to this by his own familial situation and by his interest in his sister-in-law. In my view, Freud's appraisals of this familial entanglement were affected by his own feelings of guilt for his sexual relationship with Minna. As a matter of fact, Minna, who should have stayed with the Freuds only for a couple of months, but then remained all her life (Behling, 2002), had, as a governess, played a role in Freud's children's lives. Given the closely confidential relationship that had developed between herself and Sigmund because of their protracted cohabitation, we might however allege that this role had not always been dictated by disinterested aims. Furthermore, we have seen that Freud would gladly spend long holidays with Minna, with whom he engaged in more pleasant and enticing conversations than those with his wife. It is possible that some servant might have pointed out to Martha that Freud's intimacy with his sister-in-law was inappropriate. However, because of her relationship with her sister, Martha too, in a similar manner to Dora, "would hear of nothing that might make her think ill of her relations".

As for the hypothesis that Freud had an affair with his sister-in-law during those two weeks in September 1900, we could quote Freud himself in order to support this claim. Jones (1953, vol. I, p. 125) tells us that in July 1882, a month after their secret engagement, and before joining his fiancée in Wandsbeck, he wrote:

> Journeys end in lovers meeting
> Every wise man's son doth know.

Eighteen years later, apparently, Martha no longer remembered her passionate fiancé citing this quote; otherwise she would not have eagerly consented to her husband's coach journey with her sister Minna.[6]

Freud himself was aware of the inappropriateness of this relationship, as is illustrated by the fact that he attempted not to be seen publicly too often with his sister-in-law. In the letter to Martha that he wrote from Riva del Garda during the vacation, he mentions the presence of several professors in the *Hotel du Lac* where he was staying with Minna, and says he avoided their company not only because he had not yet attained the title of "professor", but also because he was not accompanied by his wife:

> The company at the hotel comprises most pleasant people, among whom many famous university professors and high school teachers, such as Czermak (Vienna), Dimmer (Graz), Felsenreich, Jodl (Vienna), Sigm. Mayer from Prague (I should have become his assistant). Since I am no lecturer and since I am with a woman who is not my wife, I keep wide berth from them. [Tögel, 2002, p. 131]

This was the version Freud gave to his wife Martha, so as to reassure her of his discretion—he described this party as "compris[ing] most pleasant people", but he would keep away from them, as he was in the company of his sister-in-law rather than his wife. Conversely, in the letter to Fliess written only nine days later, on 14 September 1900, he describes this party of lecturers as "trouble", whom he avoided, aggrieved by the presence of colleagues who knew him, and by whom he was seen with his sister-in-law instead of with his wife, as would have been expected.

This was not the only occasion on which Freud offered his wife a modified version of the facts. With regard to his trip to South Tirol with Minna from 4–14 August 1898, he gave Martha an altered version of the real events. Franz Maciejewski (2007) has consulted the register of guests of the *Hotel Schweizerhaus* in Maloja, and discovered that on 13 August 1898 Sigmund Freud and his sister-in-law Minna slept in a double bedroom and were checked in as "Dr. Sigm. Freud u[nd] Frau/ Wien". Although the hotel was in fact a luxury establishment, Freud described it to Martha, in the postcard sent from Maloja on 13 August, as a "modest Swiss hotel". During this trip, Freud wrote to Martha using words that may lead one to infer that he was counting on the physical resemblance between the two sisters so as to avoid denigrations from strangers, and in order to have Minna pass for his wife. On 6 August 1898 he sent a letter to Martha from Landeck in which he wrote:

> Minna really does not want to leave the Hotel Post in Landeck, so much does she like it. Anyway, I will take care of calling her

to order. It is becoming clearer and clearer why people get you confused with one another. She resembles you very much and I know that after our journey she will also mutter like you. For now though, at least occasionally, she will remain enraptured. [Tögel, 2002, p. 100]

After all, Minna herself did not refrain from displaying her enthusiasm to her sister, or her coquetry towards her brother-in-law. In the same letter, she writes to her sister:

My dearest! We'd be happy to sleep every night in a different bed, which is ideal for Sigi. He is, touch wood, in *exceptional* shape and very happy, naturally very restless. [ibid., p. 101]

In the letter Freud wrote to Martha from Le Prese, dated 10 August 1898, we read, in Minna's own handwriting:

I want to tell you something, but you won't believe it. Your husband has had lunch at the *table d'hôte*, which he liked very much and tonight we'll dine there again. He seems to have changed, really, he has befriended the spa physician, he talks with everybody and he enjoys the noblesse and the comfort even more than I do [...]. Sigi has spontaneously decided to stay here one more day: so far we have travelled at a crazy pace, because we want to stay two days in Pontresina, but it's so fabulous here, a mixture of elegance and comfort and the landscape is fantastic [...]. It's busy everywhere, thus one must be really content just to find a hotel, so we're all the more razzle-dazzle. Hasn't our mother often repeated: Minna will end up collapsing during her vacations? Yet, I can assure her that she's wrong, in fact I hadn't felt this great in years and I'm experiencing everything marvellously. The wine, everywhere of high quality and inexpensive, is certainly helping [...]. Sigi has picked up wonderful flowers, which I have kept [...]. Today we have really relaxed ourselves. I can finally flaunt my flannel dress with all the jewelleries and, obviously, Sigi always finds me very elegant [...] [ibid., pp. 105–107]

It is not essential to establish whether or not Freud had an affair with Minna, that is, if she was his "sister-in-law" or his "sister-in-love".

Reading these letters, though, it appears unequivocal that the relationship between "Sigi and Minna" was a highly eroticised one.

From this, Maciejewski (2007, p. 502) deduces, with a reasonable degree of certainty, that Freud and Minna had an affair, and that, more than just sharing a bed, they "were even up to misrepresenting their relationship to strangers as that of a husband and wife". It is possible that this had become a habit for the couple and Freud might have exploited Minna's resemblance to her sister Martha in order to present her as his wife. But since many Viennese doctors were present at the *Hotel du Lac* in Riva del Garda, on that occasion the ill-matched couple kept themselves to themselves. Maciejewski (2007, p. 502) thinks this was "a subterfuge they surely then maintained whenever feasible during subsequent holidays together in faraway places". Freud's relatives and friends were unlikely to have overlooked the peculiar nature of this relationship, and it is possible that a broader part of the Viennese entourage had noticed something, considering that Freud's niece, Judith Bernays Heller, claimed that "wicked tongues had spoken of Sigmund's 'second wife'" (Hirschmüller quoted in Maciejewski 2007, p. 499). Appropriately, Maciejewski does not utilise his finding to denigrate Freud. He makes the paradoxical claim, rather, that this incestuous affair rather reveals his human nature, and should perhaps lead to a rethinking of the autobiographical origins of the oedipal theory.

Hirschmüller (2007, p. 126) has attempted to undermine the validity of Maciejewski's deductions, but his arguments are pretentious and unconvincing. The author, who is also the editor of the published correspondence between Freud and Minna Bernays, affirms: "The letters do show a relationship of mental and personal intimacy, as between siblings, but they do not in any way hint at a love affair, nor do any of the other available historical sources." We know that Freud frequently addressed Minna as his "sister", but we also know that incestuous relationships between brothers and sisters are not so rare.

According to the author, "it seems premature to take sharing a room as proof of a sexual relationship, as Maciejewski does" (ibid., p. 126). Hirschmüller observes that there is no proof that Freud and his sister-in-law deliberately shared a room on other occasions, rather than just this one, when perhaps two single rooms were not available in the hotel, which is of course plausible. He also understands, though, that their having booked two separate bedrooms does not necessarily imply they did not sleep in the same bed. The discovery of the document from the *Hotel Schweizerhaus* in Maloja seems a particularly fortunate case, says Hirschmüller, letting transpire a certain disappointment, since the other hotels where Freud and Minna stayed had either closed down, or the guest registers from that time are no longer available. Hirschmüller not only suggests the possibility, which is completely plausible, that when Freud and Minna were in Maloja the hotel only had a double bedroom available, but he also claims that two rooms would have cost more than one. The latter observation is groundless, because on that occasion, as in other trips with Minna, Freud had chosen a luxury hotel: had he wanted to save money, he would have booked two rooms in a less expensive establishment. "Whether they shared one bed or not, and what may or may not have happened in that bed, remains a matter of speculation" (ibid., p. 127). Hirschmüller's main argument to demolish the "legend *in statu nascendi*" of "a couple lingering three days in a love nest" (ibid., p. 127) is that Freud and Minna only stayed for two days, as if a day would make an essential difference. Hirschmüller (2007, p. 127) is clutching at straws to defend the reputation of the father of psychoanalysis, and his attempts do not end here: "Once they decided to share one room for whatever reason, how else should they have signed in? As 'Dr. Sigm. Freud and Frl. Minna Bernays, sister-in-law'? With the consequence that other guests might have read this entry and drawn exactly the same conclusion, as have Maciejewski and others? Furthermore, let us not forget that in those days a hotel owner renting a room to an unmarried couple could be prosecuted for procuring (*Kuppelei*), at least in Germany and in the Austrian-Hungarian Empire."

So how should Freud have behaved at the reception? Had he asked for two single bedrooms and, on being informed that only a double bedroom was available, he might have said: "Ah, all the better! We are husband and wife", and they would have checked in as "Dr. Sigmund Freud und Frau". If, in Hirschmüller's view, other guests had gossiped about the couple, in my view the hotel manager would have thought the couple rather bizarre or unhappily married. Furthermore, if the laws were so strict back then, how is it that hotel managers did not check their guests' documents, making it so easy to lie when checking in?

Also, Hirschmüller claims that the two in-laws used to send letters to Martha, in which they would enthusiastically describe their holidays: this would have been rather bold on their part, had they really been lovers. But was it not bold enough of Freud to spend his holidays with Minna? We have seen Minna's boldness and coquetry in the notes she added to Freud's letter to his wife. We have also seen that he concealed from Martha the fact that they stayed at luxury hotels, and that he took advantage of the resemblance of the two sisters to shamelessly pass Minna off as his wife. But Hirschmüller (2007, p. 128) does not consider this as boldness, and instead adds a decisive touch to his account. How could Freud be so bold as to expose Minna to the risk of a pregnancy, he who had refrained from having sexual intercourse with his wife Martha, after Anna was born, to spare her from enduring another pregnancy? This happened, in any case, after almost a decade of consecutive pregnancies (1886–1895). Thus, had not the moment arrived for Freud to interrupt his long abstinence? And since, as Hirschmüller claims, Freud thought a condom noxious, might he not have taken the risk?

CHAPTER THREE

The first trauma: a disgusting kiss

Dora's first traumatic experience, namely the scene of the kiss with Herr K.—to which her immediate response was one of violent nausea—is a rather controversial point. In regard to this experience, Freud expresses opinions, of an entirely personal nature, which I find rather debatable. These opinions betray the cultural, chauvinist, stereotypical mentality of a middle-aged man such as he was at the time. Indeed, this is a trait he shares with the other male protagonists of those events, with whom it was easy for him to identify and share emotions. Conversely, he would find it more difficult to identify with an adolescent girl.[1]

Freud immediately condemned Dora for her reaction of violent nausea to Herr K.'s kiss, and instantly judged her to be an hysteric:

> In this scene [...] the behaviour of this child of fourteen was already entirely and completely hysterical. I should without question consider a person hysterical in whom an occasion for sexual excitement elicited feelings that were preponderantly or exclusively unpleasurable; and I should do so whether or no the person were capable of producing somatic symptoms. [p. 28]

Here, the defence of the forty-three year old analyst seems to be at work, who, in identifying with the narcissistic wounds inflicted on Herr K., who "was still quite young and of prepossessing appearance" (p. 29, note 3), judges as hysterical a reaction which we may consider completely normal. In identifying with Herr K., Freud cannot tolerate the unutterable frustration arising from the possibility that a sexual advance made by a man of his age towards "a girl of fourteen who had never before been approached"—instead of arousing "a distinct feeling of sexual excitement"—might in fact instigate "a violent feeling of disgust" (p. 28). Lacan (1951, p. 217) was among the first to observe that Freud was empathising a little too much with Herr K. Decker (1982, p. 125) has observed, moreover, that "Freud's tacit acceptance of the pernicious interfamilial relationships in which Dora was enmeshed" and that "Freud's silence on these matters is more easily understood if seen as a product of his identification with Dora's father". Mahony (1996, p. 61) claims that here Freud is "flushing out the cynicism in his fantasy about pedophilia and youthful virginity". We will see below, however, that there are reasons, which are much more valid than the cultural prejudices of the age shared by Freud, to reject his stance on Dora's reaction. These are in fact the same theoretical standpoints he had expressed to his friend Fliess, not long before he took Dora in for treatment.

Yet, other factors in Dora's case might have played a part in determining her reaction of disgust. We can easily imagine that, during the numerous years the Bauers were compelled to spend in Merano because of Dora's father's tuberculosis, the little Dora had had more than one occasion to see her tubercular father coughing. Perhaps she had also witnessed episodes of expectoration. This could already have induced in the child, even at the time, feelings of nausea and disgust linked to the oral zone, which would later be reactivated by oral contact with a contemporary of her father's. As early as in *Preliminary Communication "On the Psychical Mechanism of Hysterical Phenomena"* (1893h), Freud had reported the case of a patient[2] who, among other symptoms, "regularly felt disgust at mealtimes" that had first manifested itself when, as a child, her mother had forced her to eat cold meat:

> She did so with great disgust and retained the memory of it; so that later on, when she was no longer subjected to this punishment, she regularly felt disgust at mealtimes. Ten years later she used to

> sit at table with a relative who was tubercular and kept constantly spitting across the table into the spittoon during meals. A little while later she was obliged to share her meals with a relative who, as she knew, was suffering from a contagious disease. [S. E., 3, p. 33]

Dora's father presented both of these repellent characteristics: he was consumptive and suffered from syphilis. Thus Dora, just like Emmy von N., must have had more than one occasion, during her childhood, to feel repulsion for him. After all, Dora herself was for a period of time "a poor eater and confessed to some disinclination for food" (p. 29).

If, furthermore, it were true that, in accordance with my hypothesis, Dora was a victim of sexual abuse inflicted by her father during her early childhood—when she was five or six years old, thus exactly when Philip Bauer contracted tuberculosis—and that the abuse implied oral contacts, Dora's reaction of violent nausea and disgust to a contemporary of her father's, Herr K., taking hold of her and kissing her on the mouth, would no longer be so incomprehensible. If this were the case, we would be dealing with a trauma that acts in two phases, which can be contextualised within the Freudian concept of *Nachträglichkeit*. That is, the trauma experienced with Herr K. would not have had an effect in itself, but rather in its rendering traumatic the recollection of an analogous sexual episode with the father which had occurred during Dora's early childhood. This sexual episode, though, can only be presumed. Thus, what is it that suggests such an assumption, which might be judged as arbitrary? Freud himself leads us to infer that Dora was sexually stimulated as a child, which he allows us to deduce precisely from her "hysterical reaction" during puberty. In 1896 he had claimed that:

> Sexual experiences in childhood consisting in stimulation of the genitals, coitus-like acts, and so on, must therefore be recognized, in the last analysis, as *being the traumas which lead to a hysterical reaction to events at puberty and to the development of hysterical symptoms*. [*The Aetiology of Hysteria*, S. E., 3, pp. 206–207; italics added]

This claim clearly testifies to the correctness of my deduction, which consequently leads us to agree with Freud's confirmation of the aetiology of hysteria. We can already anticipate that, step by step, Freud will lead us to unravel, behind Dora's symptoms, what a few years back he had defined as "paternal aetiology" to indicate acts of sexual seduction by the father. Freud's answer is not delayed. Speaking of Dora's persistent nervous cough, he says:

> I was led to think that this symptom might have some meaning in connection with her father. [p. 46]

Thus with her cough, Dora accused her father. Yet we are led to understand that Freud, with this theory, meant to support the deduction that, by coughing, Dora was to a certain extent reproaching her father for his oral sex with Frau K. Since I find it hard to believe that Freud had forgotten, after only four years, the theories from 1896 that he now intended to reconfirm, I am inclined to think that he meant to proceed more cautiously with Dora than he had done with previous patients, who had prematurely abandoned their treatment just before achieving the recollection of childhood scenes that Freud intended to reconstruct.[3] It is thus worth engaging in a thorough consideration here of Dora's reaction of disgust, which Freud immediately condemned as "hysterical", in order to ascertain the degree of continuity of thought that could be traced between this judgement, and Freud's antecedent assertions on this very subject.

That "reaction of disgust" was the first symptom that immediately prompted Freud to diagnose a girl just less than fourteen years of age as hysterical. As for the importance of this first impression, I would like to provide readers with the means by which to judge for themselves whether or not this conclusion was justified on the basis of the elements Freud possessed back then, and whether or not this was consequential to the theories he had elaborated up until that point on the question of neuroses. For this reason, I will need to dwell at some length on claims made privately by Freud with his friend Fliess, in relation to the connection between disgust and sexuality.

Already in the first letters, where Freud revealed to Fliess the outline of what would later become the seduction theory, the notion of disgust appears in relation with sexual trauma:

> Just think: among other things I am on the scent of the following strict precondition for hysteria, namely, that a primary sexual experience (before puberty), accompanied by revulsion and fright,

must have taken place; for obsessional neurosis, that it must have happened, accompanied by *pleasure*. [Masson, 1985, 8 October 1895, pp. 140–144]

The following week, not remembering that he had already referred his recent hypothesis to Fliess, Freud reformulates it as follows:

> Have I revealed the great clinical secret to you, either orally or in writing?
> Hysteria is the consequence of a presexual *sexual shock*.
> Obsessional neurosis is the consequence of a presexual *sexual pleasure*, which is later transformed into [self-] *reproach*. "Presexual" means actually before puberty, before the release of sexual substances; the relevant events become effective only as *memories*. [ibid., 15 October 1895, p. 144]

A few days later Freud will gain the related clinical proof:

> Other confirmations concerning the neuroses are pouring in on me. The thing is really true and genuine. [ibid., 20 October 1895, p. 147]

The year 1896 opens with the important *Draft K* (attached to the letter to Fliess of 1 January 1896) entitled *The Neuroses of Defence*, which is his most systematic writing on the theory of infantile sexual trauma and the direct predecessor of *The Aetiology of Hysteria* (1896c). Freud still expresses some doubts about the traumatic aetiology of these neuroses, and advances his aetiological hypothesis with great caution. Later on, however, this will nonetheless receive nothing but confirmation. We can also observe a partial modification to the theory announced in the letter of 15 October 1895, and already put forward in the letter of 8 December 1895, in which the *sexual shock* that was at the origins of hysteria is now substituted with a *conflict*. The neuroses of defence

> are pathological aberrations of normal psychic affective states: of *conflict* (hysteria), of *self-reproach* (obsessional neurosis), of *mortification* (paranoia), of *mourning* (acute hallucinatory amentia). They [...] lead [...] to permanent damage to the ego. [Masson, 1985, p. 162]

A precondition for their insurgence is that the reason

> is of a sexual kind and that it occurs during the period before sexual maturity (the preconditions of *sexuality and infantilism*) [...] heredity is a further precondition, in that it facilitates and increases the pathological effect [...] . [ibid., p. 162]

There is a normal tendency to defend against sorrow, but the defence becomes detrimental if:

> it is directed against ideas which are also able, in the form of memories, to release fresh unpleasure—as is the case with sexual ideas. Here, indeed, is the one possibility realized of a memory's having a greater releasing power than was produced by the experience corresponding to it. Only one thing is necessary for this: that puberty should be interpolated between the experience and its repetition in memory—an event which thus strongly increases the effect of the revival. [Masson, 1985, p. 163]

Freud here repeatedly remarks on the importance of premature sexual stimulation as a precondition for the insurgence of a neurosis of defence, although he still acknowledges the role played by heredity. While this seems to go some way in explaining why a case of sexual seduction could occur without the emergence of hysteria, hysteria cannot emerge without the indispensable precondition of a sexual seduction. After all Freud uses a rhetorical expedient to further confirm this thesis, more specifically, by validating it *a contrario*: the indispensable condition for a neurosis of defence *not* to develop is that a premature sexual stimulation has *not* occurred such as to determine, through the concomitant contribution of heredity, the appearance of neurosis. The course of these neuroses follows a common pattern, formed by a number of stages, in turn determined by the repression process:

> The course taken by the illness in neuroses of repression is in general always the same: 1) the sexual experience (or series of experiences), which is traumatic and premature and is to be repressed; 2) its repression on some later occasion, which arouses a memory of it—at the same time the formation of a primary symptom; 3) a stage of successful defense, which is equivalent to health except for the existence of the primary symptom; 4) the stage in which the repressed ideas return, and in which, during the struggle between

them and the ego, new symptoms are formed which are those of the illness proper; 5) a stage of adjustment, of being overwhelmed, or of recovery with a malformation. [Masson, 1985, p. 164]

Contrary to what one might expect, the explanation of hysteria occupies the final and shortest part of *Draft K*, but Freud himself provides us with an explanation in the words accompanying these notes, which were meant for his friend and included in the letter from 1 January 1896:

> A gentle voice has counselled me to postpone the account of hysteria since there are still too many uncertainties in it. [ibid., p. 159]

Let us see what explanation he gives of the aetiology of hysteria in *Draft K.*:

> Hysteria necessarily presupposes a primary experience of unpleasure—that is, of a passive nature [...] A further condition of hysteria is that the primary experience of unpleasure does not occur at too early a time, at which the release of unpleasure is still too slight and at which, of course, pleasurable events may still follow independently. Otherwise what will follow will be only the formation of obsessions [...] Hysteria begins with the overwhelming of the ego [...] The raising of tension at the primary experience of unpleasure is so great that the ego does not resist it and forms no psychic symptom but is obliged to allow a manifestation of discharge—usually an excessive expression of excitation. This first stage of hysteria may be described as "fright hysteria"; its primary symptom is the *manifestation of fright* accompanied by a *gap* in the psyche. To what age this first hysterical overwhelming of the ego can occur is still unknown.
> Repression and the formation of defensive symptoms only occur subsequently, in connection with the memory; and after that *defense* and *overwhelming* (that is, the formation of symptoms and the outbreak of attacks) may be combined to any extent in hysteria.
> Repression [...] take place [...] by the intensification of a boundary idea, which thereafter represents the repressed memory in the passage of thought. It may be called a *boundary idea* because, on the one hand, it belongs to the ego and, on the other hand, it forms an undistorted portion of the traumatic memory. So, once again, it is

> the result of a compromise [...] a displacement of attention along a series of ideas linked by temporal simultaneity. Should the traumatic event find an outlet for itself in a motor manifestation, it will be this that becomes the boundary idea and the first symbol of the repressed material. [ibid., p. 169]

At the time, Freud's interest was entirely focused on metapsychology. He was reading a volume by Hippolyte Taine, *De l'intelligence* (*On Intelligence*, 1870) hoping to obtain from it something useful. To this end, he claims:

> The oldest ideas are really the most useful ones, as I am finding out belatedly. [Masson, 1985, 13 February 1896, p. 172]

This statement, which may at first appear trivial and devoid of any relevance, represents, I would contend, a crucial moment in the development of Freud's thought. It is a confirmation of the conclusions reached by Masson (1984, p. 40) that "Paris provided Freud with experiences and evidence on which he built his thesis, in 1896, that real sexual traumas in childhood lay at the very heart of neurotic illness".

We must keep in mind that Freud was reading an 1870 text in the French language. Also, the claim that "the oldest ideas are really the most useful ones" did not only refer to, or at least not only to, the text he was reading at the time, but also to the texts he had had the chance to read during his Parisian stay and that he used to keep in his library. These include, as Masson (1984, p. 38) has claimed, texts by Tardieu, Bernard, and Brouardel, that is "the major French works dealing with sexual violence against children". Ambroise Tardieu's book *Etude médico-légale sur les attentats aux moeurs* (Medical and Legal Studies on the Assaults on Manners) was published for the first time in 1857 and then republished on six occasions, the last of which was in 1878 (see Masson, 1984, endnote 8, p. 207). His claim about the usefulness of long-standing ideas befitted this text, which was published thirty years before Freud's stay in Paris. Although Paul Bernard's text *Des Attentats à la Pudeur sur les petites Filles* was published in 1886, the year of Freud's sojourn in Paris, and Brouardel's *Les Attentats aux Moeurs* in 1909, these texts can be placed within the trend of medical-legal studies inaugurated by Tardieu with his 1857 book, and were thus closer to those older ideas proposed by Tardieu thirty years beforehand.

That Freud had "belatedly" realised the importance of those older ideas confirms that he is referring to these authors, because his attention to the phenomenon of sexual abuse and of its psychic consequences emerged ten years after his stay in Paris, during which he had come into contact with these ideas and had attended "Professor Brouardel's forensic autopsies and lectures at the Morgue, which I rarely missed" (Freud, 1956a [1886], *S. E.*, *1*, p. 8).

Returning from Paris, before going back to Vienna, Freud spent March 1886 in Berlin, where he had "ample opportunities for examining children suffering from nervous diseases in the out-patient clinics of Professors Mendel and Eulenburg and of Dr. A. Baginsky, and I was everywhere most politely received" (ibid., p. 14). "In Berlin, for about a month, Freud went daily to the polyclinic where Adolf Baginsky, along with paediatric private practice, also held courses for physicians and students" (Bonomi, 1994, p. 58).[4] Although Freud's acquaintance with Baginsky only lasted a month, it is plausible that, despite the lack of time, he could have become familiar with Baginsky's ideas on the issue of infantile masturbation, its consequences on the nervous system, and its causes. As Bonomi (1998b, pp. 32–33) observes, "Baginsky stated that 'masturbation appears in the earliest childhood, already in babies' [...] and conceived it as a contagious illness because 'certain external stimuli are able to produce the evil and seduction [Verführung] plays here a very big role' [...] Sometimes the sources of the evil are to be found in stimulation by worms, sometimes in lasting constipation, or finally in abuse by filthy nursemaids and nannies, who want to calm down the children by plying with their genitals" (See also Bonomi, 2007 and 2009). Furthermore, Baginsky has classified masturbation among the causes of hysteria. Here, Bonomi (2007) is recognising one of the roots of Freud's seduction theory: after all, we must acknowledge that Baginsky's ideas on sexual seduction could not avoid confirming in Freud's mind the importance and frequency of these sexual traumas, as he had learnt during his stay in Paris by reading the French texts and attending Brouardel's lectures. Paediatricians of the time identified a predisposition to nervous disorders acquired through seduction by an adult, and this idea, once perfected, will be used by Freud in 1896 to build upon the theory of sexual seduction as the specific cause of hysteria.

Back in Vienna, Freud became "responsible for the department for nervous diseases at the 'Public Institute for Children's Diseases' in

Vienna, directed by Max Kassowitz. For ten years, from 1886 to 1896, Freud worked with children three days a week, and paediatric activity effectively represented his most constant professional engagement" (Bonomi, 1994, p. 55). Although Freud had started his career as a neurologist, we must consider that a "neurologist, back then, was in charge of the diagnosis and treatment of all 'nervous ailments', and that the large quantity of cases he could study suggests that Freud also had direct experience of numerous cases of nervous and hysterical diseases in childhood" (Bonomi, 1998a). Infantile neuropsychiatry was not yet conceived of as a specific discipline, and the first specific text, *Die psychischen Störungen des Kindesalters* (Mental Disorders of Early Childhood) by Hermann Emminghaus, was published in 1887. "Until then paediatricians held the knowledge of nervous and psychic diseases in infancy, and it is very significant that even this first monograph of 1887 appears within a paediatric context (as supplement to Gerhardt's paediatric manual). Freud's choice to turn to a paediatrician was thus a forced one. After all, it is during this period that a new psychiatric knowledge comes to the fore, hence Freud's professional growth and his neuro-paediatric work, which stands between these two fields of knowledge" (Bonomi, 1998a).

Freud therefore devoted ten years to working in the public sector with children suffering from nervous diseases, though only three times a week. Surprisingly enough though, nothing of this neuro-paediatric work comes out of his correspondence with Fliess. It is difficult to comprehend how from such a lengthy experience only a few neurological writings could remain. These include: a text on aphasia dated 1888, which Freud always considered the best among his neurological writings; a comment on an hemianopsia from the same year; a work on cerebral diplegia, and one on enuresis, in 1893; and the voluminous work *Die infantile Cerebrallähmung* for Nothnagel's 1897 manual of pathology, which Freud worked on with some reluctance.

It seems plausible that this prolonged period of work experience with children suffering from nervous diseases contributed to keep alive in Freud's mind the memory of what he had learnt both in Paris and during his brief experience with Baginsky in Berlin (although the latter did not impress him as much as Charcot and Brouardel had).

It was probably over these years that the idea slowly began to form in Freud's mind that the consequences of those sexual abuses were visible not only on the anatomy table, which he had learnt at the Morgue in Paris, but also in the context of the therapeutic relation he would establish with his adult patients who had survived this type of violence during childhood. We do not know how Freud worked with these young patients for ten years, nor do we know if he investigated their family history, just as he used to do with his private adult patients. Yet it is unlikely, I think, that he kept his public and private practices so separate as to act as a neurologist with the children in the public hospital and as a psychotherapist with his private patients. As a matter of fact, though, he never revealed anything of this experience in the Public Viennese Institute to Fliess. It is possible that his experience in this clinical environment led Freud to devise the hypothesis, which he formulated at the beginning of 1897, that even infantile epilepsy could stem from an early sexual trauma [Masson, 1985, 12 January 1897, pp. 223–224].

I find it unlikely that these ten years spent at the first Public Institute for Children's Diseases in Vienna would not have made a crucial contribution to the hypotheses developed in *The Aetiology of Hysteria* (1896c). It seems, rather, that "neuro-paediatrics is a fundamental matrix of Freud's thought. The emphasis on the trauma, contagion, seduction, and on the idea of acquired predisposition at a precocious age must be considered, along with the psychic mechanism, one of the two poles from which the seduction theory originated, as the specific aetiology of hysteria, in 1896" (Bonomi, 1998a, p. 84).

At the end of February 1896, Fliess had sent Freud the manuscript of his work *Beziehungen zwischen Nase und weiblichen Geschlechtsorganen* (The Connections between the Nose and the Female Genitals) in which he argued in favour of his most famous theory, namely that of a functional connection between the nose and the female sexual organs. This work offers Freud the cue to enrich the aetiology of neurosis with a chronological element referring to the period of the sexual trauma:

> [...] I want to add that some of your random remarks really impressed me. Thus, it occurs to me that the limits of repression in my theory of neuroses—that is to say, the time after which sexual experiences no longer have a posthumous but an actual effect—coincide with the second dentition. [Masson, 1985, 1 March 1896, p. 174]

Freud had already expressed this idea in *Project for a Scientific Psychology* (1950 [1895]), thus Fliess' book had perhaps only reactivated his interest in a hypothesis left undeveloped, and then retrieved in *The Aetiology of Hysteria* (1896c).

In a subsequent passage in the letter from 1 March 1896, disagreeing with the criticism expressed by Breuer in relation to the aetiology of neurasthenia, Freud returns to a point he had already dealt with in *Draft B*, expressing his perplexities as to the weight that hereditary and traumatic factors should be assigned within the aetiology of neurasthenia. He mentions that neurasthenia arises in persons "who, it is true, never masturbated, but who nevertheless exhibit from the beginning a type of sexuality that has the same appearance as if they had acquired it through masturbation" (Masson, 1985, p. 175). This contradiction can only be solved by acknowledging a traumatic aetiology, which Freud in *Draft B* had referred to as a "sexual assault".

If we bear in mind that Freud now positions the border of repression in the period of second dentition, a traumatic theory of neurasthenia begins to take shape, which includes an episode of "masturbatory assault" in early childhood and explains the emergence of neurasthenia also in persons who do not engage in masturbation.

Of particular interest is the letter to Fliess of 14 November 1897, in which two concepts—necessary to understanding Dora's reaction to the trauma of the kiss—stand out and on which Freud focuses his observations: namely, the *emergence of disgust* and the notion of *deferred action*, concepts that are elaborated within the discussion on repression. I believe it is worth quoting Freud's considerations in full here:

> Now, *the zones which no longer produce a release of sexuality in normal and mature human beings must be the regions of the anus and of the mouth and throat*. This is to be understood in two ways: first, that seeing and imagining these zones no longer produce an exciting effect, and second, that *the internal sensations arising from them make no contribution to the libido*, the way the sexual organs proper do. In animals these sexual zones continue in force in both respects; if this persists in human beings too, perversion results.
>
> [...] A *release of sexuality* (as you know, *I have in mind a kind of secretion which is rightly felt as the internal state of the libido*) comes about, then, not only 1) through a peripheral stimulus upon the sexual organs, or 2) through the internal excitations arising from those organs, but also 3) from ideas—that is, from memory traces— therefore also by the path of *deferred action*. (You are already familiar with this line of thought. *If a child's genitals have been irritated*

by someone, years afterward the memory of this will produce by deferred action a release of sexuality far stronger than at the time, because the decisive apparatus and the quota of secretion have increased in the meantime). Thus, there exists *a nonneurotic deferred action* occurring normally, and this generates compulsion [...] *Deferred action of this kind occurs also in connection with a memory of excitations of the abandoned sexual zones. The outcome, however, is not a release of libido but of an unpleasure, an internal sensation analogous to* **disgust** *in the case of an object* [author's emphasis].

To put it crudely, the memory actually stinks just as in the present the object stinks; and in the same manner as we turn away our sense organ (the head and nose) in disgust, the preconscious and the sense of consciousness turn away from the memory. This is *repression*. [Masson, 1985, 14 November 1897, pp. 279–280]

Reassessing the scene of the kiss with Herr K., and Dora's reaction, in light of the above considerations, it seems to me that Freud was being excessively peremptory when he classified Dora's behaviour—that is, her disgust—as "already entirely and completely hysterical".[5] If Dora's reaction were the result of a deferred action, then it could be considered, according to the Freudian theory of 1897, to be a *"nonneurotic deferred action"* which "occurs also in connection with a memory of excitations of the abandoned sexual zones" and causes "an internal sensation analogous to disgust". If it were true, as the seduction theory of 1896 would require, that Dora's father sexually abused her, stimulating the child both genitally and orally thus provoking a sensation of disgust in the girl, then the experience with Herr K. would have simply reactivated the memory of an analogous sensation endured in the relationship with her father. After all, Freud himself remarks that each and every attempt of his to draw Dora's attention to her relations with Herr K. would but elicit associations with her father:

> I did not find it easy, however, to direct the patient's attention to her relations with Herr K. She declared that she had done with him. The uppermost layer of all her associations during the session, and everything of which she was easily conscious and of which she remembered having been conscious the day before, was always connected with her father. [p. 32]

Freud had already illustrated this mechanism of the trauma on two occasions in the *Project for a Scientific Psychology* of 1895, exposing the case of Emma, a hysterical patient subject "to a compulsion of not being able to go into shops *alone*" (S. E., 1, p. 353). Freud reconstructed the infantile traumatic episode that had originated this curious compulsion.

Emma explained her inhibition through

> a memory from the time when she was twelve years old (shortly after puberty). She went into a shop to buy something, saw the two shop-assistants (one of whom she can remember) laughing together, and ran away in some kind of *affect of fright*. In connection with this, she was led to recall that the two of them were laughing at her clothes and that one of them had pleased her sexually. [S. E., 1, p. 353]

Freud observed that Emma's memory was not sufficient to explain either the compulsion or the determination of the symptom. He therefore continued to investigate the patient's memories, trying to find an episode more apposite to this objective. An older memory eventually surfaced:

> On two occasions when she was a child of eight she had gone into a small shop to buy some sweets, and the shopkeeper had grabbed at her genitals through her clothes. In spite of the first experience she had gone there a second time; after the second time she stopped away. [ibid., p. 354]

A state of "oppressive bad conscience" had arisen in Emma, caused by self-reproaches for having returned to the shop a second time, as if she had wanted to provoke the shopkeeper. The associative connection between the two scenes is the laughter of the shop assistants and the sneer of the shopkeeper, and the fact that Emma was alone. The most recent memory, dating back to puberty, stirs up the oldest memory of the sexual assault and arouses in the present moment what could not have been aroused at the age of eight, namely, "a *sexual release*, which was transformed into anxiety. With this anxiety, she was afraid that the shop-assistants might repeat the assault, and she ran away" (ibid., p. 354).

Here Freud clearly illustrates that mechanism of the *Nachträglichkeit*, which will become pivotal to the pathogenesis of hysteria. The sexual release, Freud claims,

> is linked to the memory of the assault; but it is highly noteworthy that it [the sexual release] was not linked to the assault when this was experienced. Here we have the case of a memory arousing an affect which it did not arouse as an experience, because in the meantime the change [brought about] in puberty had made possible a different understanding of what was remembered.
>
> Now this case is typical of repression in hysteria. We invariably find that a memory is repressed which has only become a trauma by *deferred action*. The cause of this state of things is the retardation of puberty as compared with the rest of the individual's development.
>
> [...] Every adolescent individual has memory-traces which can only be understood with the emergence of sexual feelings of his own; and accordingly every adolescent must carry the germ of hysteria within him. [ibid., p. 356]

Commenting on Emma's case, Freud had thus observed that the germ of hysteria could be detected in all adolescents, even though only an exiguous number of them would then develop the disease. Furthermore, this germ was connected with the adolescent's sexual emotions. In the same letter from 14 November 1897 Freud had also claimed that "disgust appears earlier in little girls than in boys", subsequently further characterising the differentiation between the sexes as follows:

> But the main distinction between the sexes emerges at the time of puberty, when girls are seized by a *non*neurotic *sexual* repugnance and males by libido. For at that period a further sexual zone is (wholly or in part) extinguished in females which persists in males. I am thinking of the male genital zone, the region of the clitoris, in which during childhood sexual sensitivity is shown to be concentrated in girls as well. [Masson, 1985, 14 November 1897, p. 280]

This further confirms the fact that, at the moment of the kiss, when she was nearly fourteen, Dora could have been in the phase of "nonneurotic sexual repugnance" that marks the period of puberty: categorising her reaction of disgust as "hysterical" could consequently appear as more of an insult than a correct diagnosis by Freudian standards. However, if when he expressed this judgement Freud had had in mind what he had claimed four years before in *The Aetiology of Hysteria* (1896c)—namely, that "the reaction of hysterics is only apparently exaggerated; it is bound to appear exaggerated to us because we only know a small part of the motives from which it arises"[6] (*S. E., 3*, p. 217)—thus, we may presume, he had realised that this exaggerated reaction had to be motivated by a cause, which must have derived from the patient's remote childhood. Yet Freud says nothing of this, because he did nothing to help Dora retrieve the memory of old traumatic scenes, busy as he was trying to convince his patient of her passion for Herr K. Furthermore, Dora did not even allow him the time to do so, since she took her leave after numerous clues that the archaeologist of the psyche of *The Aetiology of Hysteria* had become a "burglar", who used with her, as he told Fliess, his collection of picklocks. It is difficult to understand why, with Dora, Freud would have dwelled on scenes from puberty if he had already known, in 1896, that these were not the scenes responsible for hysteria, given that "the consistency with which the proposition that symptoms can only proceed from memories is carried through in hysteria. None of the later scenes, in which the symptoms arise, are the effective ones; and the experiences which *are* effective have at first no result" (*S. E., 3*, p. 213). Yet in January 1899 Freud had largely, though not definitively, abandoned his seduction theory, and was elaborating his theory of the hysterical fantasies, for which episodes from puberty were acquiring importance, while infantile traumas were already being relegated to the background. On 30 January 1899, he wrote to Fliess:

> Puberty is becoming ever more central; fantasy as the key holds fast. Yet there is still nothing big or complete. [Masson, 1985, p. 342]

The letter to Fliess, herein examined, continues by taking into account the neurotic side of the issue:

> And now for the neuroses! Experiences in childhood which merely affect the genitals never produce neurosis in males (or masculine females), but only a compulsion to masturbate and libido. But since as a rule experiences in childhood have also affected the two other sexual zones, the possibility remains open for males, too, that libido

> awakening through deferred action may lead to repression and to neurosis. Insofar as memory has lighted upon an experience connected with the genitals, what it produces by deferred action is libido. Insofar as it has lighted upon an experience connected with the anus, mouth, and so on, it produces deferred *internal disgust* [...] [Masson, 1985, 14 November 1897, pp. 280–281]

To put it bluntly, and paraphrasing Freud, we can conclude that for Dora the memory of her tubercular father stank as much as Herr K., and it could only have produced *deferred internal disgust* in her, which manifested itself in a violent nausea.

If we can assign Dora, because of her gynaecophilic tendency, to the category of "masculine females" in Freud's terms, then Freudian theory would once more lead us to presume that the "deferred internal disgust" shown by Dora testifies to infantile sexual experiences connected not to the genital zone but to the other two, and perhaps especially the oral zone. If we keep in mind that Dora's father, because of his impotence, had oral sex with Frau K., we can also presume that any alleged sexual abuse of little Dora would have implied involvement of the oral zone, especially because he knew of the oral predisposition of the little "thumb-sucker", whom he claimed to have weaned off this habit. Unfortunately, we do not know how Dora's father weaned her off the habit of sucking her thumb, which continued until the age of four or five, and I will refrain from giving vent to any flights of fancy here. All we know is that

> Dora herself had a clear picture of a scene from her early childhood in which she was sitting on the floor in a corner sucking her left thumb and at the same time tugging with her right hand at the lobe of her brother's ear as he sat quietly beside her. [p. 51][7]

Yet, could this memory be just a screen memory, used to cover an older and less innocent episode of a sexual nature? Freud had inferred a possible screen memory from Dora's claim that "she had been able to keep abreast with her brother up to the time of her first illness" (p. 82, n. 1) and that she would initially keep up with him in their studies, while she would later leave behind. Freud still does not have any suspicion in relation to this memory of Dora's. He affirms that a screen memory is the fruit of a compromise: the memory does not refer to the original episode, but to another, to which it is linked by contiguity[8] (in a spatial or temporal sense): a rather banal one, which thus makes it possible to keep the element that could create conflict removed [*Screen Memories* (1899), S. E., 3, p. 307]. Hence he concludes:

> Further investigation of these indifferent childhood memories has taught me that they can originate in other ways as well and that *an unsuspected wealth of meaning lies concealed behind their apparent innocence.* [ibid., p. 309; italics added]

Dora's memory of sucking her thumb while squeezing her brother's lobe in the other hand presents all the necessary characteristics to be identified as a screen memory. It is, first of all, a memory belonging to the patient's early childhood, and a completely innocent, trivial one, which does not display any relevant element that justifies its fixation in memory in such detail. These characteristics would in themselves be sufficient to classify it as screen memory. Yet, this innocent memory of an oral, autoerotic stimulation could represent the substitute of another oral stimulation of an erotic nature, which is chronologically contiguous to the one referring to this banal event. Were this true, the traumatic memory of a sexual stimulation would have been denied access to memory, because of the resistance, which would have displaced the memory onto a temporally contiguous episode, one closely associated with it from the point of view of the content of the repressed memory. Now, in Dora's memory, the "close association" is given by the fact that this innocent and banal memory from very early childhood refers to an autoerotic oral stimulation, which presumably happened at the same time as the assumed traumatic sexual event rejected by consciousness.

After all, in *The Aetiology of Hysteria* (1896c) Freud had been bluntly explicit about the perverse sexual practices that involved children who would later develop hysterical symptoms. He also describes the perverse adult in a way that inevitably makes us think of Dora's father, especially in the references to the expedients that the impotent person uses to satisfy his own sexual desires:

> *they include all the abuses known to debauched and impotent persons, among whom the buccal cavity and the rectum are misused for sexual purposes* […] People who have no hesitation in satisfying their sexual

desires upon children cannot be expected to jib a finer shades in the methods of obtaining that satisfaction; and the sexual impotence which is inherent in children inevitably forces them into *the same substitutive actions as those to which adults descend if they become impotent*. All the singular conditions under which the ill-matched pair conduct their love-relations—on the one hand the adult, who cannot escape his share in the mutual dependence necessarily entailed by a sexual relationship, and who is yet armed with complete authority and the right to punish, and can exchange the one role for the other to the uninhibited satisfaction of his moods, and on the other hand the child, who in his helplessness is at the mercy of this arbitrary will, who is prematurely aroused to every kind of sensibility and exposed to every sort of disappointment, and whose performance of the sexual activities assigned to him is often interrupted by his imperfect control of his natural needs—all these grotesque and yet tragic incongruities reveal themselves as stamped upon the later development of the individual and of his neurosis, in countless permanent effects which deserve to be traced in the greatest detail. [*The Aetiology of Hysteria* (1896c), S. E., 3, pp. 214–215; italics added]

The obsessive character of Dora's reproaches towards her father, and the relentless repetition of the same thoughts about her father's sexual relationship with Frau K., do not arouse in Freud the suspicion that Dora wanted to unconsciously reproach her father for an older, and even more illicit relationship than the present one. Yet he had acknowledged that:

this excessively intense train of thought must owe its reinforcement to the unconscious. It cannot be resolved by any effort of thought, either because it itself reaches with its root down into unconscious, repressed material, or because another unconscious thought lies concealed behind it. In the latter case, the concealed thought is usually the direct contrary of the supervalent one. [pp. 54–55]

The conscious thought, intensely invested, Freud claims, is a *reactive thought* that has the function of keeping a repressed thought buried in the unconscious. Only by bringing the repressed contrary thought into consciousness is it possible to deprive the *reactive thought* of its intensity.

Let us see, then, what is for Freud the unconscious root of the obsessive reproaches that Dora addresses to her father:

> Her behaviour obviously went far beyond what would have been appropriate to filial concern. She felt and acted more like a jealous wife—in a way which would have been comprehensible in her mother. [p. 56]

Through her reproaches, Dora was putting herself in her mother's place and, through her cough, which was derived from unconscious fantasies of oral sex, she was putting herself in Frau K.'s. Freud deduces from this that Dora was in love with her father. He had reached this conclusion through a particular way of expressing herself on Dora's part, which he deliberately omits, concerning the fact that Frau K. only loved her father because he was "a man of means" ("ein *vermögender* Mann"). Reversing Dora's words to signify the contrary, as he frequently did during the treatment, Freud concludes that what Dora really intended to say was that her father was sexually impotent (*unvermögender*), that is "a man without means", and that with this expression she was alluding to the fact that he had oral sex with Frau K. After having ascertained that Dora knew what the practice of *fellatio* consisted of, though she could not indicate the source of this knowledge, Freud draws her attention to the fact that she was alluding to a sexual practice involving the throat and the oral cavity. That is, "precisely those parts of the body which in her case were in a state of irritation" (p. 47). Yet, "she would not hear of going so far as this in recognizing her own thoughts" (p. 48), although "if the occurrence of the symptom was to be made possible at all, it was essential that she should not be completely clear on the subject" (p. 48).[9]

Freud does not hesitate in concluding that, "with her spasmodic cough, which, as is usual, was referred for its exciting stimulus to a tickling in her throat, she pictured to herself a scene of sexual gratification *per os* between the two people whose love-affair occupied her mind so incessantly" (p. 48). Dora accepted this interpretation "tacitly", which in Freud's diplomatic language means that she did nothing to contradict it. However, she did nothing to confirm it either. Also, the fact that the cough disappeared not long afterwards could not be understood as a definite confirmation of the interpretation, "since her cough had so often before disappeared spontaneously" (p. 48). Yet the lack of confirmation on Dora's part did not discourage our "burglar" who, displaying a curiously less considerate attitude towards his patient after these alleged oral fantasies, declared to his readers and to his hypocritical colleagues who declined to deal with these so-called sexual perversions, which "are very widely diffused among the whole population" (p. 51), that:

> So it is not to be wondered at that this hysterical girl of nearly nineteen,[10] who had heard of the occurrence of such a method of sexual intercourse (sucking at the male organ), should have developed an unconscious phantasy of this sort and should have given it expression by an irritation in her throat and by coughing. [p. 51]

A factor that facilitated the formation of this fantasy in Dora's case, according to Freud, was that somatic precondition of having sucked her thumb during early childhood. Her past of "thumb-sucking" predisposed her, therefore, to a *fellatio* fantasy, which nevertheless had its remote origin in the completely innocent memory of breast-feeding and thus of sucking at the maternal nipple.

> So we see that this excessively repulsive and perverted phantasy of sucking at a penis has the most innocent origin. It is a new version of what may be described as a prehistoric impression of sucking at the mother's or nurse's breast—an impression which has usually been revived by contact with children who are being nursed. [p. 52][11]

Moi (1990) identifies in the definition of *fellatio* as an "excessively repulsive and perverted phantasy" a defensive reaction-formation on Freud's part. "It is little wonder that he feels the need to defend himself against the idea of fellatio, since it is more than probable that the fantasy exists, not in Dora's mind, but in his alone" (p. 190).

Freud situates the *fellatio* fantasy at the root of Dora's cough, immediately after having affirmed something that seems itself pre-emptively contradictory of the link between the symptom and the phantasy. He claims:

> According to a rule which I had found confirmed over and over again by experience, though I had not yet ventured to erect it into

> a general principle, a symptom signifies the representation—the realization—of a phantasy with a sexual content, that is to say, it signifies a sexual situation. It would be better to say that at least *one* of the meanings of a symptom is the representation of a sexual phantasy, but that no such limitation is imposed upon the content of its other meanings. [p. 47]

Right afterwards, he adds that "a symptom has more than one meaning and serves to represent several unconscious mental processes simultaneously" (p. 47), while nonetheless explaining that "a single unconscious mental process or phantasy will scarcely ever suffice for the production of a symptom" (p. 47). Yet Freud identified no other fantasies or meanings behind this symptom, and declared that soon after his interpretation of the symptom as *fellatio* phantasy, the cough disappeared: "But I do not wish to lay too much stress upon this development; since her cough had so often before disappeared spontaneously" (p. 48). Thus a symptom, the cough, an otherwise unlikely candidate for classification as a hysterical symptom in Freud's terms (because produced by one phantasy only), disappeared after Freud interpreted it in light of that perversion which is "very widely diffused among the whole population".

In fact, if my argument that Dora suffered sexual abuse at the hands of her father is true, her father would have himself been placing Dora in her mother's position, seeking from her those sexual gratifications denied to him by his wife. In identifying herself with Frau K., Dora was in turn reminding her father of having herself been his lover, not willingly, like Frau K., but forcedly. Freud acknowledged that Dora's oedipal inclination for her father could have become so intense "that it turns into something [...] which must be put on a par with a sexual inclination" (p. 56) because of "certain other influences, which need not be discussed here", and that he preferred to relegate to a footnote, namely *"no doubt the early appearance of true genital sensations, either spontaneously or as a result of seduction or masturbation"* (p. 57, n. 1; italics added).[12]

Freud's statement that external influences "need not be discussed here" is highly surprising, because what he had initially promised to his readers, with this case history, was, precisely, confirmation of his seduction theory, namely the fact that in the aetiology of hysteria he had identified the precocious occurrence, in the childhood of these patients, of genital sensations produced by acts of seduction.

This is the first time that Freud uses the term "seduction" in this essay, despite the fact that his declared intention was to confirm, through this case history, *The Aetiology of Hysteria* (1896c). In *Three Essays on the Theory of Sexuality* (1905d), which is contemporaneous to Dora's case history, the word seduction appears repeatedly with reference to infantile sexuality.[13] Speaking of masturbation, moreover, Freud affirms that during childhood external occasions bear great importance, especially seduction (at the hand of an adult or of another child), which introduces the child to genital satisfaction that he will later be forced to renew through masturbation. He then adds, on the question of seduction:

> I cannot admit that in my paper on 'The Aetiology of Hysteria' (1896c) I exaggerated the frequency or importance of that influence, though I did not then know that persons who remain normal may have had the same experiences in their childhood, and though I consequently overrated the importance of seduction in comparison with the factors of sexual constitution and development. [S. E., 7, pp. 190–191]

In the end, he acknowledges that infantile sexuality can also be stirred spontaneously through internal causes, though not through the intervention of seduction.

Although Freud was reading about Greek archaeology while treating Dora, he never cared to dig up the prehistory of this particular adolescent's childhood; he did not carry out any archaeological work, despite this being his favourite metaphor for defining the psychoanalytical investigation. On the contrary, drawing upon his description of the case to Fliess, one may infer that his work more closely resembled that of a burglar—with his attempts at forcing the girl with a collection of picklocks[14] representing a sexual metaphor that reveals his unconscious fantasies—than that of a scrupulous archaeologist.

Freud identifies in external circumstances, connected with Philip Bauer's numerous illnesses, the factors that favoured an intensification of Dora's relationship with her father:

> The nature of her disposition had always drawn her towards her father, and his numerous illnesses were bound to have increased her affection for him. In some of these illnesses he would allow no one but her to discharge the lighter duties of nursing. He had been

so proud of the early growth of her intelligence[15] that he had made her his confidante while she was still a child. It was really she and not her mother whom Frau K.'s appearance had driven out of more than one position. [p. 57]

Here, Freud seems too easily to overlook the fact that the father himself favoured such intimacy by "allow[ing] no one but her" at his bedside, and he does not grasp the analogy between this situation and that engendered by Herr K. in the scene at the shop, when he had suddenly managed to exclude his wife so as to remain alone with Dora. Furthermore, the father had forced Dora to precociously assume an adult role, making of her his confidante. Thus he had once more favoured a "conjugal" bond with Dora, and only the "discoverer of the oedipal complex" could see in this relationship the consequence of a "sexual inclination" on Dora's part for her father. Slipp (1977, p. 369) has observed that: "The father was a domineering, intelligent, charming, and promiscuous man, who was seductive towards Dora in his behaviour so much so that she considered herself almost as his wife".

Masud Khan (1989, p. 51), in his work *Grudge and the Hysteric* from 1974, asserts that there is "an *actual* trauma in the aetiology of hysteria but it is not of a sexual nature. It relates more to the failure of the mother to cater to the ego-needs of the child" (p. 51). If we follow Khan's hypothesis, the hysteric's grudge should be mostly addressed towards the mother, who had deprived her of the care and attention necessary during the period of her first development, hence when she needed them most, when, as Khan says, the recognition and facilitation of the ego-needs "was necessary".

Dora's grudge was not aimed at her mother, for whom she had, Freud reports, scarce consideration, and whom she even despised. Furthermore, "she had withdrawn completely from her influence" (p. 20). Dora's grudge was intended for her father, whom she had repeatedly accused and held responsible for both her psychic trouble and her vaginal leucorrhoea. There is no doubt that the description of Dora's mother is consonant with the mother figure describe by Khan, a figure unable to provide her offspring with adequate maternal care. Freud himself describes her as being affected by "housewife's psychosis", obsessively busy with her domestic cleaning, with "no understanding of her children's more active interests". If there were a reason for Dora to hold a grudge against her mother, it was for her absence, not only during the first years of her childhood and her psychosexual development, but also for the nonchalance with which she had exposed her, firstly, to paternal seduction, by ascribing her husband the task of weaning her off infantile enuresis, and, secondly, to the seduction of an "old" man, such as Herr K. would have appeared to the fourteen-year-old Dora, by letting her go to his shop alone and thus exposing her to that disgusting kiss which was the first trauma of her adolescence.

It could be maintained, following Freud's seduction theory, that an hysteric's grudge is justified by his infantile trauma and by the awareness of the absence of a helpful mother, or even by the suspicion or sense of maternal complicity with the perpetrator. The hysteric's profound mistrust is then prevalently directed towards male figures, precisely as a consequence of that basic misunderstanding of which Khan speaks, of that confusion of tongues that leads to a child's demand for tenderness being misunderstood as an erotic proposal. In Dora's case, the foremost responsibility for this misunderstanding lies with the father. He had put her in her mother's place, demanded her care only during his repeated periods of illness, made her his confidante and then exposed her, as an adolescent, to his friend's repeated, though maladroit, attempts at seduction. Dora's grudge towards her father and her repeated accusations were therefore more than justified. Khan, in his conceptualisation of hysteria, has nonetheless completely excluded the paternal figure, who held a pivotal role in Freud's seduction theory, while Freud, in his analysis of Dora, had completely excluded the maternal figure.

Freud had said: *"Hysterics suffer mainly from reminiscences"* (S. E., 2, p. 7). Paraphrasing, I think inadequately, the Freudian motto, Khan affirms that "the hysteric remembers par excellence through repetition" (p. 58), but repetition recalls the repetition-compulsion that is a typical modality of responding to the trauma. "Repetition is the mute language of the abused child" (Herman, 1992, p. 110). The hysteric's memories are written on her body, says Khan, correctly: "The hysteric remembers from early childhood largely somatic memories deriving from maternal care, which do not lend themselves to psychic elaboration and verbalisation" (p. 58). This idea that memories can neither be verbalised nor worked-through is consonant with the most recent neuroscientific theories which, as I discuss below, suggest that traumatic memories are deposited in an unrepressed unconscious that belongs to the realm of implicit memory. Yet it is equally plausible that these traumatic memories are ascribable not only to maternal negligence but also, and for good reason, to those traumatic events of a sexual nature that Freud had indicated in his earlier aetiology of hysteria.

To validate my hypothesis, I will quote Ferenczi's assertions on the crisis of the hysteric (20 March 1932) taken from his *Clinical Diary*. From the following quotation, one can deduce that Ferenczi has drawn on and developed Freud's theory of premature sexual trauma, adapting his therapeutic technique accordingly, and developing a far more empathic relationship with the patient than the ironic detachment with which Freud had greeted Dora:

> Observation of a case in which in relaxation ('trance') opistho-tonic positions did appear: [...] the position was a reaction to a feeling of painful excitation in the genital passage [...]: in this position, psychic unpleasure and defence against ardent desire are simultaneously represented. *With the help of exchange of questions and answers it could be established that this state of excitation has been implanted by the father, with the help of gentle shaking and seductive words and promises* ... a scene is reproduced in which the father takes the child in his lap and actually makes use of her. [Ferenczi, 1985, pp. 63–64; italics added]

Among the elements that led to treatment succeeding, Ferenczi lists the following factors:

> The major factor in this favorable result may well be the process of the unconscious becoming conscious, that is, the reparation of the original trauma through spontaneous elucidations and those I provide; the knowing, that is to say, the overcoming of those factors which produce not-knowing (anxiety, fragmentation) introduces a part of the trauma into the mainstream of the total personality [...]. A second, nonintellectual element or factor of the success is the patients' feeling that not only do we not despise them, [...] but we pity them and would gladly help them if it were within our power. We believe in their innocence, we love them as beings enticed into maturity against their will, and it is our aim that they should accept our compassion and understanding, admittedly an incomplete fulfilment of their hopes for the time being, until life offers them something better. [ibid., p. 65]

Unfortunately, life did not offered Dora "something better".

CHAPTER FOUR

From archaeologist to burglar

In *The Aetiology of Hysteria* (1896c) Freud specifies with precision the characters that the traumatic scene should possess in order to produce a pathogenic effect:

> For let us be clear on this point. Trácing a hysterical symptom back to a traumatic scene assists our understanding only if the scene satisfies two conditions; if it possesses the relevant *suitability to serve as a determinant* and if it recognizably possesses the necessary *traumatic force*. [S. E., 3, p. 193]

In Dora's story, there are two scenes that Freud defines as traumatic: the scene by the lake, wherein Herr K. made advances on Dora, making her understand that he was not obtaining any sexual gratification from his wife, and the scene of the kiss in the shop, which had occurred two years beforehand, when Dora was not yet fourteen, "which was even better calculated to act as a sexual trauma" (p. 27). In fact, the scene of the kiss, assuming that it possessed the *suitability as a determinant*, and that it was therefore capable of engendering a traumatic effect, surely did not possess the other precondition, namely, the *traumatic force*. As a matter of fact, in order to ascribe the necessary traumatic force to the event, Freud needs to imagine that during that passionate yet quick embrace, Dora felt the pressure of Herr K.'s erect penis on her body, to which she responded with an analogous clitoral arousal.[1]

In *The Aetiology of Hysteria* (1896c) Freud had expressed his thoughts on the matter very clearly, and was aware that reconstructing one's infantile past could be neither quick nor easy,

> and the fact that the scenes are uncovered in a reversed chronological order (a fact which justifies our comparison of the work with the excavation of a stratified ruined site) certainly contributes nothing to a more rapid understanding of what has taken place. [S. E., 3, p. 198]

Thus Freud was not satisfied with the first traumatic scene that had emerged; he was aware that behind the hysteric symptom "a chain of operative memories" was concealed, "which stretches far back behind the first traumatic scene" (S. E., 3, p. 197). And if this scene did not possess the pathogenic requirement he had indicated, he was determined

> to pursue the same path a little further; perhaps behind the first traumatic scene there may be concealed the memory of a second, which satisfies our requirements better and whose reproduction has a greater therapeutic effect; so that the scene that was first discovered only has the significance of a connecting link in the chain of association. And perhaps this situation may repeat itself; inoperative scenes may be interpolated more than once, as necessary transitions in the process of reproduction, until we finally make our way from the hysterical symptom to the scene which is really operative traumatically and which is satisfactory in every respect, both therapeutically and analytically. [S. E., 3, p. 195]

With Dora, Freud did not delve so far back in time. Rather, he was satisfied with the scene of the kiss, which he judged to be "even better calculated to act as a sexual trauma". He did not undertake to excavate older scenes, which would have been more appropriate for acting as sexual trauma, because after repudiating his *neurotica*,[2] he had also left aside his archaeologist's tools and picked up his burglar's picklocks.

In 1896, when archaeology was still his heuristic model, Freud had explained the problem of the traumatic scenes as follows:

> Eventually, then, after the chains of memories have converged, we come to the field of sexuality and to a small number of experiences which occur for the most part at the same period of life—namely, at puberty. It is in these experiences, it seems, that we are to look for the aetiology of hysteria, and through them that we are to learn to understand the origin of hysterical symptoms. [S. E., 3, p. 200]

Yet these episodes, while they share the two characters of sexuality and puberty, differ in terms of kind and importance: in some instances we have episodes with a real traumatic force, while in other cases these experiences are "astonishingly trivial" (S. E., 3, p. 200). Freud concludes that these latter episodes "lack suitability as determinants" (p. 201); thus the analyst will have to continue with the analytical work, seeking to determine symptoms in episodes even further back in time.

> [...] *In doing so, to be sure, we arrive at the period of earliest childhood,* a period before the development of sexual life; and this would seem to involve the abandonment of a sexual aetiology. *But have we not a right to assume that even the age of childhood is not wanting in slight sexual excitations, that later sexual development may perhaps be decisively influenced by childhood experiences?* [...] *Perhaps the abnormal reaction to sexual impression which surprises us in hysterical subjects at the age of puberty is quite generally based on sexual experiences of this sort in childhood, in which case those experiences must be of a similar nature to one another, and must be of an important kind.* If this is so, the prospect is opened up that what has hitherto had to be laid at the door of a still unexplained hereditary predisposition may be accounted for as having been acquired at an early age. [S. E., 3, pp. 201–202; italics added]

Freud thus comes to confirm a fundamental aetiological principle:

> We have learned that *no hysterical symptom can arise from a real experience alone, but that in every case the memory of earlier experiences awakened in association to it plays a part in causing the symptom.*

> If—as I believe—this proposition holds good *without exception*, it furthermore shows us the basis on which a psychological theory of hysteria must be built. [S. E., 3, p. 197]

Also, later, in *The Interpretation of Dreams* (1900a), Freud reiterates the link between the recent trauma and the old offence:

> A humiliation that was experienced thirty years ago acts exactly like a fresh one throughout the thirty years, as soon as it has obtained access to the unconscious sources of emotion. As soon as the memory of it is touched, it springs into life again and shows itself cathected with excitation which finds a motor discharge in an attack. [S. E., 5, pp. 577–578]

Therefore, the careful archaeological work necessary in order to bring to light important pieces of one's past will be successful only if the archaeologist retains the required constancy, and a good degree of optimistic perseverance. Proceeding with the analysis until the first childhood memories are arrived at, the patient will recollect those episodes which, as a result of their character and relation to symptoms only emerged later, and which constitute the aetiological factor of neuroses. These infantile experiences are still of a sexual nature but present a higher uniformity with respect to the puberty episodes. These are "sexual experiences affecting the subject's own body—of *sexual intercourse* (in the wider sense)" (S. E., 3, p. 203).

> I therefore put forward the thesis that at the bottom of every case of hysteria there are *one or more occurrences of premature sexual experience*, occurrences which belong to the earliest years of childhood but which can be reproduced through the work of psychoanalysis in spite of the intervening decades. I believe that this is an important finding, the discovery of a *caput Nili* in neuropathology. [S. E., 3, p. 203]

Freud will insist on the actuality of these infantile sexual scenes and on a series of elements that support them, from the intense affectivity accompanying the recollection of these traumatic memories, to the relative uniformity of these scenes, and the relation to these infantile scenes of the content of the patient's entire clinical history. Yet, he also bases the authenticity of the infantile traumatic scenes on therapeutic evidence, that is to say on the fact that:

> There are cases in which a complete or partial cure can be obtained without our having to go as deep as the infantile experiences. And there are others in which no success at all is obtained until the analysis has come to its natural end with the uncovering of the earliest traumas. In the former cases we are not, I believe, secure against relapses; and my expectation is that a complete psycho-analysis implies a radical cure of the hysteria. [S. E., 3, p. 206]

Dora's case seems to belong to the latter category, yet the failure of the therapy cannot be attributed to her premature abandonment of it, because this event itself testifies to its lack of success. Notwithstanding the brevity of this analysis, Freud could nevertheless have examined the traumatic aspects of Dora's childhood in greater depth, especially by giving due attention to the two dreams Dora had put at his disposal.

Over the course of Dora's analysis, Freud did not seek to retrieve infantile scenes and was satisfied with working, as we would say today, on *the here and now*, that is, on Dora's recent traumas, without carrying out a reconstruction of her infantile past. Mahony (1996, p. 90) has observed that by analysing "the first dream, Freud focuses to a large extent on relating Dora's lakeside trauma to her childhood, whereas in analysing the second he concentrates nearly exclusively on relating the lakeside trauma to her recent past." But even when he had gone back to Dora's childhood, the only sexual evidence he had unearthed were traces of infantile masturbation, and surely not the episodes that he had described in 1896 as "*a precocious experience of sexual relations with actual excitement of the genitals, resulting from sexual abuse committed by another person*" (S. E., 3, p. 152), episodes that had to have taken place during childhood, before the age of eight to ten.

Freud had a preconceived thesis to demonstrate, namely that Dora's passion for Herr K. (as well as for her father, and maybe also her analyst who, similarly to Herr K. and the father, stank of cigars). To achieve such a goal, he would not need the hoes, shovels, and spades indispensable to an archaeologist. A good collection of picklocks would be enough to break open Dora's "jewel-case".

In *The Aetiology of Hysteria* (1896c) Freud had reached the conclusion that:

> the aetiological pretensions of the infantile scenes rest not only on the regularity of their appearance in the anamneses of hysterics, but, above all, on the evidence of there being associative and logical ties between those scenes and the hysterical symptoms—evidence which, if you were given the complete history of a case, would be as clear as daylight to you. [S. E., 3, p. 210]

However, the *Fragment of an Analysis of a Case of Hysteria* (1905e) would also have been sufficient to unveil the associative and logical connections between Dora's symptoms and a precocious sexual trauma, if only Freud had undertaken to search for a traumatic event in his patient's childhood, instead of retreating to those episodes that occurred during puberty which, in 1896, he would have judged as "astonishingly trivial". Freud's position is even more incomprehensible if one considers the fact that, in *Heredity and the Aetiology of the Neuroses* (1896a), he had clearly expressed his opinion on the role played by sexual episodes occurring after puberty:

> All the events subsequent to puberty to which an influence must be attributed upon the development of the hysterical neurosis and upon the formation of its symptoms are in fact only concurrent causes—"*agents provocateurs*" as Charcot used to say, though for him nervous heredity occupied the place which I claim for the precocious sexual experience [...] analysis demonstrates in an irrefutable fashion that they enjoy a pathogenic influence for hysteria only owing to their faculty for awakening the unconscious psychical trace of the childhood event. [S. E., 3, pp. 154–155]

In that same work Freud had also clearly expressed the necessity of shedding some light on these traumatic episodes from childhood, in order to obtain a prompt therapeutic effect. He had also declared that working on the accessory causes, the *agents provocateurs*, meant giving up on the possibility of a radical healing. Yet the moment he took Dora into treatment, he seemed to have forgotten those suggestions he had himself repeatedly given to his colleagues throughout the year 1896:

The precocious event has left an indelible imprint on the history of the case; it is represented in it by a host of symptoms and of special features which could be accounted for in no other way; it is peremptorily called for by the subtle but solid interconnections of the intrinsic structure of the neurosis; *the therapeutic effect of the analysis lags behind if one has not penetrated so far*; and one is then left with no choice but to reject or to believe the whole. [S. E., 3, 1896a, p. 153; italics added]

[...] a consideration of these stock causes may offer lines of approach to a *therapy which does not aim at a radical cure* and is content with repressing the illness to its former state of latency. [ibid., p. 148; italics added]

When our procedure leads [...] to findings which are insufficient as an explanation both in respect to their suitability as determinants and to their traumatic effectiveness, *we also fail to secure any therapeutic gain*; the patient retains his symptoms unaltered, in spite of the initial result yielded by the analysis. [S. E., 3, 1896c, p. 195; italics added]

Had Freud remembered these observations, maybe he would not have needed to ask himself, in the *Postscript* to the case history, where he might have failed Dora. He would have immediately realised that the therapeutic failure derived from the fact that he had not gone far enough back in time to reconstruct the infantile scenes. Perhaps he would have also understood that it had been a mistake to abandon the archaeologist's tools for the easier job with the burglar's picklocks.

CHAPTER FIVE

The dream of the burning house

> *A house was on fire. My father was standing beside my bed and woke me up. I dressed quickly. Mother wanted to stop and save her jewel-case; but Father said: "I refuse to let myself and my two children be burnt for the sake of your jewel-case." We hurried downstairs, and as soon as I was outside I woke up.* [p. 64]

The dream of the burning house is a recurring one,[1] which Dora had for the first time during her holiday on the lake, presumably right after the episode involving Herr K. It was then repeated for three nights in a row. The dream later occurred once again in Vienna, during the period of her analysis, just when it *"would throw light upon an obscure point in Dora's childhood"* (p. 64; italics added).

So, on the first occasion, the dream had been instigated by the episode on the lake with Herr K., while on the second occasion, it occurred when the patient was clarifying "an obscure point of her childhood" with her analyst. As is perhaps to be expected, then, an analogy can be found between the two day residues that had engendered the recurrence of the same dream, namely, the scene on the lake with Herr K. and the obscure childhood episode.

Acting as a hypothetical opponent of his dream theory, Freud claims that Dora's dream "has shown itself in the first instance to be the continuation into sleep of an intention formed during the day" (p. 68). Freud provides Dora with the following interpretation:

> But your dream recurred each night, for the very reason that it corresponded to an intention. An intention remains in existence until it has been carried out. You said to yourself, as it were: "I shall have no rest and I can get no quiet sleep until I am out of this house". In your account of the dream you turned it the other way and said: *"As soon as I was outside I woke up."* [p. 67]

Let us put aside, for the time being, the recent episode with Herr K., and keep in mind that Freud himself draws attention to "the way in which the dream worked into the analysis as a whole" (p. 64). Therefore, we cannot avoid considering the dream in connection with what was happening in the analysis, since during the same period light was being "throw[n] upon an obscure point in Dora's childhood" (p. 64). The thought, as Freud suggests, that lies behind the manifest content of the dream is, one may imagine, precisely "the continuation into sleep of an intention formed during the day" (p. 68). However, it does not refer to the contingency of Dora's relationship with Herr K., but rather to that obscure episode from her childhood in which, according to the dream, her father is the protagonist. Freud will not satisfy the reader's curiosity on this point, as he does not reveal what he knew or had deduced about the nature of this obscure childhood episode.

A possible day residue in this dream, which could lead us to consider the figures of the father and Herr K. as corresponding to one another, can be found in what Dora had heard about the relationship between Herr K. and his wife, who had seldom spoken about divorce, "but it never took place, because Herr K., who was an affectionate father, would not give up either of the two children" (p. 37).

Hence, the fear of losing both of one's children could be attributed to both Herr K. and Dora's father's. After all, the most recent event to bring about the recurrence of the dream in Vienna was an argument between Dora's parents, caused by the mother's habit of locking the dining room at night, which was the only way out from (and into) Dora's brother's bedroom. Dora's father was annoyed by this habit because he thought *"something might happen in the night so that it might be necessary to leave the room"* (p. 65). Locking the door would not only have impeded Otto from leaving his bedroom but would also have prevented anybody from entering the room, including his father. This could perhaps be the real reason why this neurotic housewife had taken up the bizarre habit of confining her son. We also know that Otto suffered from enuresis, and for even longer than his sister. Freud's account reveals, however, that the father had only been accorded the task of weaning Dora off this habit, and not his son. If Otto had taught Dora how to masturbate, it follows, according to Freud's theory, that his habit of masturbating was most probably roused by paternal seduction. What about Dora's neurotic mother, then, with her obsessive nature and bizarre habits, whose sole concern was the cleaning of the house? One may argue that she had guessed at the occurrence of some night time intrusion by the father into Otto's bedroom and wanted to protect Otto by locking him up in his room; by means of her obsessive rituals, she had actually meant to protect her children from being infected by a syphilitic and tubercular father. Despite Freud's scornful opinion of Dora's mother, she could by no means have been unaware that by blocking all ways out of her son's bedroom, she would achieve nothing but prolong his enuresis. Yet, perhaps she considered this to be the lesser of two evils, considering the worst that could happen to her son.

In the dream, the father is in Dora's bedroom. He does not act like a father who, distressed by an imminent peril, leans on his child's bed and awakens her so as to rescue her. Rather, he stands still, like a voyeur. His attitude too closely resembles that of Herr K. for us to avoid supposing that the same thoughts were crossing his mind as had crossed Herr K.'s. The latter had entered Dora's bedroom while she was sleeping, and had observed her in silence.

But where, one might ask, does the thought presented by Freud to the patient as a latent one of her own—namely, that, "I shall have no rest and I can get no quiet sleep until I am out of this house"—come from? Considering the way in which the analyst presents it to the patient, it appears neither to be included in the manifest thoughts of the dream, nor to derive from Dora's associations. Might it belong, then, to Freud's unconscious? Had Freud unconsciously realised that the scene of the dream had something to do with that obscure episode from Dora's childhood?

Yet, since the beginning Freud had displayed a certain admiration for Dora's father, for his intelligence and the qualities of his character. He therefore could not believe that he had had the same thoughts about his daughter that Herr K. might have had, even if in his previous writings he had acknowledged the importance of "paternal aetiology" in hysteria. Freud himself had linked Herr K.'s attitude, staring at Dora while she was asleep in her bedroom, to Dora's father's manner, "standing beside your bed in the dream" (p. 66). Nevertheless, he would not carry this association any further, neither when he was faced with "a parallel line of thoughts, in which Herr K. is to be put in the place of your father" (p. 70) nor when he had pieced together Dora's thoughts in the following way: "My 'jewel-case' is in danger, and if anything happens it will be Father's fault" (p. 69).[2]

Having to choose, according to his take on enuresis, between either accusing the father of seduction or blaming Dora for her masturbatory habit, Freud chooses the latter. This is also because the first would have led him to also lay the blame on the father for his son's enuresis, which lasted even longer.

When he analyses the part of the dream that involves the jewel-case, Freud contradicts himself and utilises shifts of meaning to absolve Dora's father and inculpate the patient. Through a game of word substitution that looks more like hocus-pocus than the translation of a metalanguage, Freud comes to the conclusion that Dora was "ready to give [her] father what [her] mother withheld from him" (p. 70). Yet there is no need to juggle with the truth in order to arrive at the conclusion that, as I intend to demonstrate, the father was willing to obtain from Dora what his wife was denying him. Dora rightly asks herself why, in the dream she had at the lake, the mother is present as well, because at the time she was in fact not there. Yet, her astonishment might also derive from a dream that puts on stage the father's seduction of an infant Dora, for an abused child knows all too well that the mother is always absent from the scene and pretends not to be aware of what is going on.

It would appear, once again, that Freud is on the right track, that he is on the trail of a "pater" responsible for hysteria, as he once said to Fliess, when speaking of the dream that stands, as it were, upon two legs:

> one of which is in contact with the main and current exciting cause, and the other with some momentous event in the years of childhood. *The dream sets up a connection between those two factors—the event during childhood and the event of the present day—and it endeavours to*

re-shape the present on the model of the remote past. For the wish which creates the dream always springs from the period of childhood; and it is continually trying to summon childhood back into reality and to correct the present day by the measure of childhood. I believed that I could already clearly detect those elements of Dora's dream which could be pieced together into an allusion to an event in childhood. [p. 71; italics added]

We will later find out that Freud was, in fact, only on the trail of Dora's infantile masturbation: this could not relate to the obscure episode from her childhood, charged with consequences. Here, we are once again faced with an insurmountable obstacle which denies Freud the possibility of confirming his theories of 1896 on the traumatic aetiology of hysteria, insofar as, back then, in *Further Remarks on the Neuro-Psychoses of Defence* (1896b), he had excluded infantile *"active masturbation"* with absolute certainty from belonging to those sexual practices that played an aetiological role in hysteria. He peremptorily affirmed that: "Although it is found so very often side by side with hysteria, this is due to the circumstance that *masturbation itself is a much more frequent consequence of abuse or seduction than is supposed*" (S. E., 3, p. 165; italics added).

So if, after discovering Dora's infantile masturbation, Freud had performed the work of a scrupulous archaeologist on her case, he would have kept on digging into her psyche to track down the origins of that early trauma, that sexual seduction which could have induced the patient's masturbatory behaviour pattern. Yet, since Freud had substituted thorough archaeological work, for the hastier attitude of the burglar, he was satisfied with the first findings that came to light through the use of his "picklocks".

Beyond the possible lack of application of the psychoanalytical technique to this case history, the most recurrent impression it gives us is of an aware or unaware desire, on Freud's part, to avoid the theme of paternal sexual trauma in his interpretations. When he goes from fire to water to bed-wetting, Freud correctly remembers the habit of waking the child up in order to stop her from wetting the bed, as Dora's father does in the dream, telling his patient that: "This, then, must be the actual occurrence which enabled you to substitute your father for Herr K." (p. 72). Even more so, Dora could have substituted Herr K.'s attempts at seduction with real episodes from her childhood involving her father's seduction, and all of her symptoms in fact pointed to this.

But when it comes to investing infantile masturbation with the importance of an effective aetiological factor in Dora's hysteria, Freud begins to tergiversate and become insecure. In the end, he does not provide us with an answer:

> Instead of answering "Yes" or "No" to the question whether the aetiology of this case is to be looked for in masturbation during childhood, I should first have to discuss the concept of aetiology as applied to the psychoneuroses [...] Let it suffice if we can reach the conviction that in this case the occurrence of masturbation in childhood is established, and that its occurrence cannot be an accidental element nor an immaterial one in the conformation of the clinical picture. [pp. 81–82]

If Freud were thinking of attributing some relevance to infantile masturbation not only as a triggering factor of hysteria, but as also being somehow involved in its aetiology, because it "cannot be an accidental element nor an immaterial one in the conformation of the clinical picture", then we must conclude that, instead of "corroborating" his ideas on premature sexual traumas as aetiological factors, he had in fact regressed here to pre-psychoanalytical theories. It seems that Freud is returning here to notions he had encountered during his paediatric training in Berlin, with Adolf Baginsky, according to whom masturbation was the cause of hysteria (see Bonomi, 2009). Indeed, around the mid-nineteenth century "the nexus between hysteria, childhood and masturbation had begun to be emphasised [and] the vice is indicated as the cause of the gradual diffusion of hysteria in childhood" (Bonomi, 2007, p. 95). Here, Freud reveals himself to be "a child of his age", as he had himself confessed in a letter to Fliess, "and after all, it is known that even Freud remained persuaded that masturbation could cause organic damage" (Bonomi, 2007, p. 94). At this point, we could adopt the same metaphor Freud himself used to describe the reflux of inhibited neurotic sexuality, and argue that, in this case, the stream of Freud's ideas, blocked by the obstacle of Dora's infantile trauma, instead of flowing along the riverbed of the seduction theory, fill up the collateral—abandoned and dried-up—channel of masturbation as a cause of hysteria.

Although Freud shared ideas of his time about the ill-omened consequences of masturbation, the attentive reader cannot help but notice that the masturbation could not be the obscure episode, full of consequences, from Dora's childhood. Freud was only too aware, as he had learnt from Brouardel's lectures during his Parisian sojourn, that infantile sexual abuse bears many more consequences than mere masturbation.

Shortly after his recantation of the seduction theory, in his letter to Fliess of 21 September, with the words "I no longer believe in my *neurotica*",[3] Freud's thoughts turn to masturbation once more in his letter to Fliess of 27 October 1897. In this communication, he establishes a connection between masturbation and hysteria. Nonetheless, the issue of premature sexual experiences in childhood still occasionally inhabits his thoughts at this point. In this letter, Freud refers to the concept of resistance:

> Resistance, which finally brings the [analytic] work to a halt, is nothing other than the child's former character, the degenerative character, which developed or would have developed as a result of those experiences that one find as a conscious memory in the so-called degenerative cases, but which here is overlaid by the development of repression [...] This infantile character develops during the period of "longing", after the child has been removed from sexual experiences. Longing is the main character trait of hysteria, just as actual anaesthesia (even though only potential) is its main symptom. During this same period of longing fantasies are formed and masturbation is (regularly?) practiced, which then yields to repression. If it does not yield, then no hysteria develops either; the discharge of sexual excitation for the most part removes the possibility of hysteria. [Masson, 1985, 27 October 1897, pp. 274–275]

In this letter, masturbation is still somehow linked to premature sexual experiences, as Freud claims that it occurs in the period of longing, when the child has been deprived of those sexual experiences belonging to premature seduction. The infantile character would develop as a consequence of those sexual experiences and would manifest itself in the period of longing, that is, when they had come to an end and were repressed. Conversely, these experiences remain on the level of consciousness in degenerative cases. Freud reiterates here the thesis that he had already communicated to Fliess in his letter of 6 December 1896. In this clinical case, he formulates it as follows: "Psychoneuroses are, so to speak, the *negative* of perversion" (p. 50). Seduction still retains a central role here, because the repression of infantile sexual experiences results in infantile character and hysterical longing. In Dora's case, masturbation, for which the subject is solely responsible, is all that remains, and would act in light of the dark powers of vice.

Freud leads the reader on the track of seduction, through a series of references to Dora's childhood. These lead back to that "pater" whom he had once already found responsible for the hysteria, using the language of a "whodunit" that reminds us of some of the best works from that "period of seduction":

> The dream does in fact contain infantile material, though it is impossible at a first glance to discover any connections between that material and Dora's intention of flying from Herr K.'s house and the temptation of his presence. Why should a recollection have emerged of her bed-wetting when she was a child and of the trouble her father used to take to teach the child clean habits? [...] Her father was himself partly responsible for her present danger, for he had handed her over to this strange man in the interests of his own love-affair. [pp. 85–86]

Dora's wish, Freud tells us, is to substitute the strange seducer with her father. Had a similar situation occurred in the past,

> that situation would have become the main one in the dream. But there *had* been such a situation. Her father had once stood beside her bed, just as Herr K. had the day before, and had woken her up, with a kiss perhaps, as Herr K. may have meant to do. Thus her intention of flying from the house was not in itself capable of producing a dream; but it became so by being associated with another intention which was founded upon infantile wishes. The wish to replace Herr K. by her father provided the necessary motive power for the dream. [p. 86]

So far, we have more than one element that allows us to interpret Dora's dream as traumatic, reproducing a scene of infantile sexual seduction:

the infantile memory of the father weaning the child off enuresis and his co-responsibility in exposing her to Herr K.'s attempts at seduction; the substitution of the current seducer with her first seducer, namely, the father, which was responsible for the premature sexual enjoyment that Dora would subsequently strive to re-produce through masturbation. Then, rather, the meaning of Dora's dream could be to "again find the path to arousal" (Pontalis, 1990, p. 36), to return to her first infantile arousal and to the person responsible for it. Yet we know that Herr K.'s attempts at seduction aroused in Dora nothing but disgust and repulsion.

In *The Interpretation of Dreams* (1900a) Freud had claimed:

> The deeper one carries the analysis of a dream, the more often one comes upon the track of experiences in childhood which have played a part among the sources of that dream's latent content.
>
> [...] The general justification for inferring the occurrence of these childhood experiences from dreams is provided by a whole number of factors in psychoanalytic work, which are mutually consistent and thus seem sufficiently trustworthy. [S. E., 4, pp. 198–199]

In his analysis of Dora's two dreams, Freud made no attempt to reconstruct infantile traumatic scenes, on the basis of existing consistent material. Instead, he limited himself to reconciling all the elements of the dreams with his *a priori* thesis, according to which Dora's hysteria had originated from infantile masturbation. Using Dora's dreams, I will endeavour to display that sufficiently consistent elements emerge in order to corroborate the thesis of an infantile experience of a sexual nature, of which the father was the protagonist. Only ten years after the publication of *The Interpretation of Dreams* (1900a) Freud admitted, in an added footnote, that one of his patients "had been repeating in it the initial trauma from which her neurosis had arisen. I have since then come across the same behaviour in other patients; having been exposed to a sexual assault in their childhood, they seek, as it were, to bring about a repetition of it in their dreams." (S. E., 4, p. 185, fn. 1) This wish to bring about a repetition of the infantile trauma in the dream should be interpreted, in my view, as an attempt to invest the dream with the task of working-through the trauma.

Continuing with his interpretation, Freud seems to take a further step along the track of seduction, when he comments that:

> Dora's wish that her father might take the place of the man who was her tempter called up in her memory not merely a casual collection of material from her childhood, but precisely such material as was most intimately bound up with the suppression of her temptation. [p. 87]

Freud also adds that Dora's rejection and suppression of Herr K.'s love was due to *"her premature sexual enjoyment and its consequence*—her bedwetting, her catarrh, and her disgust". Blass (1992, p. 170) believes that Freud's considerations about Dora's masturbation are abstruse, specifically as regards his conclusions that her refusal of Herr K.'s seductive approaches had to be ascribed to her premature masturbatory enjoyment. Blass also says "it is difficult to understand why masturbation would be an ultimate cause for the rejection of a seducer", unless, I suggest, masturbation is the consequence of a premature infantile sexual seduction.

A few lines later, Freud adds that, together with constitutional factors, such a prehistory can generate, upon the erotic necessities of maturity, two types of behaviours, namely, "an *abandonment to sexuality which is entirely without resistances and borders upon perversity*; or there will be a reaction—*he will repudiate sexuality*, and will at the same time fall ill of a neurosis" (p. 88; italics added). In Dora's case, "her constitution and the high level of her intellectual and moral upbringing decided in favour of the latter course" (p. 88).

Here, Freud expounds the consequences that sexual stimulation at a premature age can have on sexual behaviour with extreme clarity: hypersexual behaviour like perversion or the rejection of sexuality. These two modalities of sexual behaviour are nowadays recognised as the effects of infantile sexual abuse and were in any case known to Freud at the time of the seduction theory. Again, we are briefly under the impression that Freud is on the trail of a "pater" who is responsible for Dora's hysterical symptoms, insofar as, speaking of "the various determinants that we have found for Dora's attacks of coughing and hoarseness" (p. 83), he claims:

> After a part of her libido had once more turned towards her father, the symptom obtained what was perhaps its last meaning; it came

to represent sexual intercourse with her father by means of Dora's identifying herself with Frau K. [p. 83]

Yet Freud's considerations come to a stop; this symptom, rooted in Dora's infantile prehistory and which denounces the sexual nature of her relationship with the father, no longer excites Freud to the point of his exclaiming "Eureka!" Only a few years beforehand, this memory of Dora's bed-wetting, along with the symptom that foreshadowed sexual intercourse with the father, would have provided Freud with the certainty of a paternal aetiology of hysteria, irrefutable proof of the father's seduction. Instead, this erotic bond with the father now serves the purpose of keeping Dora's unconscious erotic attraction for Herr K. repressed. Here, Freud prefers to use the term "masturbation" as an "exchange" that allows him to draw the reader's attention to the dead track of infantile self-eroticism, rather than to infantile sexual seduction, a track that had proved risky and overworked. Freud prefers to appreciate evidence "of her infantile love for her father".

As regards the jewel-case, a symbol of the female genitals, Freud would have us believe that in the dream, Dora is worried about her own jewel-case, when in fact it is the mother who wants to save her jewel-case from the fire, for which her husband reproaches her. The image of the fire evokes in Freud the idea that Dora is burning with love for Herr K., much as she had once been in love with her father. Truth be told, as we will see shortly, some of Dora's associations would suggest taking a completely different direction.

During the following session, Dora remembers something that had been missing from her first account of the dream to Freud: that is, the fact that every time she had woken up from a dream, she could smell smoke. Freud deduces "that the dream had a special relation to myself [...]. Dora objected, however, to such a purely personal interpretation, saying that Herr K. and her father were passionate smokers—as I am too, for the matter of that" (p. 73). Here, Freud lets himself be carried away by his unconscious fantasies of a countertransferential nature, which probably express an erotic attraction towards Dora. Even admitting that she had manifested an eroticised transference towards Freud, to the extent that—as Freud concludes—she desires a kiss from him, a kiss which tastes like smoke, he falls into the trap of flattering himself with this erotic phantasy of Dora's, for this also was his unconscious desire. Freud thinks that the perception of her own erotic desire towards the analyst has led Dora to interrupt the treatment. Freud introduced the concept of transference for the first time in *Studies on Hysteria* (1895d), in which he refers to the case of a patient who, in the transference, expressed a desire to receive a kiss from him (S. E., 2, pp. 302–303). Ten years later, Freud discovers the same transference in Dora: yet another patient who desires a kiss from him. Considering the fact that Freud had not yet formulated the concept of countertransference, are we not dealing here with a projection of the analyst's desire?

Dora remembers the smell of smoke at a later stage, not because it had been strongly repressed, or not only because of this, but because something in the relationship with Freud had allowed this forgotten fragment to surface: perhaps the unconscious perception of an erotic attraction on her analyst's part.[4] This interpretation of the transference is relegated to a footnote. In this dream, the father must be substituted with Herr K., but Freud also puts himself in the shoes of Herr K., and Dora's mother must be substituted with Frau K. In Freud's interpretation, everything is overturned and moved around, no character is in their proper place but rather occupies somebody else's, with the same promiscuity to be found in the real life relations between the Bauer and Zellenka families.

Perhaps Freud realised his emotional involvement when, just a few years later in 1909, he found himself entangled in the therapeutic relationship between Jung and Sabina Spierlein. This allowed him to observe all the erotic involvement implied by the "cure of hysteria". I would even argue that the words he addressed to Jung in a letter dated 7 June 1909 could be read as a posthumous insight into his erotic involvement with Dora:

> I myself have never actually been taken in quite so badly but I have been very close several times and had a *narrow escape*.[5] I believe that only grim necessities weighing on my work, and the fact that I was ten years older than yourself when I came to psychoanalysis, have saved me from similar experiences. But no lasting harm is done. They help us develop the thick skin we need to dominate "countertransference", which is after all a permanent problem for us; they teach us to displace our own affects to best advantage. They are a blessing in disguise. [McGuire, 1974, pp. 230–231, 145F]

I would like to return to the scene of the jewel-case. I believe that, on more than one occasion, Dora provided Freud with hints to interpret the dream correctly, but that he constantly ignored them. In the associations that follow the dream, and in the material that surfaces later on, Dora tries to take Freud back to the original version of the dream; that is to say, to the fact that the person worrying about her jewel-case was in fact the mother, and not Dora herself. Shortly after recounting her dream, Dora mentions a sojourn with her mother at Franzensbad, a thermal place where the mother had gone to treat a "vaginal catarrh":

> It was Dora's view—and here again she was probably right—that this illness was due to her father, who had thus handed on his venereal disease to her mother. [p. 75]

Dora had also formulated the hypothesis that her own leucorrhoea had been handed on by her father, who would have infected both her mother and herself. Akavia (2005, pp. 201–202) rightly observes that, "since the disease can also be acquired congenitally (though it is not inherited), Dora may indeed have contracted the disease via her mother. Freud did not bother to clarify this issue and callously dismissed Dora's 'fantasies' about being infected by her father. Furthermore, even if Dora did confuse gonorrhoea and syphilis, Freud overlooked her conviction that her father was a threatening figure who caused her mother great suffering by infecting her with syphilis."[6]

In light of these considerations, we should be more indulgent with Dora's mother and less contemptuous of Freud, because her obsession with cleaning could, as a neurotic symptom, represent a reaction to living with a syphilitic and consumptive husband; it could also be seen as a way, albeit an inadequate one, of protecting her children from contagion.[7] This could also account for the mother's aversion towards anything relating to the genitals, even though this led her to put the father in charge of weaning Dora off enuresis when he was still affected by a venereal disease.

Akavia (2005, p. 207) observes "Freud accorded only passing attention to the connection between Dora's hysteria and her father's syphilis", writing in a footnote:

> To my mind, however, there is another factor which is of more significance in the girl's hereditary or, properly speaking, constitutional predisposition. I have mentioned that her father had contracted syphilis before his marriage. Now a *strikingly high* percentage of the patients whom I have treated psycho-analytically come of fathers who have suffered from tabes or general paralysis. [pp. 20–21, fn. 1][8]

Yet one may wonder if, beyond this constitutional factor, the emergence of a neurotic disorder in his offspring, one that derives from a sexual factor, could not be the consequence of a psychic transmission from the father. His suffering from syphilis would testify to a sexual promiscuity on his part, which in turn also affects the nature of the familial lifestyle, thus involving his own children.

Freud interprets the fire in the dream as a state of burning for love (*Verbrannt sein*), but Dora suggests instead that the fire implies "inflammation", a venereal infection that caused "abdominal pains and a discharge" in her mother. The fact that the "mother wanted to save the jewel-case so that it should not be *burnt*" (p. 72) might therefore well allude to her desire to cure the vaginal infection which caused her a burning and inflammatory sensation (*Verbrannt, Entbrannt*). After all, had Freud not said that the house was the dream-symbol for the human body? The fact that, along with this memory, Dora "identified herself with her mother" (p. 75), would suggest that she shared with the latter analogous concerns, as they both suffered from vaginal leucorrhoea. Thus, within this context, Dora's repeated accusations against her father would have been correct.

The fire is probably an overdetermined element of the dream bearing manifold meanings. It also signifies the eroticisation of the relationship with the father who stands in front of the bed, and the possible, catastrophic consequences of such eroticisation—the death threat. Freud turns all of Dora's claims into their opposites, and just as he had reversed her accusations towards her father into self-accusations, he does the same with the dream-image of the fire into water, and explains to Dora that this was "another connection with 'love' (for love also makes things wet)" (*Liebe, die auch naß macht*) (p. 72). However, in the follow-up to his interpretation, this nexus, which he had so carefully illustrated, playing the role of Dora's sexual educator, must be completely abandoned, since it links the element of the "wet" not to erotic excitement but to Dora's nocturnal enuresis. If so, for what reason would Freud refer to the erotic meaning of the fire, if he did not intend to use this explanation in his interpretation?

In relation to this first dream, Benvenuto (2005, p. 13) claims that a hysteric "is unable to leave the house burning with passion, in which she participates with her soul, but not yet with her body". Now, if Dora could not yet experience the bodily erotic sensations aroused by the paternal seduction, this was because her young body was not yet prepared for it; she was not physiologically ready to turn the burning passion (*Verbrannt*) into "*naß macht*", the product of sexual excitement. Hence, her *wetting* consisted in enuresis, in bed-wetting.

It would seem, somehow, that this thought was in Freud's mind when he made a speech to Dora about "wet" as being connected not only with bed-wetting but also with love. Yet it seems to me that he never really explained to her the connection he was making, between erotic excitement and infantile enuresis. I am almost under the impression that Freud has kept most of his interpretations connected with sexual events in Dora's childhood to himself, without saying anything to his patient and without sharing them with his readers either.

Drawing again on Benvenuto's reading of this dream, I believe that my own interpretation finds support in the theory of seduction. Benvenuto (2005, p. 13) says that the hysteric, "because she has never really removed herself from her childhood, takes every sexual proposal as an attempted act of paedophilia. She's in her lost childhood up to her neck, and when she dreams of fleeing it … it's to eventually return there." Is this not the clearest evidence of Dora being traumatically fixated on her childhood? Dora experienced Herr K.'s sexual advances as traumatic, and possibly as "paedophilic assaults", in that they reactivated the infantile trauma. Herr K.'s advances activate the mechanism of *Nachträglichkeit*, originating a dream that does not stage the recent and rather banal trauma of Herr K.'s sexual harassment, but re-transcribes instead an older and deeper trauma that was sedimented in Dora's unrepressed unconscious and could become accessible only through dreams or by means of transference. After the trauma of the lake, the task of Dora's dream amounts to *nach-tragen*, that is, to registering in a second instance the traumatic meaning of an infantile experience which, when it first occurred, had not been experienced as traumatic but whose traumatic meaning can now be registered—"realised", as one may commonly say—after the scene at the lake with the maladroit paedophile seducer, Herr K. In Dora's unconscious, the paedophilic assault on Lake Garda has a revelatory function: it "relocates" in its traumatic context the remote scene of her childhood with her father standing in front of her bed; it places it in the highly eroticised scenario of a fire that threatens to destroy the entire family because of the burning up of passions engendered by the jewel-case, with its sexual symbolism. In the most delicate moment of her sexual development, when the pressure of adolescent instincts makes Dora understand that she is leaving childhood behind, Herr K.'s rough sexual advances take her back to the traumatic events of her childhood.

Drawing again on Benvenuto (2005, p. 12), I would like to relate his observations about the dream in a double register, which is also that of Freud's original theory of infantile trauma. "There's no doubt, as Freud guesses, that [Dora's] escape from her father's house plays out her desire to escape from an *erotic siege*, not only Herr K.'s, but also from her own desire. In other words, her dream plays out her desire to escape from desire, and represents the desire not to desire [...]. Dora oneirically asks her father to free her from the temptation of satisfying her father's wish ..."

Dora's father could have freed her from this desire only if he had stopped confusing tenderness with eroticism. Dora desires paternal warmth but what she receives, by contrast, are erotic stimulations. Thus, her desire cannot but amount to a desire for freedom, a desire to free herself, even, from this desire for tenderness. Only her father can free her, if he begins to speak his daughter's language. Faced with the "confusion of tongues",[9] perhaps Dora's only feasible defence is falling silent, aphonia. What Dora asks, and is still asking of her father, is to be freed from the temptation to satisfy "the father's desire", both in the sense of her father's erotic desires for her, and of her own desire for paternal tenderness. Dora's desire does not simply amount to escaping Herr K.'s erotic siege in this phase of her adolescence, but also to the erotic siege in which her father has held her during childhood. By failing to bring to light this aspect of Dora's childhood, Freud has not only profoundly disregarded his own theory of the aetiology of hysteria, but he has also contravened the fundamental principle of his *Traumdeutung*, namely, that the dream is the realisation of an infantile desire. In dealing with Dora's case, Freud does not even look for this desire.

Freud attributes Dora's leucorrhoea to masturbation, and finds confirmation of her autoerotic activity in the symptomatic act of her playing with her reticule, "opening it, putting a finger into it" (p. 76). How can we be so sure that, with this gesture, Dora was feigning masturbation?[10] Freud himself says that "the existence of such an origin and the meaning attributed to the act cannot be conclusively established. We must content ourselves with recording the fact that such a meaning fits in quite extraordinarily well with the situation as a whole and with the programme laid down by the unconscious" (p. 77). Yet "the programme" of Dora's unconscious centred on the father's guilt for her leucorrhoea, while Freud was focusing on Dora's own guilt for her masturbatory habits. It is equally plausible that, with this gesture, Dora could have been feigning acts of sexual seduction once carried out upon her, and unconsciously provoking her analyst, trying to rouse sexual fantasies in him, by both faking seduction and seducing at the same time.[11] After all, Freud claims that, "Dora's symptomatic act with the reticule did not immediately precede the dream. She started the session which brought us the narrative of the dream with another symptomatic act" (p. 78). Dora hid a letter of her grandmother's that she was reading, and Freud thought she wanted to "play secrets" with him, concluding from this with his colleagues that she wanted to keep from him the notion of her enuresis and leuchorrea in order to keep her masturbation a secret. Yet even this gesture of Dora's, her playing and keeping a secret from her analyst, was nothing other than a seductive technique, an attempt to capture the latter's interest, to become interesting in his eyes.

Let us go back to the evidence, provided by Freud, of Dora having masturbated in childhood:

> The reproaches against her father for having made her ill, together with the self-reproach underlying them, the leucorrhoea, the playing with the reticule, the bed-wetting after her sixth year, the secret which she would not allow the doctors to tear from her—the circumstantial evidence of her having masturbated in childhood seems to me complete and without a flaw. [p. 78]

Yet this could also prove, and perhaps more rightfully so, a sexual seduction carried out by the father, who during his "nocturnal visits" to control Dora's enuresis, might have touched the child's genitals to verify if she was wet. He might have also touched her beyond the call of duty, which could have woken Dora and aroused in her some pleasurable sensation. The child's feelings for these "nocturnal visits" could have easily been ambivalent: on the one hand, she could have been frightened; on the other, she could have been enticed by the pleasure she had experienced. To hide this sensation from the father and keep up "the secret" with him as well, the young Dora probably had to hold her breath so as not to betray her uneasiness. Her dyspnoea could have originated from this, and not from having heard her parents having sex during one of her father's nocturnal visits to her mother, as Freud thought.[12] It also follows that the stimulus to masturbation would have been instigated by the father, through a desire to reproduce the pleasurable genital sensations experienced during these nocturnal visits, which would confirm, as we have seen, what Freud had claimed in 1896.

Once the enuresis had ceased, there followed the onset of "asthma nervosa", dyspnoea. Enuresis and asthma appeared in a temporal sequence; asthma substituted enuresis. If, with her enuresis, Dora had intended to put out the fire of the dream, with the asthma she was signalling the presence of smoke, the smell of which she remembered when she woke up from the dream. With her dyspnoea, Dora identified with her father, who had "shortness of breath" because of his pulmonary illness. Freud comes to the conclusion that Dora's dyspnoea set in after she had heard her parents having sex. This deduction derived from "Dora's symptomatic act and certain other signs" (p. 79), of which we are not informed by Freud and that do not allow us to understand the extent to which his reconstructions were based on the "requirements of theory". As a matter of fact, he says: "Part of this material I was able to obtain directly from the analysis, but the rest required supplementing" (p. 80), which means "extracting it" from his theories on infantile sexuality. Freud goes as far as to acknowledge that Dora's cough could represent "an imitation of her father (whose lungs were affected)" (p. 82), but he concludes that this

> could serve as an expression of her sympathy and concern for him. But besides this, it proclaimed aloud, as it were, something of which she may then have been still unconscious: 'I am my father's daughter. I have a catarrh, just as he has. He has made me ill, just as he has made Mother ill. It is from him that I have got my evil passions, which are punished by illness'. [p. 82]

If these evil passions were, as Freud seems to believe, an infantile propensity to masturbation, then we would have confirmation of the claim made by Freud in 1896, namely, that infantile masturbation is the consequence of a sexual seduction carried out by an adult. Speaking of Dora's cough and catarrh, Freud observes in a footnote that because the term "catarrh" could stand for both a vaginal secretion and an oral one, this symptom "had been *displaced from the lower to the upper part of her body*" (p. 83, n. 2).[13]

Despite all these symptoms, with which Dora proclaimed the father's responsibility "to the entire world", and which in 1896 Freud would acknowledge as the discovery of the *caput Nili*, he continues to maintain the father's innocence and Dora's culpability. Yet in April 1897, he said the following to a patient who had been recovering traces of a traumatic childhood memory: "Well then, let us speak plainly. In my analyses the guilty people are close relatives, father or brother" (Letter to Fliess of 28 April 1897).

Freud continues his account of the analysis, relating the traumatic events that had distressed this patient affected by insomnia and a fear of travelling by coach:

> And it then turned out that her supposedly otherwise noble and respectable father regularly took her to bed when she was from eight to twelve years old and misused her without penetrating ("made her wet", *nocturnal visits*). She felt anxiety even at the time. A sister, six years her senior, with whom she talked things over many years later, confessed to her that she had had the same experiences with their father. A cousin told her that when she was fifteen she had had to fend off her grandfather's embraces. Of course, when I told her that similar and worse things must have happened in her earliest childhood, she could not find it incredible. In other respects it is a quite ordinary case of hysteria with the usual symptoms. Q. E. D. [Masson, 1985, 28 April 1897, p. 238; italics added]

In December 1896, Freud took on the treatment of a cousin of Fliess', Miss G. de B., and asked his friend to investigate, behind his wife's back, "who in the family or the surroundings has had a speech defect such as stuttering". We must deduce from this request that the patient Freud had started to treat suffered from hysteria. He presumed that the symptom of stammering was the consequence of a process of identification with her sexual aggressor, with the person responsible for that seduction, which was the origin of her hysteria.

Also, in *The Interpretation of Dreams* (1900a) Freud had mentioned the mechanism of hysterical identification, which "is a highly important factor in the mechanism of hysterical symptoms" and "is not simple imitation but *assimilation* on the basis of a similar aetiological pretension; it express a resemblance and is derived from a common element which remain in the unconscious". The hysteric, Freud claims, uses identification in order to express a sexual community. She prefers to identify with people with whom she has had sexual intercourse, or with people who are engaged in sexual relations with her own sexual partners. "In hysterical phantasies, just as in dreams, it is enough for purposes of identification that the subject should have *thoughts* of sexual relations without their having necessarily taken place in reality" (1900a, *S. E., 4*, p. 150).

So, here, Freud is clearly saying that hysterical identification expresses a "common sexual element". It testifies to the sexual nature of the relationship between the hysteric and the person she takes up as her model for identification. As such, Dora's identification with her father had to be grounded on this "common sexual element", and since Freud had already fully clarified that the hysteric's identification was not "mere imitation", it seems inappropriate for him to speak of "imitation of the father" when Dora's "oral" symptoms rather implied identification with him.

Again, we are briefly under the impression that Freud is thinking of a "pater" who is responsible for Dora's hysterical symptoms, because when speaking of "the various determinants that we have found for Dora's attacks of coughing and hoarseness", he affirms that:

> After a part of her libido had once more turned towards her father, the symptom obtained what was perhaps its last meaning; it came to represent sexual intercourse with her father by means of Dora's identifying herself with Frau K. [p. 83]

Thus, in light of this theory of hysterical identification, Dora's identification with Frau K. was also of a sexual nature, and reinforced the sexual community with her father in an erotic identifying triangle.

Yet Freud's considerations end here. The symptom that, rooted in Dora's prehistoric childhood, would reveal sexual intercourse with her father, can no longer excite a jubilant *eureka!* from Freud, or a *quod erat demonstrandum*. Freud asks himself why, following Herr K.'s attempted seduction, "a recollection [should] have emerged of her bed-wetting when she was a child and of the trouble her father used to take to teach the child clean habits?" (p. 86) Only a few years beforehand, this infantile memory, along with the symptom that foreshadowed a sexual relationship with the father, would have provided Freud with the certainty of a paternal aetiology of hysteria, and irrefutable proof of the father's seduction. Now, according to Freud, this erotic bond with the father serves the purpose, instead, of keeping Dora's erotic attraction to Herr K. repressed.

Freud understands "that Dora's wish that her father might take the place of the man who was her tempter called up in her memory not merely a casual collection of material from her childhood, but precisely such material as was most intimately bound up with the suppression of her temptation" (p. 87), infantile sexual material that is, which features the father as seducer, behind the pretext of educating Dora not to wet the bed. He also realises that the "reaction [of] repudiat[ing] sexuality" derives from "her premature sexual enjoyment and its consequence— her bed-wetting, her catarrh, and her disgust" (p. 87). And yet Freud sees in all this nothing but proof of "infantile love for her father" (p. 88). After claiming that Dora's dyspnoea derived from her having overheard her father panting during coitus, Freud affirms that her excitement "may very easily have made the child's sexuality veer round and have replaced her inclination to masturbation by an inclination to anxiety" (p. 80).[14]

The asthma attack (dyspnoea) occurred while the father was absent and she was thinking about him "devotedly in love". Dora "was wishing him back", and experiencing a sense of "longing" for him (p. 80). If we take a step back, we find the term "longing" in the letter to Fliess of 27 October 1897, and we can spot another inconsistency between what Freud claims at this point and what he had previously reported to his friend Fliess. In the aforementioned letter, Freud had identified resistance within the "infantile character" that develops during the period of "longing", that is, "after the child has been removed from sexual experiences", which according to the early Freud means the period when sexual seduction by the adult is over. During the period of "longing", which is the "main character trait of hysteria", fantasies are produced (not symptoms such as Dora's asthma), and masturbation is practised, which then gives way to repression. If repression does not occur and masturbation continues, "the discharge of sexual excitation for the most part removes the possibility of hysteria". Three years have passed since Freud wrote that letter, and he has changed his mind. Longing for the father generates the asthmatic symptom. Clearly, the term "longing" has now assumed a different meaning.

In its first meaning, "longing" refers to the father's lost sexual stimulations; the child compensates this loss with an autoerotic stimulation, with masturbation. In this sense, Freud could rightly claim that infantile masturbation was the consequence of the adult's seduction, like others had argued before him. If the paternal absence had created in Dora the symptom of dyspnoea, one could perhaps even think that with this symptom she was attempting to allude to her infantile "secret". Therefore, in the absence of the father and of his erotic stimulations, Dora would now repeat them and turn to the symptom of holding her breath during his "nocturnal visits", to conceal her uneasiness as well as her sexual enjoyment. In this sense, asthma could be the product of her longing for her father. In any case, through this symptom Dora would be demonstrating that her "infantile love for her father" and her being "devotedly in love with him" involved a "sexual" father, a father whose sexuality she assumes in her symptom.

Freud's analysis of this first dream follows the thread of seduction and the reader is often gratified by the idea that, sooner or later, a validation of the theory of seduction will surface, which Freud had anticipated in the foreword to this case history.[15] Again, his words introduce an achievement that will fall short of expectations:

> A special triumph is achieved if a recent situation, perhaps even the very situation which is the exciting cause of the dream, can be transformed into a infantile one. This has actually been achieved in the present case, by a purely chance disposition of the material. Just as Herr K. had stood beside her sofa and woken her up, so her father had often done in her childhood. The whole trend of her thoughts could be most aptly symbolized by her substitution of her father for Herr K. in that situation.
>
> But the reason for which the father used to woke her up long ago had been to prevent her from making her bed wet.
>
> This "wet" had a decisive influence on the further content of the dream; though it was represented in it only by a distant allusion and by its opposite. [p. 89]

He continues with interpretations that seem to refer back to the theory of seduction, but which frequently lead to disappointment instead. Freud is not looking for a "triumph" because he is not looking to go back up from to the latest circumstance with Herr K., which was the source of the dream, to an episode of Dora's childhood. Yet in the letter to Fliess (10 March 1898), he had claimed that "dream life seems to me to derive entirely from the residues of the prehistoric period of life (between the ages of one and three)"—a period that is the source of the unconscious and contains the aetiology of all neuroses. He then formulates the following: "What is *seen* in the prehistoric period produces dreams; what is *heard* in it produces fantasies; what is *experienced sexually* in it produces the psychoneuroses." He later affirms that a recent desire may produce a dream only if it can be connected with material from the prehistoric age (Masson, 1985, 10 March 1898, p. 302).

Not even this theory finds confirmation two years later, because Freud will say of Dora's dream that:

> [It] was a reaction to a fresh experience of an exciting nature; and this experience must inevitably have revived the memory of the only previous experience which was at all analogous to it. The latter was the scene of the kiss in Herr K.'s place of business, when she had been seized with disgust. [p. 92]

Therefore, instead of going back to the prehistoric phase of Dora's life, the analyst is content to find out about the traumatic sexual episode revived by the dream, which had occurred only two years beforehand. Freud had lost interest in prehistory, and was by now equipped with the burglar's "picklocks". Unearthing relics from the past was too tiring and lengthy a job, which no longer met the requirements of theory, which had to be rapidly confirmed. Freud's priority was to corroborate his more recent theory of hysterical fantasies and of infantile sexuality, which he would expound in *Three Essays on the Theory of Sexuality* (1905d). To this end, the burglar's ability was more apt than the archaeologist's patience.

Let us now go back to the dream:

> "Wet" was connected not only with the bed-wetting, but also with the group of ideas relating to sexual temptation which lay suppressed behind the content of the dream. Dora knew that there was a kind of getting wet involved in sexual intercourse [...]. She also knew that the danger lay precisely in that, and that it was her business to protect her genitals from being moistened. [p. 90]

Freud's thoughts and interpretations continue to thrive on the terrain of sexuality, but without him being able to retrieve the thread of seduction broken a few years beforehand, and which he had repeatedly tried to mend ever since. Even though he keeps on claiming that "fantasies, have stood the test splendidly" (Masson, 1985, 7 November 1899, pp. 382–383), in his clinical practice Freud continually comes upon those authentic scenes of sexual seduction that had led him to formulate his traumatic aetiology of hysteria. And yet, even though Freud remains in a field that could easily point to the theory of seduction—with its constant reminders of the paternal presence behind the multiplicity of sexual meanings—the thread remains broken. Not even after evoking the sexual meaning of "wet" and identifying for Dora the necessity "to protect her genitals from being moistened" can Freud remember the case he had defined as an "ordinary case of hysteria" and which he had described to Fliess on 28 April 1897 as an example of paternal perversion, with a father who would take his daughter in the bed and "wet" her, as we have just seen.

In a letter to Fliess of 8 February 1897, Freud had acknowledged that his father had been a pervert too:

> Unfortunately, my own father was one of these perverts and is responsible for the hysteria of my brother (all of whose symptoms are identifications) and those of several younger sisters. The frequency of this circumstance often makes me wonder. [Masson, 1985, 8 February 1897, pp. 230–231]

Speaking of his brother's hysteria, Freud acknowledged that all his symptoms suggested identification with the aggressor, and thus, in that case, with the father. It would seem, then, that in the period of February 1897 Freud's intent was to envisage a possible alternative to the formation of the hysterical symptom by conversion, considering the possibility that hysterical symptoms were the consequence of a process of identification with the sexual aggressor.

> It seems to me more and more that the essential point of hysteria is that it results from *perversion* on the part of the seducer, and *more and more* that heredity is seduction by the father. Thus an alternation emerges between generations:
> 1st generation: perversion.
> 2nd generation: hysteria, and consequent sterility.

Occasionally there is a metamorphosis within the same individual: perverse during the age of vigour and then, after a period of anxiety, hysterical. Accordingly, hysteria is not repudiated sexuality but rather *repudiated perversion* [...].

[...] Thus patients who have had something sexual done to them in *sleep* have attacks of sleep. They go to sleep again in order to experience the same thing and often provoke a hysterical fainting fit in that way.

Attacks of dizziness and fits of weeping—all these are aimed at *another person*—but mostly at the prehistoric, unforgettable other person who is never equalled by anyone later. [Masson, 1985, 6 December 1896, pp. 212–213]

Here, Freud specifies that the hysterical symptom, because it is directed towards the other, always entails a communicative intentionality. Yet when he addressed Dora's "hysterical fainting", he no longer remembered what he had himself claimed a few years earlier. Hence, he did not contemplate the possibility that this fainting might testify to sexual acts inflicted on a sleeping Dora by that "prehistoric, unforgettable other"—namely, the father.

CHAPTER SIX

The second dream

Dora described her second dream as follows:

I was walking about in a town which I did not know. I saw streets and squares which were strange to me [Later addition: *I saw a monument in one of the squares*]. *Then I came into a house where I lived, went to my room, and found a letter from Mother lying there. She wrote saying that as I had left home without my parents' knowledge she had not wished to write to me to say that Father was ill. "Now he is dead, and if you like* [Later addition: *There was a question-mark after this word, thus: 'like?'*] *you can come". I then went to the station* ["Bahnhof"] *and asked about a hundred times: "Where is the station?" I always got the answer: "Five minutes." I then saw a thick wood before me which I went into, and there I asked a man whom I met. He said to me: "Two and a half hours more." He offered to accompany me. But I refused and went alone. I saw the station in front of me and could not reach it. At the same time I had the usual feeling of anxiety that one has in dreams when one cannot move forward. Then I was at home. I must have been travelling in the meantime, but I know nothing about that. I walked into the porter's lodge, and enquired for our flat. The maidservant opened the door to me and replied that Mother and the others were already at the cemetery* ["Friedhof"]. [Later additions: *I saw myself particularly distinctly going up the stairs* and *After she had answered I went to my room, but not the least sadly, and began reading a big book that lay on my writing-table*] [p. 94. Later additions added by author]

Freud wrote that, after the resolution of this dream, the analysis was broken off. Yet, the dream had not been completely solved; he himself added that "it cannot be made as completely intelligible as the first" (p. 94) and that "the whole of it was not cleared up" (p. 95). The second dream, Freud claims, bears a relation to the interruption of the treatment. Dora had this dream three days before the conclusion of the analysis, and since Freud immediately started to write the clinical account, it seems incomprehensible that he would have shown hesitations and mnemonic lacunae about it. Such difficulties had not emerged with the first dream, which Dora had narrated a few weeks beforehand. He declares: "I am not equally certain at every point of the order in which my conclusions were reached" (p. 95), and warns the reader that: "I shall present the material produced during the analysis of this dream in the somewhat haphazard order in which it recurs to my mind" (p. 95). Were we to employ Freudian parameters to judge this behaviour, we would have to conclude that we are dealing with a case of "resistance". The analysis of this dream is shorter than the previous one, and not only because Dora broke off the treatment, even though the second dream is richer in details than the first.

The dream occurs at a stage in the analysis when "Dora herself had been raising a number of questions about the connection between some of her actions and the motives which presumably underlay them. One of these questions was: 'Why did I say nothing about the scene by the lake for some days after it had happened?' Her second question was: 'Why did I then suddenly tell my parents about it?'" (p. 95).

Therefore, at this stage, Dora was questioning why she had not spoken about the trauma immediately. These questions could have had something to do not only with the recent trauma but also, and even more pertinently, with the childhood episode evoked in the first dream. Thus, while Dora was somehow trying to work through some fragments of her recollections relating to her infantile trauma, Freud considered that: "Her having felt so deeply injured by Herr K.'s proposal seemed to me in general to need explanation" (p. 95). I should point out here that, conversely to what should happen within a psychoanalytical session, the patient was a step ahead of her analyst. It is also surprising that Freud should ask himself such a question, insofar as he had already envisioned an appropriate explanation four years before, when, in *The Aetiology of Hysteria* (1896c), he wrote that:

> You will remember the mental 'sensitiveness' which is so frequent among hysterical patients and which leads them to react to the least sign of being depreciated as though they had received a deadly insult [...] It is not the latest slight—which, in itself, is minimal—that produces the fit of crying, the outburst of despair or the attempt at suicide, in disregard of the axiom that an effect must be proportionate to its cause; *the small slight of the present moment has aroused and set working the memories of very many, more intense, earlier slights, behind all of which there lies in addition the memory of a serious slight in childhood which has never been overcome.* [S. E., 3, p. 217; italics added]

Consequently, Freud's surprise at Dora's reaction reveals the neglect, on the analyst's part, of his own theories, formulated a few years beforehand, theories that he had also claimed he would confirm with the exposition of this case history.

Freud identifies in the dream allusions to the male and female genitalia, and a reference to her father's and her own death, which she threatened to bring about in a letter intended to alarm her father. Dora wanted to convince her father that had he persisted in his erotic relationship with Frau K., she (Dora) would have died as a consequence. It was, therefore, a destructive erotic relationship for her, while in the dream it is Dora's father who dies.

This second dream is the continuation of the first one; even Freud acknowledges this. Here, Dora has finally managed to realise the intention formulated in the first dream, that of leaving the paternal house. Finally, she is no longer required to take her mother's place in compensating for her father's sexual frustration. Just as she had been the only person her father would allow to look after him during his illness, in the day residue of this second dream she has to serve him a glass of brandy to help him sleep, to counter his insomnia deriving from his sexual frustration.[1] Dora acts as intermediary to compensate for her father's sexual frustration. Here, a day residue appears that connects this dream to the first one. In order to take the brandy to her father, Dora needs the key to the pantry, which is in her mother's possession. Engrossed in the conversation, she had not heard Dora asking, about a *"hundred times"*, "Where is the key?" The key, beyond its obvious phallic meaning, is also linked here to sexuality in another way. She needs the key in order to open the pantry and provide the father with the shot of brandy that will help him sleep, sedating his sexual frustration: Dora "understood very clearly what it was that her father needed when he could not get to sleep without a drink of brandy" (p. 98). The (vanished) key to Dora's room in the lake house protects her from Herr K.'s illicit intrusions, just as the key to Otto's bedroom is perhaps necessary to protect him from his father's nocturnal intrusions.

In the dream, Dora receives a letter from her mother communicating to her that her father has died, and that, if she wants, she can now go back home: "If you would like? to come" (p. 98). Freud remarks upon the similarity between the mother's letter and the one from Frau K. in which she invites Dora to the lake, with the same curious question mark, thus taking us back to the second traumatic scene by the lake. Furthermore, the wood in the dream also reminds us of that period, inasmuch as it can be read as a reference to the wood surrounding the lake. Thus, we have confirmation that the second dream is a continuation of the first one, and represents a step forward in Dora's working-through of her infantile trauma. In *The Interpretation of Dreams* (1900a), in an added footnote of 1909, Freud specified that some dreams re-enact the infantile trauma from which the neurosis had developed. Regarding the dream of a patient of his, he observed that:

> It was not until later that I learnt that she had been repeating in it the initial trauma from which her neurosis had arisen. I have since then come across the same behaviour in other patients; having been exposed to a sexual assault in their childhood, they seek, as it were, to bring about a repetition of it in their dreams. [S. E., 4, 185, n. 1]

In the second dream, the mother assumes a more active role towards Dora, and by referring to the father with the assertion, *"Now he is dead, and if you like [?] you can come"*, she reveals that she knows that Dora had left the house because of her father. Hence the mother, who in the first dream was solely concerned with saving her jewel-case, in the end makes it clear to her daughter that she had always been aware of the erotic games her father plays with her (Dora), and admits to having always kept quiet, just as Dora had done. Now that the father is dead, Dora is out of danger and can go back home. Thus in the sentence, "if you would like [?] to come", we can read an ambiguous sexual reference that betrays this knowledge on the mother's part.²

The first component of the dream-situation, which Freud identifies as a revenge phantasy against her father, is accompanied by a second component, which emerges, as Freud claims, from "a symbolic geography of sex" (p. 99). Dora referred to having experienced a feeling of anguish in the dream, when, in attempting to reach the station, she had found herself in a condition of paralysing impossibility, unable to continue walking her path. She experiences a feeling that, in my view, is akin to an experience of surrender and paralysis before a precocious sexual trauma. Yet, Freud overturns this subjective experience of Dora's as well, transforming it into a "phantasy of a man seeking to force an entrance into the female genitals" (p. 100). This would therefore represent "a phantasy of defloration" wherein Dora's experience of paralysis is transformed into the experience of a rapist, incapable of bringing penetration to completion. Freud does not realise that by using these precise words to define this second meaning of the dream, he is taking us back to the time of childhood referred to in the first dream. The man attempting to penetrate Dora's genital organ is certainly not Herr K., because the effort implied in the dream indicates an anatomical incompatibility. Perhaps Dora is still too young and her genital organ too small, and perhaps the man's penis is not sufficiently erect, and would thus belong to Dora's father, who was impotent. It seems that, albeit perhaps unwittingly, Freud is leading us to deduce a sexual seduction undergone by Dora at her father's hand. Whether Dora's father did attempt to deflower his daughter, or whether he merely touched her genitals, or masturbated her, we cannot say. Yet, after so many clues, the recognition that Dora had been the victim of sexual abuse seems unavoidable, and in her hysteria one must recognise a paternal origin in line Freud's repeated claims in his 1896 writings.

At the end of the dream, Dora goes back home and the maidservant who opens the door informs her *"that Mother and the others were already at the cemetery"*. In the course of a session, Dora adds a missing fragment to this account: *"After she had answered I went to my room, but not the least sadly, and began reading a big book that lay on my writing-table"* (p. 94, n. 4). Freud hurriedly supposes here that the big book Dora is reading is a dictionary of sexual education, and adds: "Children never read about forbidden subjects in an encyclopaedia *calmly* [...] Dora's father was dead, and the others had already gone to the cemetery. She might calmly read whatever she chose" (p. 100). Yet Dora could also calmly read anything she wanted to not only because her father was dead, but also because she was no longer a "child". By referring to children generally, Freud reveals that, at least unconsciously, he was not interpreting Dora's dream merely within the context of the present moment, but was rather envisioning it against the background of Dora's childhood, though this unconscious perception did not make it into his draft of the case history.

Now that her father was dead, Dora could take care of her own sexual education without the obstacle of "paternal initiation". "If her father was dead," says Freud, "she could read and love as she pleased" (p. 100). Yet why would Dora have needed to wait for her father's death to "read and love as she pleased", if not because he had been her lover and sexual initiator when she was a child? And if, as Freud claims, Dora had been truly in love with him, why so much indifference upon learning of his death? Why does Dora, "not the least sadly", indulge in sexual readings on the day of her father's funeral?

I will now attempt to clarify a misunderstanding surrounding this entangled story, namely, the nature of the sources from which Dora obtained her sexual knowledge. What Freud says about it stands in stark contrast with what he will write in *Three Essays* (1905d) wherein, speaking of the neurotic's sexuality, and referring to the hysterics taken as models for all neurotic patients, he claims that:

> The character of hysterics shows a degree of sexual repression in excess of the normal quantity, an intensification of resistance against the sexual instinct (which we have already met with in the form of shame, disgust and morality), and what seems like an instinctive aversion on their part to any intellectual consideration of sexual problems. As a result of this, in especially marked cases, the patients remain in complete ignorance of sexual matters right into the period of sexual maturity. [S. E., 7, p. 164]

In another passage from *Fragment*, he affirms that:

> For where there is no knowledge of sexual processes even in the unconscious, no hysterical symptom will arise; and where hysteria

is found there can no longer be any question of "innocence of mind" in the sense in which parents and educators use the phrase. With children of ten, of twelve, or of fourteen, with boys and girls alike, I have satisfied myself that the truth of this statement can invariably be relied upon. [p. 49]

In this respect, Strong (1989, p. 16) asserts that: "In a sense, the Freudian hysteric falls ill from too much sexual knowledge [...] That the 'innocent of mind' will not fall ill implies that sexual knowledge is dangerous to a woman's health" (p. 16). An unbridgeable contradiction can be found here between the sexual knowledge that produces hysteria, and the hysterical character that is conjugated with an utter sexual ignorance, at least until the age of sexual maturity. Dora was not yet even fourteen at the time of the kiss in the shop, and she had confessed to Freud that, back then, she did not possess the necessary sexual knowledge. However, despite her "innocence of mind", Freud had judged her "entirely and completely hysterical".

According to Freud, Dora's sexual knowledge would derive from Mantegazza's *The Physiology of Love* (1887). Let us ascertain whether or not this claim is plausible, or whether Dora's sexual knowledge derived, rather, from experiences suffered on her skin, as is the case with abused children.

As we will see below, Freud had met Paolo Mantegazza at the time at which he was conducting his studies on cocaine, and had read the essay published in 1859, entitled *On the Hygienic and Medicinal Properties of Coca Plant and on Nervin Nourishment in General*, a work in which Mantegazza uncritically lauded the positive properties of coca leaves. It is hard to believe that Freud read other texts by Mantegazza, either the *Fisiologia del piacere* (*The Physiology of Pleasure*) or the aforementioned *The Physiology of Love*, because he would have easily realised that Dora's sexual knowledge could not derive from these sources. Decker (1991) informs us that *The Physiology of Love* was largely popular and widely read, and that at the end of the eighteenth century Mantegazza was one of the major authorities in the field of modern sexual life. His books were translated into many Western languages worldwide. The author rightly claims that, had Dora only read *The Physiology of Love* (1873), she would have received very limited notions of sexual education.[3]

Mantegazza's book deals with sexuality in the tone of the most decadent romanticism, and very often uses metaphors from the vegetal and animal world, just as Little Hans' father had done in his attempts at sexual education, which had not helped him prevent his son's neurosis. Rather than finding in this book, as Herr K. would have us believe, an opportunity that would stimulate her sexual fantasies to the point where she would fabricate his attempts at seduction, it is more likely that Dora would have found in it useful suggestions to remain alert in the face of her seducer, and for evaluating her feelings for Herr K. more appropriately.

Mantegazza claims:

> To distinguish in others the true love from the false, my study of physiology will be of service to you; to explore your own heart, a moderate attention to the phase of your sentiments will surface. [Mantegazza, 1887 [2007], p. 134]

Thus, before providing her with sexual instructions, Mantegazza invites the girl, to whom the book is addressed, to distinguish between true and false love. Even before this, when speaking of adolescence and of the strong sexual impulse that leads teenagers to pursue the other sex in that developmental phase of sexuality that he defines as "the hysterical period of life" (p. 119), he warns the girl against the risk that the growing sexual instinct might push her into the harms of the "first come" (p. 241), somebody who cannot live up to her adolescent's fantasies of a

> winged man with nothing of earthly save two lips to imprint on hers a kiss. [...] Instead of this angel there appears before her a man in trousers, with moustaches, who smokes excessively and betrays women; perhaps his hair is already grey, he may be a husband and father—but he is a man! [p. 120]

Thus, from Mantegazza's work, Dora could have easily identified her seducer, Herr K., acknowledging his marked dissimilarity to the one who might have fulfilled her juvenile fantasies, provided that Dora fit this late romantic stereotype of an adolescent. In any case, she had been warned, by Mantegazza, that the "first come" with a moustache stinking of smoke, already a husband and father, could not offer her the love that she would fantasise about as an adolescent. Yet the power of the sexual instinct might have induced the girl to welcome this "first come" as the one who was meant to satisfy her pressing sexual needs, hence prompting her to idealise a base individual:

> A heart of a grocer in the body of a porter! But he is pallid, and the dullness of his gaze seems to her sentimental languor; he is ill, and his illness appears poetic; he is robust, and for her he is the god of strength; he is arrogant, but she thinks him passionate; he is an egotist, and so much the better, for he will love but her, who alone knows how to make him happy [...] Woe to him if seduction unites itself to all this tissue of lies with which first love too often weaves its nest! Woe if to the inexperienced maiden the aged libertine knows how to say in accents acquired from long practice in the art, "I love you!" [...] Then the fire is lighted, the flames arise, and the first object loved is placed on the altar, choruses of eternal oaths chanted to it perfumed by the incense of the maddest, most licentious idolatry. [pp. 120–121]

Thus, before any sexual teaching, Mantegazza delivers to young female adolescents lessons of self-defence, and Dora would have recognised in these words her experience with her clumsy seducer.

In yet another passage of the book, Dora could have easily recognised her first experience with Herr K. in Merano, the stolen kiss on the shop doorstep:

> To have possessed before having loved, to have been possessed before having given the kiss of love! What ignominy! What baseness! And yet love is such a magician that, at times, it can perform the prodigy of being born of lechery. [p. 131]

Therefore, Dora had been warned several times by this reading about the unseemliness of Herr K.'s behaviour: Mantegazza's moral judgement would probably have been acknowledged as an authoritative source. Certainly Mantegazza's words must have seemed much more convincing to Dora than her analyst's, which were revealing of a dubious morality, as he wanted to convince her, despite the repeated negations, of her unconscious love for Herr K., that "first come, already husband and father, stinking of smoke".

From another fragment added to the account of the dream, we learn that Dora sees herself "particularly distinctly going up the stairs". In *The*

Interpretation of Dreams (1900a), Freud attributes to this act a meaning of a sexual nature, namely, he interprets it as the symbolic representation of coitus. Furthermore, we know that in the dream Dora was trying to get to the station in order to return home by train, and she also reports finding herself at home without realising how she got there (*Then I was at home. I must have been travelling in the meantime, but I know nothing about that*). Referring once more to the "dream book", we know that the train journey also has a sexual meaning, and similarly alludes to the coitus. Thus, we are presented here with another two, clear, sexual references: the first to a sexual activity of which the dreamer is perfectly aware (*I saw myself particularly distinctly going up the stairs*), and the second to a sexual activity (achieved or suffered) in a condition of dissociation of consciousness (*I must have been travelling in the meantime, but I know nothing about that*).

Through a series of associations connected with the act of "going up the stairs", Freud reconstructs the genesis of a new hysterical symptom of Dora's, namely, "the dragging of one leg" as a consequence of an appendicitis, having arisen "nine months" after the scene by the lake. The conclusion seems obvious: appendicitis pain and menstruations, nine months, thus, the "phantasy of *childbirth*" (p. 103). Yet Freud adds:

> I am convinced that a symptom of this kind can only arise where it has an *infantile* prototype [...] I scarcely dared hope that Dora would provide me with the material that I wanted from her childhood [...] [p. 103]

Dora punctually brings this material to the attention of her analyst. When the Bauer family lived in Merano, Dora had misplaced one of her feet when going down the stairs (the same one that would later become lame as a result of "somatic compliance"). We read that, "this had been a short time before the attack of nervous asthma in her eighth year" (p. 103).

Thus, Dora had already developed hysterical symptoms (nervous asthma) by the age of eight, which reveals two more contradictions in her analysis. In *The Aetiology of Hysteria* (1896c), Freud affirms that:

> In our *severe cases* the formation of hysterical symptoms begins—not in exceptional instances, but, rather, as a regular thing—at the age

of eight, and that the sexual experiences which show no immediate effect invariably date further back, into the third or fourth, or even the second year of life. [*S. E.*, 3, p. 212; italics added]

Therefore, according to this criterion, Dora's case should have been classified as "severe hysteria", and not as a "petite hystérie" as Freud had defined it.[4] Considering the eighth year of age as a "boundary line" for hysteria, he claims that:

> I must assume that this time of life, the period of growth in which the second dentition takes place, forms a boundary line for hysteria, after which the illness cannot be caused. From then on, a person who has not had sexual experiences earlier can no longer become disposed to hysteria; and a person who *has* had experiences earlier, is already able to develop hysterical symptoms. [ibid., p. 212]

Therefore, since Dora had already developed hysterical symptoms when she was eight years old, she must have had precocious sexual experiences that could be situated between the ages of two and four, and which were responsible not only for the emergence of these symptoms, but also for the predisposition to hysteria which appeared during her adolescence.

After the death of her dearest aunt, Dora had an appendicitis episode that subsequently left her with a slight claudication, a lame right foot. This appendicitis had developed "nine months" after the lake scene. Thus, claudication is a hysterical symptom, Freud thinks, deriving from the idea of having taken a "false step" during the walk by the lake, the consequence of which, nine months later, would have been the appendicitis, revealing a birth-giving fantasy. Yet Dora had shortly before spoken with Freud of oral sex, masturbation and vaginal lubrication. Hence, she could not be considered so unprepared an adolescent as to be under the impression, even in a fantasy, that Herr K.'s advances could magically make her pregnant. This would have been more plausible on the occasion of the first trauma, the scene of the kiss, had Dora read Mantegazza's book back then, when she was not yet fourteen. This is however implausible two years later, when she is at the lake house. From reading *The Physiology of Love* Dora could have deduced that Herr K.'s kiss and his vigorous embrace could have not only deprived her of her virginity, but also made her pregnant. With respect to the kiss that impregnates, Mantegazza says:

> Where an intimate contact of two kisses creates a new existence, an unknown current transmits to the new man, together with the sparks of life, all the treasures of past voluptuousness. [p. 190]

Let us consider then, the appalling consequences of a reciprocal bodily contact according to Mantegazza:

> Touch, in love, is always excited by voluptuousness, it is always deeply sensual, it is always a positive possession, without contrast, or possibility of contrast. Woman can deceive herself, she can believe herself pure of all virile contact when the hand of man has never touched but the hem of her garments; but when skin has touched skin, when a finger has touched another finger, something is already lost of that waxen varnish with which nature covers the virgin fruit, still odorous with the perfume of the tree that nourished it. [...] Whoever believes himself or herself a virgin after a kiss given and returned is a hypocrite, and is somewhat like him who believes that the studied reticence of lechery can still leave something to attain. O women, who have the dangerous fortune to be beautiful and desired, stay all your adorers at the handshake, in rare cases arrive at the given kiss; but remember that a kiss returned is a tremendous bill of exchange which one should never sign [...]. [pp. 191–192]

Dora's hysterical claudication, which emerged nine months after the lake trauma when she was 17 years old—just like her hysterical cough and the dyspnoea—is an unconscious attempt to disclose to "the whole world" that the trauma she was dealing with was not simply that of the lake. It was an older one, which dated back to when she was eight years old or even younger, when between the domestic walls lurked passions so burning they could have set the house on fire. Yet her analyst understood nothing of this, or did not want to, because he was still convinced that had Dora yielded to temptation at the lake, "this would have been the only possible solution for all the parties concerned" (p. 108).

Freud would have therefore wanted to rearrange these two married couples, with Dora being married to Hans (Herr K.) and Philip (her father) to Peppina (Frau K.). Considering his way of dealing with complicated family arrangements, perhaps Breuer was right to warn Fliess' wife against Freud, claiming that the latter was used to ruining other people's marriages.[5]

Freud enthusiastically exposed to Dora his interpretation of the second dream, which is to say his belief in her indestructible, though unconscious, love for Herr K., her child-birth fantasy, and her vengeance fantasies against her father. To his enthusiasm, though,

> Dora replied in a depreciatory tone: "Why, has anything so very remarkable come out?" [p. 105]

Freud takes pride in the fact that his patient did not express any objection to his interpretation. Yet this is not to say that he had been particularly convincing; Dora showed no opposition simply because she had already decided to quit the treatment. The day after, on 31 December 1900,

> she said good-bye to me very warmly, with the heartiest wishes for the New Year, and—came no more. [p. 109]

Freud could have predicted this failure as well as Dora's subsequent relapses, if he had only remembered what he had written four years beforehand in *The Aetiology of Hysteria* (1896c), as previously quoted:

> I will add that in a number of cases therapeutic evidence of the genuineness of the infantile scenes can also be brought forward. There are cases in which a complete or partial cure can be obtained without our having to go as deep as the infantile experience. And there are others in which no success at all is obtained until the analysis has come to its natural end with the uncovering of the earliest traumas. In the former cases we are not, I believe, secure against relapses; and my expectation is that a complete psycho-analysis implies a radical cure of the hysteria. [S. E., 3, pp. 205–206]

When Dora announced to Freud her decision to break off the treatment, she justified it by declaring: "I shall wait no longer than that to be cured" (p. 105), as if she had predicted that continuing to ignore her infantile traumas would lead her nowhere, just as in her dream the hope of reaching her goal—that is, the station—had been deferred. Freud, though, considered her decision to end the treatment to have happened "so unexpectedly, just when my hopes of a successful termination of the treatment were at their highest, and her thus bringing those hopes to nothing" (p. 109). The break off was seen as an act of vengeance on Dora's part. Yet, when Dora returned, fifteen months later, to continue her treatment, Freud did not take her seriously and this time *he* dismissed *her*, in retaliation against her act of "vengeance", which had made him deeply frustrated in his therapeutic ambitions. Freud had accused Dora of having behaved like a "governess" with him, giving him two weeks' notice when she had communicated her intention to break off the treatment.[6] Freud, though, forgot that not only the governess, but also the employer must give fifteen days' notice. This would have motivated Freud's vengeance and his refusal to welcome Dora back into treatment, judging her request insincere. Lewin (1973, p. 529) draws our attention to the fact that this was a case of rationalisation on Freud's part. There were no other reasons to refuse the treatment. From his letters to Fliess, it appears that during the period when Dora had asked him to be readmitted into treatment (1 April 1902)[7] Freud had very few clients and had just revoked his consent for the publication of the *Fragment* from the publishing house.[8] Thus, it would have been an opportune moment to continue not only Dora's treatment but also the related case history, to transform it from a fragment into a complete analysis, as he had himself assumed he would do, writing in the postscript: "Dora came to see me again: to finish her story and to ask for help once more" (p. 120). In a letter to Fliess dated 11 March 1902, he communicates to his friend:

> When I came back from Rome, my enjoyment of life and work was somewhat heightened and that of martyrdom somewhat diminished. I found my practice had almost melted away; I withdrew my last work from publication because just a little earlier I had lost my last audience in you.

CHAPTER SEVEN

Confusion of tongues and the traumatolytic function of the dream

Thirty-two years after Freud had taken Dora into treatment, Ferenczi presented a paper at the *12th Congress of the International Psychoanalytical Association* in Wiesbaden, with the title *The Passions of Adults and Their Influence on the Sexual and Character Development of Children*.[1] In this essay, Ferenczi emphasises the "traumatic factors in the pathogenesis of the neuroses which had been unjustly neglected in recent years" (p. 225).[2] He explains how, facing "the almost hallucinatory repetitions of traumatic experiences" (p. 225), he had found himself in need of modifying the psychoanalytical technique, discarding "the restrained coolness, the professional hypocrisy" (p. 226), which essentially reproduced the conditions of the original trauma. In this way, a condition of trust could be created between patient and analyst, which was "necessary for the patient in order to enable him to re-experience the past no longer as hallucinatory reproduction but as an objective memory" (p. 227). Ferenczi says that this new technique had enabled him to confirm the "supposition that the trauma, especially the sexual trauma, as the pathogenic factor cannot be valued highly enough" (p. 226), a thesis he had already advanced in *Child Analysis in the Analysis of Adults* (1931a) the preceding year. Ferenczi goes so far as to confirm all that Freud had claimed when elaborating his "seduction theory", and his words seem to recall the Freudian language of the time:

> Even children of very respectable, sincerely puritanical families, fall victim to real violence or rape much more often than one had dared to suppose. Either it is the parents who try to find a substitute gratification in this pathological way for their frustration, or it is people thought to be trustworthy such as relatives (uncles, aunts, grandparents), governesses or servants, who misuse the ignorance and the innocence of the child. The immediate explanation—that these are only sexual phantasies of the child, a kind of hysterical lying—is unfortunately made invalid by the number of such confessions, e.g. of assaults upon children, committed by patients actually in analysis […]. A typical way in which incestuous seductions may occur is this: an adult and a child love each other, the child nursing the playful phantasy of taking the role of mother to the adult. This play may assume erotic forms but remains, nevertheless, on the level of tenderness. It is not so, however, with pathological adults, especially if they have been disturbed in their balance and self-control by some misfortune or by the use of intoxicating drugs. They mistake the play of children for the desires of a sexually mature person or even allow themselves—irrespective of any consequences—to be carried away. The real rape of girls who have hardly grown out of the age of infants, similar sexual acts of mature women with boys, and also enforced homosexual acts, are more frequent occurrences than has hitherto been assumed. [p. 226]

In the rest of this paper, Ferenczi illustrates all the consequences of these abuses on the child's psychical evolution, from a split of consciousness to effects on his or her sexual, emotional and cognitive development, and from a sense of guilt to an identification with the aggressor. Within his reflections on the trauma, Ferenczi wrote *On the Revision of the Interpretation of Dreams* (1931), in which, in a rereading of Freud's work, he envisaged a traumatolytic function for the dream, besides that of wish-fulfilment. I quote below the most significant parts of Ferenczi's theory, which endorse my thesis that Dora's two dreams reproduce her infantile trauma, while constituting an attempt at riding it out (to which Freud did not concede to listen):

I think, however, that the recurrence of the day's residues in itself is one of the functions of the dream. While following up the connexions, it strikes us more and that the so-called day's (and as we may add, life's) residues are indeed repetition symptoms of traumata. As is known the repetition tendency fulfils in itself a useful function in the traumatic neuroses; it endeavours to bring about a better (and if possible a final) solution than was possible at the time of the original shock. [...] Thus instead of 'the dream is a wish-fulfilment' a more complete definition of the dream function would be: every dream, even an unpleasurable one, is an attempt at a better mastery and settling of traumatic experiences, so to speak, in the sense of an *esprit d'escalier* which is made easier in most dreams because of the diminution of the critical faculty and the predominance of the pleasure principle. [...] The state of unconsciousness, the state of sleep, favours not only the dominance of the pleasure principle (wish-fulfilling function of the dream), but also the return of unmastered traumatic sensory impressions which struggle for solution (traumatolytic function of the dream). In other words: the repetition tendency of the trauma is greater in sleep than in waking life; consequently in deep sleep it is more likely that deeply hidden, very urgent sensory impressions will return which in the first instance caused deep unconsciousness and thus remained permanently unsolved. [Ferenczi, 1949, pp. 238–242]

I will not indulge in commenting on Ferenczi's words, which I believe to be sufficiently clear. Also, I think that the points in common between Ferenczi's thesis on the traumatolytic function of the dream, and my reading of Dora's dreams, are rather apparent. Both imply an effort to bring to light events that are more traumatic than those highlighted by Freud, the same events that would have emerged had Freud kept his initial promise.

Speaking of the *fascination of the dream*, Pontalis (1990) mentions the *traumatic dream*, in the following terms:

The traumatic dream is a "flash-back" and a block of the image: it represents nothing but the event. It makes it present again, it repeats it or, better still, it re-produces it, and thus confers on it an even greater intensity than that which it had had in reality. [pp. 21–22]

Freud did not identify Dora's dream of the burning house as a traumatic one. Instead, he interpreted its recurrence as the effect of an intention that urged for its realisation. In *The Interpretations of Dreams* (1900a), Freud had even connected anxiety-dreams to wish-fulfilment and up to that point he had never questioned the general principle according to which the main function of a dream is that of wish-fulfilment. Only twenty years after Dora's dreams would Freud return to the question of the true nature of traumatic dreams and the reasons for their recurrence, in his *Beyond the Pleasure Principle* (1920g). Freud had recognised

> the probability that in dreams too the transformation of thoughts into visual images may be in part the result of the attraction which memories couched in visual form and eager for revival bring to bear upon thoughts cut off from consciousness and struggling to find expression. On this view a dream might be described as *a substitute for an infantile scene modified by being transferred on to a recent experience*. The infantile scene is unable to bring about its own revival and has to be content with returning as a dream. (S. E., 5, p. 546)

In light of these claims, and of other quotations by Freud on dreams, how was it possible for him to really believe that the "infantile scene" behind the dream of the burning house was a recollection of Dora's masturbation? One could also object that in an adult, or even in an adolescent such as Dora herself, the memory of masturbation in childhood is not so traumatic an event that it would need to be repressed deeply, alongside those "earliest memories of childhood" that are "not obtainable any longer as such" and that are therefore replaced by transferences and dreams. An infantile scene that cannot impose its re-enactment through memory, and must re-emerge instead in the form of a dream, must constitute a much more traumatic event than masturbation, and belongs to an "unremembered experience" from that unrepressed unconscious of which I will speak below. "The hysteric is a visual type", Freud had said. Thus, what could be better than Dora's two dreams to reproduce those infantile traumatic scenes, which are sometimes so difficult to access? So complaisant had Dora been with her analyst that she had provided him, during the brief period of her analysis, with two dreams rich in material, which would have been sufficient to reconstruct the infantile traumatic scenes and corroborate the aetiology of hysteria, a task that Freud hoped to achieve through this case history.

Drawing on Paul Valéry's *Cahiers*, Pontalis asserts that the visual aspect of the dream leads back to the "thought's activity, which goes on day and night" (p. 30): "dream and thought are made of the same substance". Valéry states that "the dream is a sentence. Whatever could its purpose be?" (p. 33)

For Freud, Dora's first dream was indeed a phrase, a proposition, a sentence repeated over and over again to reveal to the dreamer the urgency of such proposition, namely, the necessity of leaving the paternal abode. Dora later carries out this intention in the second dream.

Over a century has passed since the publication of *Traumdeutung*, and our understanding of the function of the dream has deepened beyond the limited Freudian conception of wish-fulfilment, thanks to the contributions of post-Freudian psychoanalysis (Mancia, 2006b). The notion of the unconscious has itself been subjected to revision, as a result of the contributions of neuroscience. While for Freud the unconscious was strictly associated with the concept of repression, neurosciences applied to psychoanalysis have stressed the existence of an unrepressed unconscious stored in the implicit memory. Mancia (2007, pp. 43–45) defines this "unrepressed unconscious" as "a series of traumatic events of differing severity that were never repressed but were stored in implicit memory; as preverbal, presymbolic representations they never reached the level of consciousness but their effects are nevertheless felt throughout adult life. They surface in the transference, and particularly in dreams, which are memory's very own theatre. [...] Memories deposited in this system cannot be 'remembered' as such, in contrast to those stored in explicit, declarative memory. As they are not conscious, they obviously cannot be rendered in words and can be represented only in dreams or lived in the analytical relation or in the patient's relations with his or her body, through preverbal modalities."

Meares (2013, p. 89) likewise draws our attention to the bodily inscription of traumatic memories, "At the earliest or most severe level, the traumatic memories will be wordless and perhaps imageless, recorded in a largely bodily way, as affects and impulses to act". As such, the phenomenon of somatic conversion of the hysteric becomes a signal of the re-emerging of old traumatic memories.

Neuroscientific discoveries relating to implicit memory have given rise to a revision of the Freudian concept of "infantile amnesia". Solms and Turnbull (2002, pp. 147–148) claim "*conscious* and *unconscious* memory are two entirely different things. *The activation of a memory trace is not at all synonymous with conscious remembering*. The fact that you are not consciously aware and mindful of the events of early childhood does not therefore mean that the traces they left are not constantly being activated."

The encounter between psychoanalysis and neuroscience has generated a broader conception of the unconscious, associating the Freudian dynamic unconscious, which is based on repression and deposited in the explicit, or autobiographic, memory, with an "unrepressed unconscious", which is deposited in the implicit memory and not directly accessible to the memory. However, in this new theory of the mind, the *dream* still remains the *royal road* to access this unrepressed unconscious.

In the dream, "memory" enters the frame, which leads us to relive the past under different forms and renders the implicit and explicit memory the bridge between present and past experiences, "so dreams too—which emerge from implicit memory—bring the past up into the present (in the transference); this permits a *reconstruction that makes it possible to move the present back into the past*" (Mancia, 2007, p. 84; italics added). The dream thus becomes an "historic event" that gives meaning to the traces of the past, reuniting them in a series of relationships including the present. The knowledge derived from the dream also depends on the fact that, "taken in the right context and viewed in the here and now of the analytical setting [...] dreaming makes it possible to bring early experiences to the surface and give them new meaning, to 'up-date' them to the present. Thus the dream can be seen as the most credible and reliable tool in what Freud called *Nachträglichkeit*, referring to the reassigning of significance to some past experience, even if it was preverbal and presymbolic, by rewriting the memory (with or without the actual recollection)" (Mancia, 2006b, p. 312).

This neuropsychoanalytic revision of the dream advances a vision of the dream-work which places it in continuity with the daily thinking activity. "Freud (1900) did not consider the dream as a thought process, but as a sort of distortion that could be decoded by interpretation. This revealed a tendency to separate the work of the night from that of the day. We now are more likely to consider that the dream expresses its own truth, without distortion, and that this thought process is a continuation of our thinking while awake. We therefore tend to combine the night and day as a single form of thought" (Mancia, 2007, pp. 85–86).

These conclusions had already been achieved by Ogden (2001) before the contribution from neuroscience. Ogden formulated this same thought on the continuity between night and day, attributing a poetic quality to it, which is characteristic of his writing:

> The internal conversation known as dreaming is no more an event limited to the hours of sleep than the existence of stars is limited to the hours of darkness. Stars become visible at night when their luminosity is no longer concealed by the glare of the sun. Similarly, the conversation with ourselves that in sleep we experience as dreaming continues unabated and undiluted in our waking life. [Ogden, 2001, p. 5]

Actually, Freud did not really consider dreaming activity to be firmly separated from waking activity, because in *The Interpretation of Dreams* (1900a) he claims:

> The unconscious wish links itself up with the day's residues and effects a transference on to them; this may happen either in the course of the day or not until a state of sleep has been established. A wish now arises which has been transferred on to the recent material; or a recent wish, having been suppressed, gains fresh life by being reinforced from the unconscious. [S. E., 5, p. 573]
>
> With our knowledge of the dream-work, we could not possibly agree that it only covers the period of awakening. It seems probable, on the contrary, that the first portion of the dream-work has already begun during the day, under the control of the preconscious. [ibid., p. 575]
>
> Certain personal experiences of my own lead me to suspect that the dream-work often requires more than a day and a night in order to achieve its result; and if this is so, we need no longer feel any amazement at the extraordinary ingenuity shown in the construction of the dream. [ibid., p. 576]

I believe it to be extremely important, nowadays, to valorise the relation between dreams and traumatic memories, taking the courage to amend the Freudian principle according to which the dream solely amounts to wish-fulfilment. To this end, neurosciences are giving credit to what Ferenczi had anticipated, determining the traumatolytic function of the dream, and confirming its polyvalent value. Nowadays, we can no longer disavow the traumatolytic function of the dream prefigured by Ferenczi.

I am convinced that Dora's two dreams took her to that infantile traumatic area that neurosciences now acknowledge as belonging to the implicit memory and to the unrepressed unconscious. Yet Freud had already attained this knowledge in his *Traumdeutung*, when, as we have seen, he explained to the patient who had dreamt of the butcher that "the earliest memories of childhood were '*not obtainable any longer as such*', but were replaced in analysis by 'transferences' and dreams" (*S. E.*, 5, p. 668).

Neuropsychoanalysis focuses mostly on memory, trauma, and dreams. Within these areas of interest, it has found much to confirm Freudian theories, and has broadened our knowledge of the unconscious and of traumatic memories with respect to Freud and his important intuitions. This is happening simultaneously with various trends and sectors of psychoanalysis that continue to discredit Freud's seduction theory and the importance of infantile sexual traumas, accusing Freud of having carried out arbitrary reconstructions, and of having suggested to his patients traumatic memories that emerged within the treatment. Many authors have objected that the sexual scenes were not spontaneously referred by the patients, but were rather generated by Freud's own reconstructions. Because infantile sexual traumas had been repressed, they could only reach consciousness through fragments of memories, dream images, screen memories, and could not be the object of conscious accounts by the patient. Freud affirms that the traces of infantile traumas were never present in the conscious memory (*Further Remarks on Neuro-Psychoses of Defence*, 1896a, *S. E.*, 3, p. 166), and when the memory of the seduction scene was preserved, there was no hysteria. Thus, no patient who lay on Freud's couch was able to refer the conscious memory of an infantile sexual trauma, because in that case he would not have developed hysteria, and would not have crossed the threshold of Freud's consulting room.

It is discouraging to ascertain how much is still written today to prove that Freud disavowed his seduction theory, and that the latter no longer holds any scientific credibility. This is happening even as research on trauma confirms the pathogenic value of precocious sexual traumas and demonstrates its basically ubiquitous presence in many personality disorders, starting with borderline and other personality disorders.

My reference to neuroscience and neuropsychoanalysis simply derives from the wish to confirm my reading of Dora's two dreams with reference to recent theories on traumatic memories. Yet it is not essential to my argument, because the main goal of my work has been to demonstrate—drawing exclusively on the knowledge available to Freud at the time, and on his own theories—that Dora's analysis could have led to her precocious traumatic experiences being unearthed, and that this would, in turn, have confirmed Freud's seduction theory, just as he had promised to do through the exposition of this case history. At no point in this study have I made any reference to notions of which Freud would only have acquired any knowledge after the publication of the case history. I deem irrelevant those readings of Dora's case that rely on Freud's subsequent discoveries, conducted with hindsight, in light of successive psychoanalytical notions, or even drawing on contemporaneous ones.

My objective has also been limited by my desire to demonstrate—though in the most complete and documented way possible, at times perhaps bordering on pedantry—that Freud had the chance to keep his initial promise with which he had enticed the readers of this "clinical novel", having them believe they were going to find confirmation of his traumatic aetiology of hysteria.

I believe I have carried out this task, with an abundance of evidence provided by Freud himself.

CHAPTER EIGHT

Conclusions

If Dora were abused as a child, she must have perceived the overbearing intrusiveness of Freud's interpretations, as well as his burglar technique armed with a "collection of picklocks", as yet another abuse. This may have been the main reason why she abandoned therapy.

The context of Dora's first dream, falling as it did after the traumatic scene by the lake, suggests that this episode had reactivated an infantile recollection so far kept dormant. This memory manifested itself in the dream with characteristics of intrusiveness and repetitiveness, to be read as indicators of an elevated apprehension towards the recent traumatic scene with Herr K., responsible for having activated the oneiric memory of a repressed infantile trauma. There is a high probability that the dream stages a sexual abuse perpetrated by Dora's father, dating back to the patient's early childhood. Yet Freud was either unaware or unwilling to acknowledge the childhood trauma, despite his initial declarations of wanting to confirm, through this case history, his 1895–96 theory of the aetiology of hysteria. Freud no longer wanted to acknowledge the fault of the fathers, including his own father, and refused to recognise Dora's repeated accusations of her father, converting them into self-accusation.

Before concluding, I would like to mention Marie Balmary (1982), who has dedicated an entire volume to the faults of Freud's father.

According to Balmary, "those who have been sexually violated—by seduction—have tried to express—through hysteria, through the negation of sexuality—what they underwent. How would those whose thought and discourse have been violated tell what has been done to them if not through a condition where one no longer has either thought or speech? How would they try to escape if not by making use of a language that could not be understood, but which could also not be taken away from them? And those who, though not killed, had their lives taken from them, how could they fail to see in suicide the only act through which they could, paradoxically, recapture their lives?" (Balmary, 1982, p. 155). Dora tried to acknowledge her trauma and her father's fault by referring two dreams to her analyst, because, according to Balmary, to "become conscious—in order to cure—is to rediscover the witness for what we had known alone. It is to share with another the hitherto disrupted knowledge of something hidden. It is to be recognized as knowing" (ibid., p. 162). Freud did not acknowledge this awareness in Dora, not even in her dreams, which he was unable and unwilling to decipher, so much so in fact that he sometimes appears to have forgotten what he had written in his *Traumdeutung* on the technique of the interpretation of dreams, and to have lost his knowledge of the dream and of the trauma.

Balmary (1982, p. 162) claims that the way to "reorient ourselves toward otherness—an otherness better disposed to understand manifest the buried knowledge of a fault [...] is [...] by transferring it to somebody who will be able to recognise it". Consequently, "the analytic session can be rethought in this sense; the analyst no longer listens only for the patient's repressed desires but also for forgotten knowledge, which is at first represented through symptoms, then realized in the transference to the analyst. In this way, two Freudian discoveries are articulated which have never been reunited in theory: the traumatic memory and the transference. When Freud discovered the transference, he had, in effect, abandoned his theory according to which events causing neurosis were real."

This leads me back to the beginning of my discussion, namely the assertion by Freud that I have taken as the core of my argument: "The earliest memories of childhood were not obtainable any longer as such, but were replaced in analysis by 'transferences' and dreams." Yet not even in the transference, which by his own admission he could not manage successfully, could Freud reconstruct Dora's earliest infantile memories, nor could he acknowledge her father's faults, even if he knew that Dora had operated on him a paternal transference. "If the analyst does not refuse it, he can be taken in the unconscious transference that his patient makes toward him, for the one at fault whom the patient never dared to denounce, and of whose fault he is probably even ignorant, at least as a fault. From this place where the patient puts his analyst, (who accepts without really occupying it), it will be possible for the analyst to seek the meaning with his patient. Because he is taken for another, the author of an unrecognized fault, the analyst enables his patient to rediscover the trace of that lost knowledge" (Balmary, 1982, pp. 162–163).

Yet not only did Dora put Freud in her father's place, as being guilty of an unacknowledged fault that Freud the archaeologist could not bring to light, she also put him in Herr K.'s place, whose fault had conversely been recognised. In the postscript, Freud recognised this twofold transference:

> At the beginning it was clear that I was replacing her father in her imagination, which was not unlikely, in view of the difference between our ages. She was even constantly comparing me with him consciously, and kept anxiously trying to make sure whether I was being quite straightforward with her, for her father 'always preferred secrecy and roundabout ways'. But when the first dream came, in which she gave herself the warning that she had better leave my treatment just as she had formerly left Herr K.'s house, I ought to have listened to the warning myself. "Now" I ought to have said to her "it is from Herr K. that you have made a transference on to me. Have you noticed anything that leads you to suspect me of evil intention similar (whether openly or in some sublimated form) to Herr K.'s? Or have you been struck by anything about me or got to know anything about me which has caught your fancy, as happened previously with Herr K.?" Her attention would then have been turned to some detail in our relations, or in my person or circumstances, behind which there lay concealed something analogous but immeasurably more important concerning Herr K. And

when this transference had been cleared up, the analysis would have obtained access to new memories, dealing, probably, with *actual events*. [p. 118; italics added]

It was not just a matter of resolving the transference of Herr K. onto Freud, but also that of the father onto Freud, because only through this second transference could Freud have accessed those remote infantile memories that he had not deciphered in Dora's dreams. New material would thus have surfaced, that is, those *real memories* Freud mentions, memories that could have confirmed his discovery of 1896, which he had compared to the discovery of the *caput Nili*: namely, the paternal aetiology of hysteria. Yet, from the dual position of culpability where Dora had situated him, Freud was able to lead Dora to no other knowledge than that of her own fault: infantile masturbation.

I wish to conclude my reading of Dora's case by quoting the new motto which Freud had communicated to Fliess in the letter of 22 December 1897:

"What has been done to you, you poor child?"

Enough of my smut.
See you soon.

PART II

THE COUNTERTRANSFERENCE

CHAPTER NINE

Dora's analysis and her analyst's vicissitudes: a frame for Freud's countertransference

In the first part of this book, more precisely in Chapter Two, I formulated the hypothesis that Dora's analysis had begun in approximately mid-September 1900. Trying to establish the exact time of the beginning of Dora's treatment is not merely an exercise in pedantry because it helps us to place it within a frame that includes not only the events of the patient's life, but also those concerning her therapist's life. I believe that a more precise temporal collocation of Dora's treatment also allows new perspectives to emerge on Freud's countertransference. In turn, this knowledge might lead to establish a new collocation of Dora's therapy within the mental space of her analyst, and allow us to make precise references to those memories and vicissitudes stirred up by his encounter with Dora.

I do not intend, through my observations, to establish the relevance of Freud's countertransference in this treatment for the history of psychoanalysis. I will deal, rather, with chronicling daily life, offering a few useful suggestions for delineating a frame of Freud's life experiences, within which his countertransference towards Dora can be placed. I will not go into the clinical aspects of the countertransference, nor will I formulate hypotheses in this sense.

Although my viewpoint consistently differs from Lokoff and Coyne's interpersonal and linguistic perspective (1993, p. 12), I agree with the question they ask themselves: "Since an analysis is a transaction between two real people, not merely a discussion between a patient and his or her intrapsychic constructs, how does the analyst's mood and personality affect the outcome of a therapeutic relationship?" In this chapter, my analysis will focus on this aspect, and I will try to show how Freud's personal vicissitudes might have affected his patient's treatment.

What happened then, between Freud and Dora, in the consulting room?

> Nun ist die Luft von solchem Spuk so voll
> Dass niemand weiß, wie er ihn meiden soll.
> [Now fills the air so many a haunting shape
> That no one knows how best he may escape.][1]

Yet these are not Dora's phantasies, but rather the even more disquieting ones of her analyst. Two stories came together in the consulting room: that of a seduced adolescent, caught up in the erotic plots of two middle-aged men, and that of her analyst, who had just put an end to a long-lasting friendship and had also infringed, perhaps, upon his equally prolonged conjugal fidelity by seducing his sister-in-law. What kind of impact did Freud's personal vicissitudes, and the events that had distressed and continued to disturb him during Dora's treatment, have on his own interpretations? To what extent did Freud's personal life experiences pollute his judgement?

I have shown that Dora's treatment occurred, temporally, immediately after two significant events in Freud's life that had taken place in the summer of 1900: the first fractures in his friendship with Fliess, and, probably, an erotic relationship with Minna.[2] Even if this erotic relationship did in fact never occur, Freud nonetheless spent two undeniably intense weeks on holiday with his sister-in-law, which stimulated him erotically. I therefore completely agree with Rudnytsky's remark that "if Freud did engage in a sexual affair with Minna [...] the effects of this primordial boundary violation would not have been confined to Freud's 'private' life, but would, rather, have extended to the professional sphere in manifold ways, and would, indeed, haunt the entire history of psychoanalysis" (2011, pp. 13–14).

The new date I proposed for the beginning of Dora's treatment locates it even closer to the encounter in Achensee during which Freud and Fliess had an argument, giving rise to the beginning of the end of their friendship. Thus, in light of my observations, we can claim that the traumatic impact of the break-off in friendship deeply affected Freud's analysis of Dora. Moreover, ten years would pass before its shock wave ceased to affect him.

These personal vicissitudes and affective experiences were still fresh in Freud's mind when, two years after the first, swift encounter they had had in her father's presence, the not-yet-eighteen-year-old Dora knocked on his office's door. She was "in the first bloom of youth— a girl of intelligent and engaging looks". In relation to this patient's treatment, unlike the others, Freud offers his friend Fliess only a meagre and equivocal communication, priding himself on having metaphorically deflowered her with his "collection of picklocks". When he writes these lines to his friend, Freud still seems to be under the euphoric effects of his revelries with Minna. Thus it is incongruous to assume that Dora's tales of erotic plots between the Bauer and Zellenka families did not repeatedly stir up, in her analyst's imagination, the memory of those intimate moments, when he "luxuriat[ed] without regrets" with his sister-in-law.

We must keep in mind that, when he was treating Dora, Freud was also conducting his own self-analysis—which he had started with *The Interpretation of Dreams* (1900a), and was now continuing with *The Psychopathology of Everyday Life* (1901b)—for which he was still gathering material of a largely autobiographical nature. Furthermore, a fracture in his friendship with Fliess had just occurred, right before his vacation with Minna. It has been argued that Freud entertained a relationship of the transferential type with Fliess. He therefore had to work through his mourning over the loss of his analytical alter ego.

Mahony (2005, p. 38) has asserted that when this "distressed female teenager mustered a formidable challenge to the middle-aged Freud", he "enjoyed being at the zenith of his intellectual powers of observation, concentration, judgement, and memory" (p. 38). Actually, his letters to Fliess from this period portray a different picture of his circumstances during Dora's therapy. His long-term friendship with Fliess was coming to an end, he had just come out of an alleged erotic relationship with his sister-in-law, and he was both intellectually and professionally unsatisfied. We will see below that, throughout Dora's treatment, a constant preoccupation with Minna's precarious health is detectable in Freud. The changes in his relationship with Fliess caused this to worsen. Already before their meeting in Achensee, Freud describes a rather disappointing personal situation:

> I have already become rather dull, irritable, and morose and respond to everything that does not go smoothly, as with my main case, with all-too-intense a resonance. In addition, the heat these days is killing. It is time to stop. [Masson, 1985, 1 July 1900, p. 420]

He then offers Fliess a prediction of his state of mind at their meeting in Achensee:

> You will see me at the height of exhaustion and ill humor [...]. I am totally exhausted by my work and everything connected with it that is germinating, enticing, and threatening. [Masson, 1985, 10 July 1900, p. 421]

From the intellectual and scientific perspective, the situation was no better:

> The big problems are still wholly unresolved. Everything is in flux and dawning, an *intellectual hell*, with layer upon layer; in the darkest core, glimpses of the contours of Lucifer-Amor. [Masson, 1985, 10 July 1900, p. 421; italics added]

Furthermore, one can note an underlying disappointment on his part as a result of the negative reception of *The Interpretation of Dreams* (1900a), even if he does claim that:

> Whether or not people like the dream book is beginning to leave me cold and I am beginning to bemoan its fate. (Masson, 1985, 10 July 1900, p. 422)

In early August 1900, he met with Fliess and the two friends engaged in a violent argument. The only positive note during this period were the two weeks that he spent with Minna on vacation, from which he had returned to Vienna "feeling outrageously merry and well" (Masson, 1985, 14 September 1900, p. 424).

His intellectual activity continued to disappoint him:

> I myself am writing the dream [essay], without real pleasure and am becoming a professor by way of absentmindedness while collecting material for the "Psychopathology of Everyday Life". [Masson, 1985, 14 October 1900, p. 427]

Even his fantasies were pessimistic in this period:

> Otherwise I am reading Greek archaeology and reveling in journeys I shall never make and treasures I shall never possess. [Masson, 1985, 14 October 1900, p. 427]

On 23 October, he sends his birthday wishes to Fliess, and writes: "I am having a quieter time." Fliess only answers a month later and in the meantime, on 21 November, Freud says:

> As for me, nothing but monotony, not without worries. [Masson, 1985, 21 November 1900, p. 428]

On 25 November 1900, his intellectual and professional pessimism appears to reach its apex:

> In my work I am not exactly at a standstill; on a subterranean level it is probably proceeding quite well, but it is certainly not a time of harvest, of conscious mastery. There probably will be no more surprising findings at all. The [main] viewpoints probably have been put together. All that is missing is the organization and the detailed elaboration. I do not see any prospect of substantially shortening the duration of treatment; it will scarcely be possible to widen the scope of indications. [Masson, 1985, 25 November 1900, pp. 429–430]

While he was expressing this moral and intellectual pessimism, Freud was also occupied with Dora's treatment. To illustrate how Freud's personal vicissitudes and the ensuing affective states played a part in the treatment, mainly by polluting his countertransference towards his young patient, I will draw on the concept of "unanalysed residues" introduced by Lucio Russo (2003). Russo affirms that a "reading of Freud which also takes into account his implicit way of thinking involves the conclusion that psychoanalytic measure can exclude neither the tendency to objectify the unconscious nor the presence of the analyst's unconscious fantasies in the interpretation of the patient's material" (ibid., fn. 3).

Russo continues his argument by claiming that countertransference, in all its manifold versions, always remains a reaction to the transference, and that, as such, the analyst must make good use of it in order to interpret the patient's unconscious. While countertransference allows the analyst to keep the un-analysed and the un-thought of the patient within himself, self-analysis is the continuation of the analyst's analysis when communication between the two apparatuses, the protagonists of the analysis, enters a crisis. Through self-analysis, the analyst continues to produce analytic work by himself and with himself, even if the space of intersubjective communicative is now lacking. Then, "the capacity to self-analyse one's inner world, which the analyst has acquired in the course of his training analysis," is continually performed "in the analysis of his patients […]. In my view, the elements showing that the capacity to self-analyse has been attained are essentially tied to how mourning works, to the psychic experience related to the end of the training analysis, and to the introjection of the analytic function. These processes consist in the introduction, into psychic experience, of unanalysed residues, or what remains from the training analysis which enables the analyst to remain alive and open to investigating his own unconscious" (Russo, 2003). Any concluded analysis leaves behind remains of sensations, intimate parts of the analyst available for self-analysis, since they are activated by the analytic relationship with a particular patient. The "unanalysed residues" constitute "an 'unconscious reserve' which contains in the guise of a shadow the subjective parts which were already analysed but which might be used in new contexts" (ibid.).

When he was about to begin his treatment of Dora, Freud's "unanalysed residues" were his relationship with Fliess, which was charged with ambivalence and homosexual nuances, and his relationship with Minna, bursting as it was with erotic connotations. How did these "unanalysed residues" play a part, an unconscious one, in the conduction of Dora's analysis and in her analyst's countertransference? Let us start with the Freud and Fliess relationship.

Schur (1972, pp. 75–76) has insisted on the transferential aspect of Freud's relationship with Fliess. Although their friendship was prevalently epistolary, and they only met a few times during the long seventeen years of their written correspondence, Schur (1972, p. 40) claims that the "intimate exchange of letters with Fliess during this period came often very close to the free association in an analytic session". Anzieu (1986, p. 109), on the other hand, stresses the eroticised aspect of "the correspondence between the two men" which "gradually became, for Freud, a substitute for his love letters to his fiancée", where passion feeds on latent homosexual tendencies.

Schur (1972, p. 77) identifies a number of fundamental aspects of the Freud-Fliess relationship that he believes to be the markers of a relationship of the transferential kind: a) "extreme overvaluation of the object"; b) "exaggerated need for approval and praise"; c) "alternation between submission and defiance"; d) "sudden eruptions of hostility"; e) "eroticisation of the relationship". Precisely because Freud's relationship with his friend from Berlin was of a transferential nature, it is not surprising that, for Freud, the existence, not to mention the intensity, of a conflicting ambivalence in their relationship remained unacknowledged for many years (Schur, 1972, p. 78). Anzieu (1986, pp. 550–551) affirms that "Fliess played the role of psychoanalyst for his friend: he gave him interpretations. But Fliess clearly lacked any psychoanalytic insight, and his interpretations were more than once inaccurate or laden with 'counter-transference.'"

Therefore, one may say that Freud never fully worked through the transferential aspects of his friendship with Fliess, and only much later would he be able to recognise its homosexual undercurrents. Thus, the relationship remained until the end, and continued into Freud's old age, charged with "unanalysed residues". "The unavoidable dissolution of the transference-like element in his relationship was to be a slow and difficult project. What made this last aspect of his effort so painful and caused it to have lingering repercussions was the fact that, in contrast to the normal process of analysis, this dissolution was both enhanced and complicated by external events and therefore resulted eventually in a total break" (Schur, 1972, p. 89).

The break in their friendship occurred in August 1900, during their last "congress" in Achensee, which was also the last time they saw each other. The two friends had a harsh argument, and accused each other of producing scientific work of little value (Gay, 1988, p. 93). Speaking of this last encounter, Fliess described a very violent Freud. The latter was convinced that his friend wanted to invalidate his psychoanalytical discoveries through his theories, also ascribing the variations in the patient's state during the course of analysis to periodic changes. Freud believed that his friend wanted to question *tout court* the results of psychoanalysis; and although Fliess tried to reassure Freud of the contrary, the latter saw in this gesture an act of hostility on Fliess' part.

Freud was still under the influence of these emotions when he perceived in Dora a hostile attitude and a vindictiveness that did not belong to her. Begel (1982, p. 167) argues that "the revenge motive is prominent in Freud's life", and reminds us how Irma's dream "refers to the motive of revenge", and many other dreams in the *Traumdeutung* contain it.[3] Another proof of the centrality of this theme in Freud's thought can be found in the letter to Fliess of 1 July 1900. Here, he builds a narrative wherein the value of his works and that of his friend must finally be acknowledged, concluding that: "Such spiteful glee, such satisfied thirst for revenge plays an important role in my case; so far I have savoured too little of this delicious fare."[4] Thus, this was affecting Freud more than Dora, particularly in this moment of his life, when an old friendship was being torn apart and an erotic relationship with his sister-in-law was on the cards, offering a reward for his frustration, not only of a sexual nature.

Freud was focused on the revenge theme once again when Dora went back to him on April Fool's Day, 1902, such an inopportune day to seek help from a superstitious analyst, who had just written an essay on the unconscious meaning of the small gestures of everyday life. He only needed to look her into the eyes to understand that her request was not to be taken seriously. Just as Dora "took her revenge" against Herr K.'s family—"she had not resumed her relations with the family" (p. 121)—so too was Freud now taking his revenge on her, by refusing to treat her. We can find confirmation that the revenge motive was still present in Freud's thoughts in the period of March–April 1902, in a "remarkable coincidence" referred to in *The Psychopathology of Everyday Life* (1901b). A few days after the title of *Professor Extraordinarius* had been bestowed upon him, Freud met by chance the parents of a former young patient of his, who had opted to interrupt the analysis with Freud, and had sent their daughter to a luminary. Freud formulates a fantasy in which these parents bring the girl back to him after having learnt of his appointment as Professor,[5] thus giving him the chance to avenge himself for the previous offence by refusing to treat the girl. Dora knocked on his office door less than two weeks after he had indulged in this "childish phantasy of revenge" (S. E., 6, 263), thus giving him the opportunity to take the revenge that a few days before he had but daydreamed.

Freud clearly admits that, when Dora came to him the second time, he could not figure out what kind of help she wanted from him. One may thus wonder whether or not on the first occasion, when she was brought to the consulting room by her father, he had understood what kind of help he could offer his patient, since back then it was the father who put forward the request, and she formulated no spontaneous question. I would be inclined to answer this question negatively, since, during Dora's analysis, Freud had abandoned the initial aim of reducing her, at her father's request, to a more docile attitude, and had embraced the idea of solving the whole question by convincing Dora to marry Herr K. Furthermore, Freud remarked to Marie Bonaparte: "The great question that has never been answered, and which I have not yet been able to answer, despite my thirty years of research into the feminine soul is: 'What does a woman want?'" (Freud, quoted in Jones, 1955, p. 468) These words lend further weight to my negative response.

His question "*What does a woman want?*" (*Was will das Weib?*) inevitably leads us back to the initial query and encourages us to consider the issue more broadly. Freud had not understood Dora's requests and needs, and after this admission that he could not figure out what women want, another question arises, namely, what needs had Freud addressed in treating women during so many years of therapeutic activity with hysterical or, more generally, neurotic patients? In this analysis, two figures meet (or, better still, collide), both of which themselves pose a question. On the one hand, we have an adolescent who, borrowing Lacan's words (1981), finds herself wondering: *What is to be a woman?* On the other, we have an analyst who asks himself: *What does a woman want?* Arguably, neither of them found an answer to their questions, nor did they provide one for one another. We can certainly say that Freud, while he was unable to unravel Dora's enquiry, would by no means have been able to answer his own question.

This said, let us now resume the thread of the topic. Not long after the Achensee encounter, which initiated the break off of a long-lasting friendship and a transferential relationship lasting thirteen years, Freud spent two weeks with his sister-in-law Minna. Their intensely eroticised relationship may have been a way for Freud to forget about the quarrel with his friend, who had for years been his "audience", his alter ego, and his transferential object. These two events, the break-off of his friendship with Fliess and his relationship with Minna, are probably not only linked chronologically. They are interconnected, and acquire meaning within Freud's attempt at resolving his transference with Fliess. I believe this to be consonant with Anzieu's (1986, p. 527) claims in this regard: "The most likely hypothesis is that the break with Fliess was offset by the crystallisation of his affection for Martha's sister Minna, who lived with the Freuds and was at that time the only person in the family with the ability to follow Sigmund's work closely: available, intelligent, capable of deep empathy with her brother-in-law, responding internally to his secret incestuous desire, shielded from having to respond physically, by her moral uprightness and attachment to her dead fiancé, and constantly present in the household, Minna gradually came to provide Sigmund with greater creative stimulation than Fliess—a fact which must certainly have helped Freud to withdraw from Fliess." Thus, Minna helped Freud to substitute his homosexual passion for Fliess with a heterosexual one, on which I will now dwell in further detail.

It is a well-known fact that Jung was the one to gossip about Minna Bernays' affair with Sigmund Freud, on the basis of an alleged secret revelation of Minna's to Jung in 1907. This hypothesis has been reclaimed and refuted on several occasions. For instance, Kurt Eissler (1994) has dedicated an entire chapter of his *Three Instances of Injustice* to the refutation of this theory and the rehabilitation of Freud's reputation. Swales (1982), moreover, has strived to find proof of this erotic relationship in Freud's private life, and in his writings.

Swales (1982) refers to Chapter Two of *The Psychopathology of Everyday Life* (1901b). Here, Freud describes the forgetting of the word *aliquis*, attributing it to a hypothetical travel companion, as he had already done through an autobiographical fragment in *Screen Memories* (1899a). Swales demonstrates that this account is also autobiographical in nature, and that the slip is connected with his erotic relationship with his sister-in-law. According to him, she was pregnant in the summer of 1900 and, at the end of her vacation with Freud, the latter left her in Merano not to treat the recurrence of her juvenile tuberculosis, but to interrupt her pregnancy. Freud interprets his travel companion's forgetting of the word *aliquis*—a companion whom Swales proves to be Freud himself—as an interference due to the anxious wait for his sexual partner's menstruations. Mahony (1996, 2005) has underlined how the entire clinical exposition of Dora's case is marked throughout by several references to liquidity, identifying in these recurrent allusions to fluidity a reference to Fliess' repressed presence (*Fliessen* in German means "to flow"). I think that, with an equal or an even higher degree of reliability, we can read in this constant recurrence of terms defining fluidity and flux the emergence of a repressed thought which occupied Freud's mind in that period and had also caused the *aliquis* slip, namely, Freud's anguished wait for Minna's menstrual flow.

Were this the case, Freud's state of mind when he began treating Dora would have to have been particularly troubled by these recent episodes. Minna's return to Vienna would certainly not have improved it, since her health conditions were somewhat precarious and perturbing. In a letter to Fliess dated 25 November 1900, Freud describes his sister-in-law's condition as follows:

> Not everything about her condition is entirely clear, nor is the degree to which worries are justified. I do not want to fill this letter with the details; after all, we shall soon have the answer. The most striking feature is that her pulse rate is 130 and beyond. [Masson, 1985, 25 November 1900, p. 429]

In a letter dated 25 January 1901, he writes:

> A veil has lifted from Minna's illness. In connection with a strophantus[-induced] diarrhea she developed stomach and abdominal pains last week; during one of the following nights she had an especially severe attack of pain localized in the left transverse colon, so that the whole thing reminded me of an awful case of embolism of the mesenteric artery that I once saw in a cardiac patient [...] There is no doubt of the existence of an intestinal ulcer. But was it really an embolism? Rie claims to have noticed impure heart sounds throughout those days. She takes only milk now; pain rules her days. I have all sorts of fears about what the future will bring. [Masson, 1985, 25 January 1900, p. 433]

Under the effect of such intense emotions as these, Freud had carried out Dora's analysis and later drafted the case history, which he completed the night before he communicated his worries about Minna to Fliess. As a matter of fact, in the same letter of 25 January 1901, he writes:

> I finished "Dreams and Hysteria" yesterday, and today I already miss a narcotic. It is a fragment of an analysis of a case of hysteria in which the explanations are grouped around two dreams; so it is really a continuation of the dream book. In addition, it contains resolutions of hysterical symptoms and glimpses of the sexual-organic foundation of the whole. It is the subtlest thing I have written so far and will put people off even more than usual. [Masson, 1985, 25 January 1901, p. 433]

More information on Minna's health follows, in the letter from 30 January 1901:

> As to Minna's condition, I know the following: without doubt there is an ulcer; but nothing whatsoever indicates that it is duodenal. In view of the blood and the pain, Oscar's consultant, B. Hammerschlag (who, by the way, is confused by all this), even wanted to induce us to localize it in the rectum. I believe it is in the colon (flexus). It started with an embolism; but a tbc [tubercular] ulcer apparently can be excluded. [...] No one really has a clear picture, but it is beginning to dawn on us that it might be a cardiac affliction, the origin and significance of which are still unknown, but which could involve endocardiac changes [...] Her general condition has greatly improved during the past days and consequently we are in better spirits. A functional or neurotic illness surely cannot be diagnosed. The whole business is uncanny. [Masson, 1985, 30 January, p. 434]

Yet, if he had left Minna behind, in Merano, not for a "pulmonary apicitis", as he had claimed to Fliess, but, rather, to interrupt her pregnancy, the "whole business" should not have appeared so puzzling to Freud. After all, a tubercular ulcer had been excluded, which would have been plausible if Minna's illness had been the resurgence of her juvenile tuberculosis. Rather mysteriously, Freud believes he has a better understanding of the situation than the two internists who had visited Minna and thinks that if there is an ulcer, it should be found in the *flexus* of the colon. Was he in possession of further knowledge to advance these diagnostic suspicions?

Whatever the truth is, it is possible that Freud felt particularly guilty about Minna's precarious health condition, because a few days later he was no longer capable of looking back on his "luxuriating" by Lake Garda "without regrets". These concerns led to the day residues of the dream Freud had at the time, and which I will examine in greater detail in the next chapter, that's the dream of "Company at table d'hôte". At first, this dream appears "unemotional, disconnected, and unintelligible", but in the course of the analysis it reveals itself to be charged with "intense and well-founded affective impulses" (S. E., 5, 640). Freud individuates his desire for a "love that cost me nothing" as being one of the main motives of the dream.

All things considered, therefore, it is not surprising that, as he confided to Fliess, Freud wrote not only *Psychopathology of Everyday Life* (1901b) but also *Fragment of an Analysis of a Case of Hysteria* (1905e) in "a certain gloomy heaviness":

> The "Psychology of Everyday Life" will also be finished in a few days, and then both essays will be corrected, sent off, and so on. All of it has been written with a certain gloomy heaviness, traces of which it will not be possible to hide. [Masson, 1985, 15 February 1901, p. 436]

The same day he reports reassuring news about Minna's health:

> I cannot give you any further explanations of Minna's illness. No new insights have turned up; the intestinal ulcer seems to have healed properly; she is eating solids again; her general condition fluctuates; her pulse is still quite variable and can rise to 130 merely from talking. *I perceive no trace of anything neurotic.* On the whole, there is a definite improvement over the last weeks. [Masson, 1985, 15 February 1901, p. 437; italics added]

Freud's remark that he did not perceive "anything neurotic" in his sister-in-law's pathology did not derive from the evidence that Minna manifested organic symptoms. We know that, five years beforehand, Freud had defined Emma Eckstein's haemorrhages as "hysterical", when they were in fact the consequence of Fliess' maladroit surgery.[6]

Beside the fact that, according to Roazen (1975), Freud assumed that no member of his family could be afflicted by neurosis, the memory of a regrettable episode was probably still fresh in his mind. Swales (1982) associates this incident with the forgetting of the word *aliquis*, specifying that it was connected to feelings of guilt related to the death of a fourteen-year-old girl, who died as a result of abdominal cancer, and whose symptoms Freud had wrongly diagnosed as deriving from a pathology of the hysterical kind (p. 21).[7]

While Swales (1982) has tried to unearth in Freud's writings the events that troubled him during the summer of 1900, I will attempt to expose the traces, at least those that are germane to my analysis, that might have been left by these events in the *Fragment of an Analysis*, bearing in mind that the resonance of these events also manifested itself in Freud and Dora's therapeutic relationship, and must have left clues in the analyst's countertransference.

Still with reference to Freud's alleged travel companion, and the latter's associations regarding the word *aliquis*, the reading of a journal article is mentioned, which is entitled "What *St. Augustine* Says about Women". Swales notes that there is also a concealed reference to St. Augustine in Dora's case history, wherein Freud quotes his passage on birth, which is generically attributed here to a "Father of the Church": "*Inter urinas et faeces nascimur*". This reference, in my view, provides evidence that Freud was still focused on the consequences of his relationship with his sister-in-law, which would inevitably have interfered with his relationship with Dora and his related interpretation.

Moreover, the word "relics", which is improperly used at the beginning of the case history—following his favourite metaphor for the psychoanalytic investigation—to refer to archaeological findings, belongs to the free association of the "traveller". Likewise, rather than reincarnations, the words "new editions" are pronounced by the alleged travel companion, and later resurface in Dora's case when Freud speaks of the transference using the metaphor of "reprints" (Swales, 1982, p. 21). These are only clues, obviously, but if we accept that it was on the basis of just such hints that Freud had based his construction of the *Psychopathology of Everyday Life* (1901b), we must acknowledge that these clues represent a manifestation of the unconscious.

Still in the analysis of that slip, when the made-up young man mentions the names of saints and fathers of the Church, Freud, adds the name of Origen by his own initiative. The name of this father of the

Church is, however, then forgotten and does not appear in any other associations within Freud's analysis. The main reason why Origen is famous, Timpanaro (1974, p. 40) explains, is his self-castration. Must we then presume that Freud was formulating unconscious thoughts of self-punishment through castration for his sexual affair with Minna, which had led him to anxiously await her menstruations? I would be inclined to answer in the affirmative, since this is the only association that is neither developed nor interpreted. One of the main themes of the "Company at table d'hôte" dream is the feeling of being "*schuldig*", an adjective which in German means both indebted and guilty. Furthermore, it is perhaps not by chance that in this period, after returning from his holiday, Freud had read Rieger's book, *Die Kastration in rechtlicher, sozialer und vitaler Hinsicht betrachtet* (Castration studied from juridical, social, and vital perspectives), which was published in the same year, 1900. Even if Freud had read this book before the summer, it is still significant that he remembered it after returning from his holiday. He suggested it to Fliess in a short letter from 24 September 1900.

Dora had the misfortune of knocking on Freud's door at the time when the analyst was afflicted by the "sudden" breaking off of a bond that had lasted for thirteen years, and which was at once a long-term friendship, a homosexual love, a transference, and an intellectual exchange. Also, he had just experienced a feeling of outrageous merriment following his intriguing two-week vacation with Minna. These were certainly not ideal conditions in which to begin the analysis of a young adolescent who, in turn, had been subjected to sexual assaults perpetrated by a man of the same age as her analyst, and whose father was having a sexual affair with her suitor's wife. Had Dora been aware of her analyst's recent life experiences, perhaps she would not have walked through the door of *Berggasse* 19. And had Freud told Dora about the dream that had occurred during her analysis, the "Company at table d'hôte" dream—a countertransferential dream the central element of which was the desire for a "love that cost[s] me nothing"—she would probably have withdrawn from treatment long before the end of the year. It must be noted that Freud wrote *On Dreams* (1901a) in October 1900, in which he analyses that dream in various phases, gradually bringing to light the true nature of the conflict that was bothering him (Swales, 1982). This conflict was therefore active during Dora's analysis, and might have affected Freud's countertransference towards his patient.

I will now dwell some more on Russo (2003, pp. 13–14), in order to show that at this time of his life, when Freud met Dora, he was loaded not only with "unanalysed residues" but also with "unanalysable residues" insofar as the responsible events had occurred too close to Dora's analysis, leaving him with no time to work through them properly. "During a given day's work, in his relationship with his patients, the analyst sometimes feels bored, distracted or blocked by his desire to analyse for reasons that concern his own life, such as illness or death, psychic suffering, failures or conflicts. *Life also produces in his mind influences similar to patients' transferences.*" (italics added)

In the months of August and September 1900, which Freud spent between the Achensee and the Garda lake, two cases of "transferential life", as Russo calls them, took place, which were so emotionally demanding that Freud could not leave their luggage of unelaborated emotionality outside of the consulting room, where he was about to hear the story of his young patient. If, as Russo claims (2003, p. 8), "the elements showing that the capacity to self-analyse has been reached are essentially tied to how mourning works, to the psychic experience related to the end of the training analysis, and to the introjection of the analytic function", then in autumn 1900 Freud was certainly in no such condition. The break with Fliess, his "analytical object", was too recent not only for Freud to have worked through the mourning, but also to have assessed its intensity and thus the emotional impact it would have on him in the future. Actually, we know that, even ten years after the episode, Freud had still not fully worked through his relationship with Fliess (Gay, 1988, p. 274). That Dora's analysis and the drafting of the case history were conducted under the influence of the abrupt change in the relationship with Fliess is demonstrated by what Freud himself writes to Fliess on 11 March 1902:

> I withdrew my last work from publication because just a little earlier I had lost my last audience in you. [Masson, 1985, 11 March 1902, p. 456]

Also, Freud's ambivalence towards Dora's alleged homosexuality appears to have been dictated by the recent vicissitudes involving Fliess. According to Mahony (1996, p. 26), "Dora and Fliess both found themselves dealing with Freud's repressed homosexuality and feminine identification". This difficulty was connected, I believe, at this time in Freud's life, to problems in his relationship with Fliess, and to the resurgence of a latent homosexuality of which he was only beginning to form a vague awareness at this stage, and which he only had the courage to acknowledge when he was an older man. In a letter to Fliess from 7 August 1901, he writes:

> I do not share your contempt for friendship between men, probably because I am to a high degree party to it. In my life, as you know, woman has never replaced the comrade, the friend.[8] [Masson, 1985, 7 August 1901, p. 447]

As for his relationship with Minna, we have seen that after those two weeks of revelries, Freud had returned to Vienna by himself, leaving her behind in Merano so that she could undergo treatment. He then developed feelings of guilt about having abandoned his beloved sister-in-law while she was suffering from a precarious health, so much so that he may have formulated an unconscious punishment fantasy involving castration.

Dora's case history contains a comment that could be considered to be self-analytical. In the last lines of the case, before the *Postscript*, Freud makes a few observations about the opposition between reality and fantasy in the neurotic:

> Incapacity for meeting a real erotic demand is one of the most essential features of a neurosis. Neurotics are dominated by the opposition between reality and phantasy. If what they long for the most intensely on their phantasies is presented to them in reality, they none the less flee from it; and they abandon themselves to their phantasies the most readily where they need no longer fear to see them realized. Nevertheless, *the barrier erected by repression can fall before the onslaught of a violent emotional excitement produced by a real cause*; it is possible for a neurosis to be overcome by reality. But we have no general means of calculating through what person or what event such a cure can be effected. [S. E., 7, 110; italics added]

Perhaps the intimacy with Minna over their two-week vacation and the violent excitement it caused helped Freud demolish the barrier erected by repression and overcome his neurosis, leaving him surprised by this cure issuing from reality, and leading him to claim that no means were available to determine how such a cure could be brought about. After all, this cure by reality allowed him, the following year, to overcome his inhibition to visit Rome. To do so, he first had to pass by Trento, that is, he needed to refresh the memory of those places that had been the site of his erotic relationship with Minna, which had led to the collapse of the barrier erected by repression and of the incest taboo.

It is worth dwelling here on a few observations in relation to this point by Silverstein (2007), who has contributed to the controversy surrounding the relationship between Freud and Minna through a number of highly pertinent reflections, which are equally distant from hagiography and iconoclastic temptations. Silverstein's considerations follow a similar procedure to the one I have adopted in this book, that is, he seeks to confirm a hypothesis in Freud's work while keeping in mind that real life events of emotional relevance could not have failed to leave a trace in his writings.

Therefore, Silverstein (2007, p. 286) assumes that if the relationship between Freud and Minna assumed a sexual nature, a few considerations by the former following the event must be read as a self-justification for his having broken a fundamental aspect of the social structure, namely, the incest taboo.

Silverstein claims that, by means of his *psychoanalytical insight* about the taboo of incest, Freud felt himself absolved from observance of the demands of a taboo that would have otherwise limited his sexual freedom. In *Draft N*, which is included in the letter to Fliess from 31 May 1897, he had written:

> The horror of incest (something impious) is based on the fact that, as a result of communal sexual life (even in childhood), the members of a family remain together permanently and become incapable of joining with strangers. Thus incest is antisocial—civilization consists in this progressive renunciation. Contrariwise, the "superman". [Masson, 1985, *Draft N*, p. 252]

Silverstein (2007) remarks that this affirmation was made only a few months after his confession to Fliess that his marriage had come to lack sexual excitement, and a year before his trip with Minna to Switzerland, in Maloja, where Maciejewski found the hotel logs for a double room under the names of "Dr. Freud und Frau". Silverstein maintains that Freud identified with this "Superman" by daring to infringe upon the incest taboo, and in this regard, he quotes a passage from *Civilized Sexual Morality and Modern Nervous Illness* (1908d), which could bear an important autobiographical resonance:

> The man who, in consequence of his unyielding constitution, cannot fall in with this suppression of instinct, becomes a "criminal", an "outlaw", in the face of society—unless his social position or his exceptional capacities enable him to impose himself upon it as a great man, a "hero". [1908, p. 187, quoted in Silverstein, 2007, p. 286]

We must not forget that Freud had defined himself as a *conquistador*;[9] how could a conquistador accept the repression of his instincts? In *On the Universal Tendency to Debasement in the Sphere of Love* (1912d) Freud says:

> It sounds not only disagreeable but also paradoxical, yet it must nevertheless be said that anyone who is to be really free and happy in love must have surmounted his respect for women and have come to terms with the idea of incest with his mother or sister. [*S. E., 11*, p. 186]

Then, in a letter to Marie Bonaparte dated 30 April 1932, Freud affirms that in certain exceptional, singular circumstances, incest could be innocuous. It is possible, Freud claims, that for somebody capable of subtracting themselves from the influence of phylogenetic repression, incest could occur without any harm being done. Yet one can never be sure.

Silverstein (2007, p. 288) reads these affirmations as self-justifications on Freud's part. At the same time, he claims, these comments sound like an indirect confession that he had engaged in an incestuous relationship with his sister-in-law. He concludes that: "If we have learned anything from Freud, it shows easily passion can trump reason. If Freud found himself in a passionate, heat-of-the-moment situation with a less than passive Minna, it is not impossible that, given his cumulative sexual frustration, he might have given in to the pressure of his sexual drive, hoping that, maybe, for once, he could have pleasure without cost. If Freud regarded Minna as a 'mistress', he may not have displayed the same inhibitions and restraints he observed toward his wife."[10]

Silverstein's conclusion allows us to attain a further insight, when reading the case history, into the influence of Freud's personal vicissitudes on the conduction of Dora's analysis. When, on 31 December, Dora announced to Freud that this was going to be their last session, her analyst asked her:

- When did you come to this decision?
- A fortnight ago, I think.
- That sounds just like a maidservant or a governess—a fortnight's warning.
- There was a governess who gave warning with the K.'s, when I was on my visit to them that time at L—, by the lake.

At this point, Dora says that Herr K. had made "violent love" to the governess, who had eventually yielded, but that after a while he had ceased to show any interest in her. Freud then asks a question about the epilogue of this *love affair*:

- And what became of the girl?
- I only know that she went away.
- And she did not have a child as a result of the adventure?
- No. [S. E., 7, pp. 105–106].

Let us examine how Freud's personal vicissitudes influenced the questions he posed to Dora, and his interpretations. Freud had accused Dora of having shown an interest in Herr K.'s children only to obtain their father's approval. In the Freud household, Minna, as the governess, looked after Freud's children, and with sincere interest. Yet, this does not mean that she was not equally interested in their father. Freud demonstrates an inconvenient curiosity for this governess, asking Dora if her adventure had left her pregnant. Freud's question was in no way pertinent to Dora's treatment, and could by no means, and in fact did not, produce any useful material for the analysis. This would lead us to deduce that Swales was right in claiming that Freud had left Minna in Merano to interrupt her pregnancy, and that his thoughts were still focused on the consequences of his adventure with her. Freud repeatedly underlines that two weeks have passed by before Dora tells him of her decision to interrupt the treatment. Two weeks also pass, moreover, before she tells her mother about the scene by the lake and about

Herr K.'s advances. Thus, could we not say that these two weeks, which bring to mind the governess' notice, also correspond to the two weeks of vacation Freud spent with Minna, the governess?

Glenn (1986, p. 592) has specifically dealt with Freud's countertransference towards Dora, who "pictured herself as a maid",[11] claiming that "Freud's difficulty with Dora stemmed from this countertransference", that is, from Freud's countertransference towards his childhood governess Monica Zajic, who was his "instructress in sexual matters" and played an important oedipal role in Freud's life.[12] Glenn argues that, during Dora's treatment, a sexual countertransference was active in Freud (p. 593). He also observes that Freud's comparison of Dora to a nursemaid, a servant, and a governess implies a close association of these three figures in his mind (p. 599). Thus one may agree with Glenn, when he claims that Freud treated Dora "like a maid when he told her she was free to stop at any time, but that day they would go on with their work. This seems more appropriate to say to a maid than to a patient" (p. 603). Glenn claims that since Dora was, besides a member of her family, also a servant, a governess, and a maid, Freud wanted to get rid of her in order to avoid experiencing any oedipal, incestuous feelings, and, as a result, the punishment merited by these forbidden feelings. Yet, to me, this observation seems to relate much more closely to Minna than to Dora. As a matter of fact, Minna was at the same time a member of Freud's family, and a sort of governess and nursemaid, and it was to her that Freud's incestuous desires were addressed. Over the course of many years, Freud had never missed an opportunity to be alone with her, even spending his vacations with her. These may have turned out to be much more enjoyable than the holidays he would spend with his wife Martha, after sexual attraction had become lacking in their marriage.[13] If it is true that Dora reactivated in Freud the memory of his childhood governess, then it is all the more likely that the erotic entanglements of the Bauer and Zellenka families reactivated in him the memory of his two-week vacation, "luxuriating without regrets" with "Minna, the governess".

It would certainly be wrong to judge Freud's analytical work in Dora's case in retrospect, with our current knowledge of countertransference and of the analyst's emotional participation in the treatment. Yet we must acknowledge that Freud was completely unaware that his emotional experiences, stemming from recent vicissitudes, had in all probability influenced his *choice of contents* for his interpretation, as well as the *moment* at which he would interpret them and the *clarity* with which he would present his interpretations. This could account for the scepticism and emotional indifference with which Dora acknowledges the majority of her analyst's interpretations, as well as for her patent and critical refusal of them.

In the *Postscript* to the case history, Freud makes many contradictory claims regarding Dora's transference; it seems particularly implausible that "the transference took me unawares" (p. 119). Actually, he had himself on more than one occasion offered examples of Dora's transference towards him. Freud, who had just come out of an erotic relationship with his sister-in-law, cannot understand the "unknown factor" in which he reminded Dora of her seducer. This is all the more surprising, since in his analysis of the first dream, Freud had also fantasised about Dora's desire to be kissed by him, and had described Dora's analysis to his friend Fliess as an easy rape, to be conducted with his "collection of picklocks". Freud thinks that this "unknown factor" had to be money, and sees Dora as an opportunistic girl, perhaps because Herr K. used to give her expensive presents. Actually, Freud was the one concerned about money in that period, since he had paid for Minna's treatments. This preoccupation had emerged in the "Company at table d'hôte" dream, in which he had expressed his fear of becoming poor, and his desire for a love that would cost him nothing, a "love which would call for *no* expenditure". This thought would be inevitably reinforced by Dora's story, which showed that K.'s courtship was as expensive as it was as unsuccessful. Freud is not aware that this interpretation is not rooted in Dora's story, but rather in his own recent personal history, and derived from the thoughts that were worrying him at this moment in his life. This lack of awareness seems to be confirmed by the certainty with which Freud claims that, for a physician, "it need make no difference to him whether he has to overcome any particular impulse of the patient's in connection with himself or with someone else" (p. 117), as if he were disregarding the self-analytical commitment involved through a reference to the physician. After all, Freud himself confirms that he failed to understand the nature of that "unknown factor", which had led Dora to bring about the transference from Herr K. onto him. Freud thinks that this factor, the "unknown factor", has something to do with either money or jealousy.

Goretti (1997, p. 637) has observed that with Dora Freud frequently adopted "an interpretative approach based on the theoretical concept of projection". I believe, however, that he was unable to analyse his own projections onto Dora with an equal degree of clarity. In this regard, we might recognise here what was arguably Fliess' one sensible observation over the course of so many years of friendship with Freud, and which had the most shattering effect on a relationship that was already highly compromised. It represents, I would contend, the last nail on the coffin of their friendship. Fliess observed that "the reader of thoughts merely reads his own thoughts into other people".[14] If we take this remark, put it in perspective and try to deprive it of the brunt of hatefulness with which it was probably imbued—motivated as it was by Fliess' will to devalue Freud's work—then we could argue that, in many of his interpretations in the Dora case, Freud behaved like a "reader of thoughts".[15] I believe that, over this period, the strong emotional impact of personal events prevented Freud from acknowledging his own countertransference and from analysing it, especially, in such a way as to promote a self-analytical work. To those who would object that Freud only discovered the countertransference in 1910, I would respond, borrowing Charcot's words, that: "*La théorie c'est bon, mais ça n'empêche pas d'exister*" (*Theory is good; but it doesn't prevent things from existing*).

CHAPTER TEN

Spinach, cocaine, and countertransference in a dream of Freud's

The Freudian dreams that are most often associated with the theme of cocaine are the "Irma's injection" dream, the "Non vixit" dream, and the dream of the "Botanical monograph". Bernfeld (1991, p. 182) claims that the episode of cocaine surfaces in many other dreams interpreted by Freud during his self-analysis. Yet, these other dreams form part of *The Interpretation of Dreams*.

There are clues to suggest that Freud felt guilty about having initiated Fleischl to cocaine, in a dream that he interprets in a completely different way from what we might have expected. It is a very short dream, and Freud produces many associations in response to it, which represents the specimen dream of *On Dreams* (1901a): the dream of the "Company at table d'hôte". This dream has not been listed among the ones that refer to cocaine, even though, I believe, there are apparent and manifold references to it. To the best of my knowledge, only Kuhn (1999a, p. 943) has classified this dream as "a cocaine anniversary dream dredging up a sixteen-year grudge against Martha and the recently elevated Professor Königstein, both of whom Freud still held responsible for his failure to best Koller in discovering the anaesthetic properties of cocaine in eye surgery". Yet before examining this particular dream, we will first give some consideration to the most important events from the cocaine chapter in Freud's life.

The passion for cocaine[1]

Constantly broke during the early years of his career, Freud sought to make a discovery that might bring him celebrity, glory, and money: only then would he be able to marry Martha Bernays. For this reason, he dedicated himself to the study of cocaine. Despite never enjoying any of the glory brought about by the discovery, he had understood its anaesthetic properties. Credit for this was in fact attributed to his friend and colleague Carl Koller, as Freud was away and had thus put his research on hold to in order to visit his fiancée.

At the same time, Freud had also discovered other properties of cocaine, such as the effect of euphoria that he had experienced when directly experimenting on himself: "I take very small doses of it regularly against depression and again indigestion, and with the most brilliant success" (Jones, 1953, vol. I, p. 89). Enthusiastic about the euphoric effects of the substance, Freud appeared to not be too bothered about his missed opportunity for glory, and started pushing the drug among relatives and friends. He even sent a small amount to Martha, a toot, "to make her strong and give her cheeks a red colour" (Jones, 1953, vol. I, p. 89). He also gave some to his sisters, to lessen their hunger, since they were poor and lived in miserable conditions, and to alleviate their depression, which was brought about by their still being unmarried. To Martha, he spoke of cocaine as a "therapeutic experiment":

> I am also toying now with a project and a hope which I will tell you about; perhaps nothing will come of this, either. It is a therapeutic experiment. I have been reading about cocaine, the effective ingredient of coca leaves, which some Indian tribes chew in order to make themselves resistant to privation and fatigue. A German has tested this stuff on soldiers and reported that it has really rendered them strong and capable of endurance. I have now ordered some of it and for obvious reasons am going to try it out on cases of heart disease, then on nervous exhaustion, particularly in the awful condition following withdrawal from morphine (as in the case of Dr. Fleischl). [Freud (1873–1939), letter to Martha, 21 April 1884]

Freud's "obvious reasons" were, apparently, neither clinical nor research-related, but strictly personal; that is, he was attempting to cure his own cardiac neurosis and neurasthenia. Even worse, he also encouraged his friend Fleischl, who was already a morphine addict, of which he took high doses to alleviate his violent neuralgic pains, to try cocaine. Fleischl became addicted to cocaine, thereby winning, with Freud's help, the unflattering record for being "the first cocaine addict in Europe", as Bernfeld (1981, p. 174) has put it. Fleischl tragically died from cocaine intoxication, of which he used to take one gram a day (see Jones, 1953, p. 100). Freud seems to have quickly recovered from the initial guilt over his friend's death, at least at a conscious level, perhaps because this allowed him to rid himself of one of his many creditors, as well as a possible rival who was obstructing him from gaining a position at the Physiology Institute?

Jones himself, who is usually not very inclined to acknowledge Freud's dark side, admits that on this occasion the latter "was rapidly becoming a public menace" (Jones, 1953, p. 89), as he had started to enthusiastically give the drug to relatives and friends. Freud was so thrilled about this substance producing in animals "the most gorgeous excitement" (ibid., p. 90), that he came close to addiction himself.

Freud used to take the drug to cure his periodical depression and neurasthenia, and to help him deal with the troubles affecting his sexual potency. When he found out about the effects of cocaine on virility, he quickly completed his report on the substance, and got ready to leave for Wandsbeck (ibid., p. 120), announcing to his fiancée that she should expect "a big wild man who has cocaine in his body" (letter to Martha, 2 June 1884, in Jones, 1953, p. 93).

He also used cocaine to increase his intellectual vivacity. At the time Freud's scientific production was scarce, though, and amounted especially to his epistolary writings. He also used it to gain courage, taking a small dose when he went to a party at Charcot's house with his colleague Ricchetti: "R. was terribly nervous, myself quite calm with the help of a small dose of cocaine" (Freud, 1873–1939, letter to Martha, 20 January 1886). Jones would have us believe that one "needs a special disposition to develop a drug addiction, and fortunately Freud did not possess that" (Jones, 1953, vol. I, p. 89). This idea is consonant with similar opinions formulated by pharmacologists who resolutely defended the importance of their discoveries, claiming that the abuse of pharmacological substances "is more likely to be due to some personality characteristic of the abuser and not to some attributes of these drugs" (Berger, quoted in Byck, 1974, p. xxxiii). This is a half-truth, because addiction would not develop if the substance did not possess those characteristics that make it suitable for a use of the addictive kind.

Freud, in truth, never became an addict, unlike his friend Fleischl, only because he did not have enough money to purchase sufficient quantities of cocaine; he even struggled to pay for the single gram of the substance that he had used for his studies, for his relatives, and for himself.

Yet, this was not the only time that Freud used stimulating substances to deal with his depression. In his letters to Fliess, he reveals that in low-spirited moments and during periods of intellectual asthenia, he had turned to "Friend Marsala".[2] This confirms his predisposition to the use of stimulating substances, and that financial issues during those years were the real obstacle to his developing an addiction to cocaine. "Nevertheless, Freud continued to take the drug long after its dangers were known. One has to suspect that cocaine played a part in his interest in Fliess's curious theories about the nose" (Roazen, 1993, p. 172). Freud's use of cocaine through inhalation probably increased his curiosity about Fliess' theories on the effects of cocaine on nasal mucosae and nasal nerve endings. It is also possible that a variety of ailments from which Freud was suffering were the direct consequence of chronic use of the substance. First, his recurrent nasal troubles might have been caused by the localised effect of cocaine on the nasal mucosae: chronic nasal congestion, perforation of the nasal septum and an ensuing heightened sensitivity to infections. We know that Freud was affected by recurrent purulent rhinitis, and that he underwent two nasal surgeries performed by Fliess.

Also, his recurrent cardiac problems (palpitations, arrhythmias, *angina pectoris*), which his personal physician Schur ascribed to a heart condition, could be partly interpreted as the effect of a repeated and prolonged use of cocaine. Freud was a chain smoker, which certainly contributed to his cardiac conditions, so much so that his friend Fliess diagnosed him as suffering from nicotine-induced intoxication. Actually, we cannot exclude the possibility that cocaine was at least partly responsible for the persistence of these ailments. Then, Freud's periodic depressions, as periodic as his use of cocaine, could also be connected to an exogenous factor, particularly the fading of the effect of euphoria produced by this substance.

Freud's paper *On Coca*, in *Cocaine Papers* (1884e), in which he sings the praises of this substance, was the first time the father of psychoanalysis did something which led to humanity sustaining serious damage, and it was his first grave mistake. His contemporaries accused him of having introduced, after alcohol and morphine, the "third scourge of humanity" (Jones, 1953, vol. I, p. 93), from which we still have not freed ourselves.

The publication became available on 1 July 1884. At the time, Freud was still taking cocaine, and was also planning on making use of it on his train journey to Hamburg, before meeting with Martha. "I won't be tired because I shall be travelling under the influence of coca, in order to curb my terrible impatience" (Freud, 1873–1939, letter to Martha, 29 June 1884). Here, Freud alludes to his impatience to be with his fiancée, but we cannot exclude the possibility that he also took cocaine to control his fear of travelling by train, since a long journey awaited him before he could set foot in Hamburg. On this occasion, Freud's behaviour reminds us of the Indian described by Mantegazza,[3] who writes that when an Indian "is faced with a difficult journey, when he takes a woman, or, in general, whenever his strength is more than usually taxed, he increases the customary doses" (Freud, 1975, p. 51).

As regards Freud's missed opportunity for glory, on the topic of cocaine, he only had himself to blame, because on this occasion Martha had expressed her worries: she did not wish to hinder his professional career, and was willing to renounce their weeks together, so that he could continue his work. Yet Freud reassured her, and followed his "impulses". At no point after all, did he abandon his belief that he had been the first to identify the anaesthetic properties of cocaine; in the conclusion to his essay *On Coca* he spoke of its strong anaesthetic properties, which would suggest using it as a "local anaesthetic". He also claimed that such anaesthetic properties could be useful in many other different ways (pp. 80–81). Yet it was Koller, not Freud, who gained success and became popular for having discovered the anaesthetic properties of cocaine.

It is not surprising that in the *On Coca* paper Freud only marginally, and in the last lines of his essay, envisaged the possibility of using cocaine as an anaesthetic. In this work, Freud seems principally interested in the possibility of justifying his personal use of the drug through a scientific discourse, and especially in understanding if cocaine could lessen his symptoms, as well as curing his friend Fleischl's addiction to morphine. Among the effects that a drug produces on a healthy organism, Freud focuses on its stimulating effect, the capacity of coca to eliminate the effects of physical tiredness and, overall, to increase intellectual efficiency, although it could not boost mental acumen.

Among the therapeutic effects of cocaine, Freud is interested in its possible uses as an antidepressant, and in order to alleviate the functional disorders currently grouped under the name of "neurasthenia". Furthermore, the possibility of using this drug for gastric digestive troubles was of personal interest for Freud, since he frequently suffered from dyspepsia. The use of coca to treat asthma was of interest to him for its possible application in the case of other vagal neuroses involving a reflex stimulus, such as cardiac neurosis, from which he himself suffered. He argues that coca should also be considered for treating other vagal neuroses.

Last, but not least, Freud's interest in the aphrodisiac properties of the substance derived from the fact that, when only twenty-eight years old, he was probably suffering from some virility issues, while "the *coqueros* sustain a high degree of potency right into old age" (*On Coca*, p. 73). This is deducible from the fact that he felt the urge to join his fiancée when still under the effects of the drug, and that when he was forty years old he confessed to Fliess that he was almost impotent.

Robert Byck claims that Freud made continuous use of cocaine and that from *The Interpretation of Dreams* (1900) we learn that he "was still using the drug in 1895" (Byck, 1975, p. xvii). Actually, in a letter to Fliess from 26 October 1896, in which he tells his friend about the death of his father, we know that Freud had just stopped using cocaine: "The cocaine brush has been completely put aside." This event would lead us to presume that his father's death had reactivated a sense of guilt over his friend Fleischl's death, and that this new loss had eventually induced him to forsake his use of the drug.

The dream of "Company at table d'hôte"

> "Company at table or table d'hôte ... spinach was being eaten ... Frau E. L. was sitting beside me; she was turning her whole attention to me and laid her hand on my knee in an intimate manner. I removed her hand unresponsively. She ten said: 'But you've always had such beautiful eyes' ... I then had an indistinct picture of two eyes, as though it were a drawing or like the outline of a pair of spectacles ...".

This was the whole of the dream, or at least all that I could remember of it. It seemed to me obscure and meaningless, but above all surprising [...] The dream-process was not accompanied by affects of any kind. [S. E., 5, pp. 636–637]

This dream elaborates elements (day residues) from the previous night, which was probably the one spent with other friends at the Königsteins', whom Freud described as "the only warm friends we have here" (Masson, 1985, 16 June 1899, p. 356), where a "small party" used to gather to play with tarock cards.

Freud's interpretation is entirely centred on the theme of money, because "the friend whose guests we were yesterday has often put me in his debt",[4] and explicitly says that he was an oculist, to whom he had given a present, "an antique bowl, round which there are *eyes* painted: what is known as an *'occhiale'*, to avert the *evil eye*" (S. E., 5, p. 639). Here, Freud completely neglects the numerous references to the eyes, and the setting of the dream, namely, his friend the oculist's house. These elements would inevitably lead us back to the period when he was studying cocaine, when a "small party" of friends (some of whom were the same ones who used to gather to play Tarock), including Freud, Königstein and Koller, attempted to swindle one another in their pursuit of notoriety, as might be gleaned from Bernfeld's (1953) narrative. Koller pretended that Freud's research on cocaine was contemporaneous with his own experiments; Königstein gave a talk on his experiments without quoting Koller, who had anticipated his work, and Freud was convinced he had been the one to reveal the positive properties of coca.

Freud does not get the gist of the dream, namely, the fact that *spinach was eaten* at the "table d'hôte". On this point, his associations are rather banal; they might mark the starting point of his resistance. He speaks of one of his children, the one with beautiful eyes, who would refuse to eat spinach. But is it not strange that at the guests' table, in professor Königstein's house, this "small party", who were probably playing Tarock, ate only spinach? This would not be enough for a dinner, and not adequate for a game of tarock among old friends.[5] Every Saturday, Freud gladly immersed himself in games of tarock with a few old friends of his, at Dr. Königstein's house. There, he also meets with his Tarock companions and merrily dines with them. The meal is often abundant and the soirée usually ends very late (Flem, 1986, pp. 220–221). The frugal meal in the dream also contrasts with Freud's recent gastronomic experiences during his summer vacation, as described in a letter to Martha sent from *Riva del Garda* on 5 September 1900:

> After the first night, spent in a noisy and suffocating hotel in the city centre, the next morning we found a divine accommodation, the annex of another hotel 20 minutes from Riva. It comes with two rooms at the front with lake view, plenty of electric light, beams from the lighthouse reaching even the bed, a garden or—better still—a park all around, above the Lovrana one, and in the adjacent hotel we can have *meals at the table d'hôte, rich and delicious, as light and at the same time mouth-watering* as I've never experienced anywhere else. That with all this Minna is flourishing again is quite understandable. [Letter to Martha, 5 September 1900. Quoted in Tögel, 2002, p. 130; italics added]

These "mouth-watering" meals at the table d'hôte with Minna during their vacation could represent a recent dream-source. Is the spinach in the dream not after all light and tasty, rich and juicy? I would argue that it was as juicy as the coca leaves bolus in the *coqueros'* mouth, which they would chew repeatedly to extract every drop of its juice, so that they needed nothing else to eat other than that handful of leaves. Likewise, the cheerful party of which Freud was part did not need any other food than spinach.

Thus, the spinach may conceal something more precious and more fitting to both the moment and the company. In fact, these friends were not merely savouring spinach, but were also chewing coca leaves, according to the custom of South American Indians as described by Freud in the first pages of his paper on coca.

A friend is missing from this table d'hôte; the main spinach-coca consumer of the entire party, Ernst von Fleischl, who paid with his life for Freud's enthusiasm for coca. Unaccountably, something is missing from this dinner at the wealthy Prof. Königstein's house, which is unusual for an Austrian meal, that is, a plentiful helping of meat (in German: *Fleisch*).[6] Apparently, dream-censorship did not even allow the dreamer an indirect allusion to his friend, through the food that is homophonous with his name. Yet, it is precisely this omission that allows us to spot the censorship.

Fleischl was the first friend of Freud's to have any direct experience of his strong affective ambivalence. Fleischl was his friend, his superior at Brücke's Institute of Physiology, and also his professional rival, since Freud hoped to take his place as Brücke's assistant. "Freud confessed in later years how he had secretly cherished the thought that his advancement would be favoured by Fleischl's death, but afterwards he was shocked at hearing his successor in the Institute, Paneth, openly voicing the same wish" (Jones, 1953, vol. I, pp. 68–69).

This professional rivalry, Freud's ambition, and his cynicism towards his rivals, might have all played a part in the carefree way in which Freud gave cocaine to his friend Fleischl, who later died of intoxication.

Fleischl had been Freud's first ideal, and he spoke of him with admiration in a letter to Martha from 27 June 1882. He possessed all that Freud wanted, both materially and morally. In another letter to Martha, Freud speaks of his intellectual passion for his friend Fleischl, in a way that arouses suspicion as to his alleged, latent homosexuality:

> I admire and love him with an intellectual passion, if you will allow such a phrase. His destruction will move me as the destruction of a sacred and famous temple would have affected an ancient Greek. I love him not so much as a human being, but as one of Creation's precious achievements. And you needn't be at all jealous. (Freud, quoted in Jones, 1953, p. 99)

This sort of aesthetic contemplation, through which Freud intends to minimise the sexual component of his passion in Martha's eyes, along with the reference to Greek culture, actually serve to stress the unconscious homosexuality of this "intellectual passion". I am convinced that this homosexual element was an important, and recurrent, component in all of Freud's male friendships, and also played a primary role in destroying and transforming them into obstinate enmities. It is important to note that, whenever these intense friendships came to an end, the person would not become insignificant for Freud; on the contrary, he would become the object of violent attacks and sarcastic scorn. This demonstrates how the passionate element of the relationship was maintained, though it would change in time to become its opposite.

Freud centres the majority of his associations prompted by the dream of "Company at table d'hôte" on the idea and fear of being damaged. In truth, however, we can identify in this dream proof of his sense of guilt over the damage he had inflicted on others, especially on his friend Fleischl. Returning home after the joyous night spent with the small party of friends, Freud accepts a ride home in a carriage from a member of the group; the friend[7] chooses a carriage with a taximeter. In his associations prompted by the dream, Freud says that the taximeter "keeps on reminding me of what I owe". We know that Freud did not pay his debts eagerly, nor would he hurry to do so, and we have proof of this precisely from this dream. He tells us he is indebted to his friend, the oculist Königstein, whom he has failed to repay though a chance had presented itself (S. E., 5, p. 639).

Considering how nonchalantly Freud used to delay repaying his debts, which was the case with Breuer, we should assume that his irritation in recognising the taximeter as a constant allusion to his debt has something to do with a debt he could no longer square, namely, that with Fleischl, who had died before his friend could repay him. Freud draws an association, "somewhat discursively", between the thought of the debt, and the following verses from Goethe's *Wilhelm Meister*:

> Ihr führt ins Leben uns hinein/Ihr lasst den Armen schuldig werden.
> [You lead us into life/You make the poor creature guilty.]

Because the German word *schuldig* means both "guilty" and "debtor", the second verse could also be translated as follows:

> You make the poor man fall into debt.

If, remembering the debt owed to his friend, Freud also felt a sense of remorse over his death, then his reference to Goethe's verse would appear all but "discursive", and the term *schuldig* brilliantly alludes to both the financial debt and the dreamer's moral guilt, the double debt that Freud could no longer repay.

As for the theme of the carriage journey, Freud even claims that the *free cab drive* offered by his friend the night before is also the motive of the dream, that is, the day residue from which it originates. Also, this element of the dream appears to have a dual connotation. First, we grasp a further reference to Freud's debt to those friends who had financially helped him, an allusion to the fact that Freud had *come a long way thanks to his friends' generosity*, who had made his achievements possible. This meaning, though, clashes so strongly with the dreamer's pride that was unable to acknowledge it, or, even if this had been, he could not have brought himself to admit it publicly. As a matter of fact, Freud's interpretation stands in complete contrast to it. From Frau E. L.'s remark about the *beautiful eyes*, Freud gleans the possibility that she meant to say: "People have always done everything for you for love; you have always had everything *without paying for it*", yet he rejects this interpretation, and claims instead: "I have always paid dearly for whatever advantage I have had from other people."[8]

Actually, Freud spent the first years of his career relying on the financial assistance of friends and colleagues, because his father, "still full of projects, still hoping" (Freud, 1873–1939, letter to Martha, 10 January 1884), had been unable to provide for his family since moving from Freiberg to Vienna. Thus Freud found himself in the situation of providing by himself for his "very large family" (Masson, 1985, 29 August 1888, p. 24), which comprised not only his parents, but also his many unmarried sisters and, later, also his sister-in-law. Considering this situation, it seems understandable that he should be obsessed with poverty, even when he was a mature man. At the beginning of his career, though, this obsession was so strong that, empowered by the vast self-esteem his mother had transmitted to him, he shamelessly crossed all boundaries of decency in asking for financial help, to the point that the first person he distastefully pressed for money was "his old school teacher, Hammerschlag, a man who was himself very poor and subsisted on a small pension" (Jones, 1953, vol. I, p. 175).

Young Freud did not really know what being grateful meant, and had probably maintained the mind-set acquired when he was a child— little Sigi, his mother's favourite—believing that everything was due to him in light of his superiority and intelligence, and that his benefactors would undoubtedly be recompensed for their generosity not by his gratitude, but rather by reading his works, and by the awareness of having contributed to the birth of psychoanalysis.

At this point, we can go back to Freud's associations, as prompted by Frau E. L.'s words, without discerning any discontinuity in the unfolding of the matter:

> If a person expects one to keep an eye on his interests without any advantage to oneself, his artlessness is apt to provoke the scornful question: "Do you suppose I'm going to do this or that for the sake of your *beaux yeux* [*beautiful eyes*]?" That being so, Frau E. L.'s speech in the dream, "You've always had such beautiful eyes" can

only have meant: "People have always done everything for you for love; you have always had everything *without paying for it*." [*S. E.*, 5, p. 638]

Yet is this naive person not the dreamer himself? If there are still doubts as to Freud's belief that he deserved the favours and generosity of his acquaintances only because of his *beautiful eyes*, another passage from a letter to Martha, where he again mentions Hammerschlag, provides definitive proof:

Today the Hammerschlags, the dear people, are celebrating their silver wedding. Yesterday I sent them a photograph of myself. [Freud, 1873–1939, letter to Martha, 14 August 1884]

Thus, after his old professor helped him financially, despite himself barely being able to make ends meet, on the occasion of the Hammerschlags' silver wedding, Freud could find no better way of thanking his professor than giving him a picture of himself, which appears to me just another way of admitting that people should do him favours because of his *beautiful eyes*.

As for the carriage journey, this element of the dream does not appear to be deprived of (homo)sexual connotations. Freud associates the drive with his friend, with memories of numerous carriage journeys with a relative who, according to Swales' reconstruction (1982), appears to be Minna, with whom Freud might have had a sexual relationship in the summer of 1900. Freud, though, does not say that the journey with his friend reminded him of other journeys with a "dear person" from his family, which nevertheless emerges in his memory by way of association. He says, rather, that the "drive in a cab free of cost" with his friend reminded him of his "connections" with another person, a relative of his (*S. E.*, 5, p. 657).

I find it unlikely that this day element (the free cab drive with his friend), which stimulates the dream, is really as "indifferent and trivial" as Freud claims. I also believe that the thesis according to which the day residue is usually insignificant is also debatable:

We rightly speak of the dream as carrying on with the significant interests of our waking life. As a rule, however, if a connection is to be found in the content of the dream with any impression of the previous day, that impression is so trivial, insignificant and unmemorable, that it is only with difficulty that we ourselves can recall it [...] If the content of a dream puts forward some indifferent impression as being its instigator, analysis invariably brings to light a significant experience, and one by which the dreamer has good reason to be stirred. This experience has been replaced by the indifferent one, with which it is connected by copious associative links [...]. The indifferent impression which becomes a dream-instigator owing to associations of this kind is subject to a further condition which does not apply to the true source of the dream: it must always be a *recent* impression, derived from the dream-day. [*S. E.*, 5, pp. 655–657]

Mertens (2000, p. 20) has stressed Freud's contradictory viewpoint with respect to the day residue: "On the one hand, he claims that certain day residues are chosen by the dreamer because they are deprived of emotional meaning; on the other, he also claims that important events are frequently responsible for stimulating the dream itself." According to the more recent psychoanalytic interpretations of dreams, "the day residue is often a defensive substitution with respect to an important but anguishing day event, which as such must be actively removed from the dream. Censoring activity would already be at work in the choice of day residues for the dream, and not during the dream-work itself. [...] Defensive substitutions can be understood according to the principle of screen memories [...]. Integrating this idea, which Freud explicates elsewhere, into the theory of dream genesis, incongruities pertaining to the role of the day residue could disappear. A trivial day residue in the dream would thus always derive from a displacement defence. The lived experiences or the thoughts at its basis are never trivial, but conflictual, in a number of ways" (Mertens, 2000, p. 20).

In the day episode that stimulates Freud's dream, Freud mentions that his friend "offered to take a cab and drive me home in it" (*S. E.*, 5, p. 637). Freud here assumes a feminine role in regards to his friend, since his passivity in accepting the ride is prolonged during the journey as the friend invites him to spend the time observing the taximeter. A few lines later, Freud remembers the dream about Irma's injection, and the reference to the propylaea, as we will see below, also reminds us once more of his ambivalent relationship with Fleischl. In the interpretation of the dream of Irma's injection, Freud associates the word "propyl" with

Fleischl through the word "propylaea". These can be found not only in Athens, but also in Munich, a city where Fleischl regularly used to stay for two months a year. Yet it would not be necessary to even mention the Munich's propylaea to retrieve a reference to Fleischl, because, in a letter to Martha, Freud had spoken of the pain caused by his friend's destruction, comparing it to the way the destruction of a sacred and famous temple would have affected an ancient Greek. Thus the association between his friend and the propylaea was already contained in his announced bereavement. This had been repressed and thus could not have emerged as one of the free associations in the dream, giving the floor to the much more trivial and neutral reference to the architecture of Munich. Thus, if the free cab drive with his friend could represent a banal day residue, the life experiences or thoughts that the journey might have aroused in the dreamer, also when he was awake, were certainly not as trivial. In a letter to Fliess from 7 May 1900, Freud mentions two topics that resurface in this dream: the fear of poverty, and his need for a male friendship:

> On the whole—except for one weak point, my fear of poverty— I have too much sense to complain and at present I feel too well to do so; I know what I have and I know, in view of the statistics of human misery, how little one is entitled to. But no one can replace for me the relationship with the friend which a special—possibly feminine—side demands, and inner voices to which I am accustomed to listen suggest a much more modest estimate of my work than that which you proclaim. [Masson, 1985, 7 May 1900, p. 412]

Freud's associations with the "Company at table d'hôte" dream highlight his concern with "a considerable sum of money on behalf of a member of my family" (S. E., 5, p. 656), a sum he had had to spend a few days beforehand. He is speaking here of the 300 crowns he will mention in *The Psychopathology of Everyday Life* (1901b), when discussing writing slips. This expenditure was connected with his fear of poverty. I find it interesting that, despite all these references to poverty, his fear of being damaged ("at a table d'hôte I can't avoid feeling in a comic way that I'm getting too little, and must keep an eye on my own interests", "*as though I were getting the worst of the bargain at the table d'hôte*" [S. E., 5, pp. 637–638]), and his displeasure over the money spent on behalf of a family member, Jones would claim that "Freud's attitude towards money seems always to have been unusually normal and objective" (Jones, 1953, vol. I, p. 169). Actually, Freud himself acknowledged his concern with money and how his mood depended on his earnings on more than one occasion. He also acknowledged that the fear of poverty never abandoned him (Masson, 1985, 21 September 1899, p. 374).

Tögel (2002b) informs us that Freud's financial position in 1900 was in actual fact far from precarious. On the contrary, it was such that he was able to afford a long summer vacation with frequent stays in luxury hotels, which I will discuss below. Also, his worries about the 300 crowns he had to spend for his sister-in-law appear unwarranted, all the more so because, as we will see later, Freud had left Minna in Merano with sufficient money to stay there an extra week or two. Freud returned to Vienna on 10 September, and from a letter to Fliess from 23 October we learn that at that point Minna had already returned to Vienna. She must therefore have left Merano between 15 and 23 October, having remained there for five or six weeks. Since Freud had left her in Merano with sufficient money to stay on for one or two weeks, he must have then paid for the additional four weeks. That is, a sum of money which amounted, at the time, to two days of psychoanalytic work for Freud. Why did Freud not take the money from his professional earnings, rather than the returns from selling his books? Perhaps the money was not intended for Minna, but was destined instead to reach the other side of the ocean, to end up in the savings of the Parke-Davis company in exchange for a quantity of cocaine? Were this the case, it would be understandable that Freud's Super-Ego prevented him from subtracting that sum from the family budget, and that he would opt, instead, to sacrifice a few books, an extremely self-punishing gesture for a bibliophile like Freud. In *The Psychopathology of Everyday Life* (1901b) he tells us that he had 4,380 crowns in his postal account, and withdrew 438 instead of 380 as he had decided to bring the account back down to 4,000 crowns (S. E., 6, p. 119). Freud interprets this withdrawal, amounting to ten per cent of the total sum, as the librarian's ten per cent discount, because a few days before he had offered his librarian medicine books for 300 crowns, but the latter had considered the request to be excessive, hence Freud's decision to withdraw the money from his postal savings. The fear of poverty was certainly at the basis of his preoccupations, although once he had realised the scale of his savings, Freud initially decided to withdraw 80 crowns more, leaving a round figure of 4000 crowns in his account. Yet the fear of poverty eventually got the better of him, and he instead decided to withdraw a sum that corresponded to the first three figures of his savings—(4380). Therefore, visually, nothing would remain in his account but the final number, namely, zero: thus, a confirmation of the fact that the withdrawal was impoverishing him. This appears to me much more plausible than his own interpretation, although at this point he had nothing left to hide besides what he had already censored, the "absent relative for purposes of medical treatment". My reading is also more in line with the fact that his fear of poverty briefly overcame him. Yet Freud's fear of suffering a loss must have been connected not only with money, but also with his professional credibility. As a matter of fact, the cocaine incident had cost him credibility and affected his reputation, and he had been the object of much criticism.

More than one of Freud's associations, in my view, leads us from the spinach to the cocaine and, then, to his friend Fleischl. At a certain point, Freud observes how various elements of the dream are now gathered together through a new connection. This new connection involves the *theme of the eyes*, in manifold ways: the antique bowl Freud had given to Königstein, and on whose circumference eyes are depicted; the oculist himself, his friend; and a patient to whom Freud had recommended the latter's services for lens prescription. The theme of the eyes takes us back to Königstein's and Koller's experiments with cocaine, and to their paternity disputes over the discovery of the anaesthetic properties of cocaine.

We can even hypothesise that, on this occasion, Freud was demanding an opportunity for revenge from his father, to finally belie old Jacob's paternal verdict, when Sigmund was seven years old, that nothing good was to be expected from the boy. Perhaps Freud wanted to finally demonstrate his value to his father, what good had come from his study of cocaine, and how thanks to those studies he would now be able to alleviate his father's pain, finally ridding himself of that pessimistic paternal verdict.

Immediately after he notes this new connection, Freud asks himself, "why *spinach*, of all things, was being served in the dream" (S. E., 5, p. 639)? His answer is rather disappointing and unworthy of the author of *The Interpretation of Dreams*:

> The answer was that spinach reminded me of an episode which occurred not long ago at our family table, when one of the children—and precisely the one who really deserves to be admired

for his beautiful eyes—refused to eat any spinach. I myself behaved in just the same way when I was a child; for a long time I detested spinach, till eventually my taste changed and promoted that vegetable to one of my favourite foods. My own early life and my child's were thus brought together by the mention of this dish. [...] Thus I was reminded of the duties of parents to their children. [S. E., 5, p. 639]

Freud cannot find any association to the spinach other than the memory of one of his children, the one with beautiful eyes, who had an aversion to eating it. I would infer that he is speaking of his son Ernst here,[9] which would lead us again to Ernst Fleischl through an "unsaid", as in the case of the missing food. Thus his child Ernst's refusal to eat would allude to the fact that Fleischl did not follow Freud's instruction to take cocaine orally, but took it, instead, through subcutaneous injection. Freud seems to be in search of a way to exculpate himself for his friend's death, as if the latter's demise should be attributed to a failure to follow precise instructions for taking cocaine. We should note an analogy with the dream of "Irma's injection": the patient Mathilde (who had the same name as Freud's daughter) is recalled in this dream through the injection; she had died of intoxication because Freud had repeatedly prescribed her a medicine he thought to be innocuous. In the dream, this death elicits worries over his own daughter Mathilde's health. Similarly, in analysing the "Company at table d'hôte" dream, we can go from his son Ernst, to whom Freud refers through associations with spinach, from spinach to coca leaves, and finally to Ernst Fleischl. After all, we learn from Freud himself that he had intended to make of his children "revenants" of important figures from his past.

What possibilities did the dreamer have open to him to allow coca leaves to appear in the manifest content of his dream? Spinach could serve this purpose, not so much because of the vague resemblance of the leaves, but rather because this vegetable had become a favourite dish of Freud's, who had also used cocaine for twelve years.

Continuing his work of interpretation and further developing his associations concerning the dream, Freud comes to formulate two ideas that he defines as "intermediate thoughts":

In carrying out the analysis I came upon the following thought: *"I should like to get something sometimes without paying for it."* But in

> that form the thought could not be employed in the dream-content. It was therefore given a fresh form: "*I should like to get some enjoyment without cost* ['*Kosten*']". Now the word "*Kosten*", in its second sense fits into the "table d'hôte" circle of ideas, and could thus be represented in the "*spinach*" which was served in the dream. When a dish appears at our table and the children refuse it, their mother begins by trying persuasion, and urges them "*just to taste* ['*kosten*'] *a bit of it.*" It may seem strange that the dream-work should make such free use of verbal ambiguity, but further experience will teach us that the occurrence is quite a common one. [S. E., 5, p. 650]

Freud's relationship with cocaine had also begun with his "tast[ing] a bit of it", but he had then found the substance to be so pleasant, as much as the spinach, that this tasting continued for twelve years. What is more, for his friend Fleischl the spinach-coca became his favourite course, so much so that his life came to an end because of cocaine intoxication. Hence, if we consider these intermediate thoughts, keeping in mind the entire cocaine affair, we can claim with some certainty that Freud could not have enjoyed the benefit of cocaine *without cost*, that is to say, without bearing throughout his life the weight of guilt over his friend Fleischl's death (the feeling of being *schuldig*). After all, as I mentioned earlier, he also paid for this incident on a professional level, because his reputation remained completely compromised for some time.

If, as Freud claims, dreams represent wish-fulfilments, this wish being almost always an infantile one, what link is to be found between this dream and Freud's childhood? What childhood feelings could we link with his fear of taking a loss and the feeling of being *schuldig*? In my view, it is with a sense of infantile jealousy typical of the firstborn, because Freud himself confesses to having experienced his little brother Julius' death with strong feelings of guilt and to having acknowledged his birth with jealousy (see Masson, 1985, 3 October 1897, p. 268).[10] This was probably connected with his being "afraid of getting the worst of the bargain", and of losing both his position as his mother's favourite and the privilege of being the only one to receive her care and attention. Freud had himself made a comment about his voracity and infantile avidity, which would chime with this fear of suffering a loss, of not receiving enough food at the *table d'hôte*. Yet this voracity appears to me to be the displacement, at the oral level, of his fear of losing his mother's love.

Thus it is perhaps within this frame—which is not the banal frame Freud creates by making a connection, through spinach, between his and his child's youth—that he says:

> Thus I was reminded of the duties of parents to their children. Goethe's words
>
> > Ihr führt ins Leben uns hinein
> > Ihr lasst den Armen schuldig werden
>
> gained a fresh meaning in this connection. [S. E., 5, p. 639]

A sole woman among too many men

A mysterious woman appears in the dream, E. L., who addresses Freud thus: "*But you've always had such beautiful eyes.*" This sentence seems to present an allusion to a characteristic Freud did not possess "but" whose lack was compensated by his having always had "beautiful eyes". The reference to the eyes could have something to do with Brücke, or it could represent Freud's identification with him, since in 1899 he would describe himself as a pupil of Brücke, the physiologist (see Roazen, 1975), as well as of Charcot. In *The Interpretation of Dreams* (1900a), Freud speaks of Brücke in the following terms: "No one who can remember the great man's eyes, which retained their striking beauty even in his old age, and who has ever seen him in anger, will find it difficult to picture the young sinner's emotions" (S. E., 5, p. 422).

Another element then leads to Brücke and to the thought that Mrs. E. L.'s words indicate the missed opportunity for success in the cocaine affair. In relation to this unattained glory, Jones writes that Freud "might have consoled himself with the reflection that his revered master, Brücke, had suffered a similar fate. In 1849, he recognized that the red reflex from the eye came from the retina, but had not the wit to put a lens in front of it so as to focus its vessels. In the following year his friend, Helmholtz, did so, and thus was hailed as the discoverer of the ophthalmoscope" (Jones, 1953, vol. I, p. 87). Thus, just like Freud, Brücke, the mentor with strikingly beautiful eyes, had also missed an opportunity to become famous.

The writings *On Dreams* (1901a) and *The Psychopathology of Everyday Life* (1901b) are contemporaneous. In the latter, Freud analyses a *lapsus calami* of his as he was writing a cheque for 300 crowns intended for an "absent relative for purposes of medical treatment", of which I have already spoken. During this analysis, which focused on the "fear of growing poor", he tells us of "a dream [of a] few days before which called for the same solution" (S. E., 6, p. 120). In a footnote, he adds that: "This is the one which I took as the specimen dream in my short work *On Dreams*" (1901a). Thus the dream in question precedes the slip described in *The Psychopathology of Everyday Life* (1901b) by a few days. To locate this dream temporally, I will follow Swales' indications (1982), who concludes that in both situations the person in question is Minna Bernays. Then, I will also consider a possible alternative to this dating of the dream.

According to Swales' reconstruction, the dream would date back to early September 1900. One may find it unlikely that Freud would have had a dream about cocaine four years after he had stopped taking it. Yet, I think it is safe to assume that Freud had developed a strong psychological addiction to the drug, analogous to his addiction to smoking, which lasted throughout his life.[11] Moreover, are we so sure that he did not have a relapse in the summer of 1900, continuing to use the substance in the following months? Starting on 14 September, Freud enjoyed a period of incredible productivity that lasted five months (see Swales, 1982). He wrote *On Dreams*, *The Psychopathology of Everyday Life* and *Dream and Hysteria*, which would then become *Fragment of an Analysis of a Case of Hysteria*. We must also bear in mind that during the period before this, which had been particularly prolific on the scientific front, Freud had undertaken so many travels, that they would have been stressful even for a present-day traveller. Freud travelled continuously for two weeks, making use, first and foremost, of a horse-drawn coach, and sometimes of trains. It is here worth reading Freud's description to Fliess (in the letter of 14 September 1900) of the long journey he and his travel companions had embarked on, after they had parted:

> After we [Fliess and Freud] parted, we [Martha and Freud] drove to Trafoi [...] Then we travelled—*all our intermediate trips took place during thunderstorms and under other aggravating circumstances*—to Sulden [...] We then went via Merano for a stopover to the Mendola, were we met Lustgarten and other Viennese friends [...] Martha then left for home via Bolzano and absolutely insisted that I follow Lustgarten to Venice to act as his guide [...] *I was right in the swing*

of tramping around and was amenable to everything [...] Finally—we have now reached August 26—came the relief. I mean Minna, with whom I drove through the Puster Valley to Trentino, making several short stops along the way. *Only when I was completely in the South did I begin to feel really comfortable*; under ice and snow something was missing, though at the time I could not have defined it [...] From Trentino we made an excursion to the extraordinarily beautiful Castel Toblino [...] Minna wanted a taste of a high-altitude sojourn; therefore we went over a spectacular mountain road to Lavarone (1,200 meters), a high plateau on the side of the Valsugano [...] The nights began to be cool, however, so I headed directly for Lake Garda [...] We finally stopped for five days at Riva, *divinely accommodated and fed, luxuriating without regrets, and untroubled*—unless the meeting of the Society of Professors at the Hotel du Lac is to be regarded as a "trouble" [...] We kept away. Two long boat trips took us one time to Salo and the other to Sirmione [...]

On September 8 I took Minna to Merano, where she is supposed to stay for either a few weeks or a few months to cure her pulmonary apicitis [inflammation] [...] [that] casts a shadow on the immediate future. I arrived *feeling outrageously merry and well* in Vienna, found my family in good spirits, and *on the very same day was back in harness*. [Masson, 1985, 14 September 1900, pp. 422–424; italics added]

If we consider that the twenty-eight-year-old, neurasthenic Sigmund visited his fiancée in Wandsbeck while hooked on cocaine so as to be able to endure the long journey and overcome his impatience, how could the forty-year-old, still neurotic Freud have endured six intense weeks without being physically and psychologically affected, without suffering from some of the various ailments by which he was periodically afflicted? The reasonable suspicion arises, therefore, as to whether or not Freud was able to endure this physical tiredness, and the intellectual fatigues of the months to come, which were marked by an intense scientific productivity, because he was using cocaine again. This would further endorse the view that cocaine entered the manifest content of the dream through the curious presence of spinach, a dream-image only apparently insignificant but in truth charged with disquieting references. When quoting from the letter to Fliess, I stressed in italics those passages that appear to confirm my bold, but nevertheless not groundless, hypothesis: we get the impression that we are dealing with a maniacal Freud, who is enduring a tiring and uncomfortable journey with continuous and reckless transfers, without being in the least affected. His state of mind is clearly euphoric, he is open to all suggestions and external stimuli, *amenable to everything and even* willing to "luxuriate" "untroubled" and "without regrets". He returns to Vienna *"feeling outrageously merry and well"* even if he has just left his beloved sister-in-law in Merano in poor health conditions that cast *"a shadow on the immediate future"*. The very day of his arrival in Vienna, he *"was back in harness"*. It seems to me that there is more than one reason to suspect that, during his summer vacation and the following months, Freud indulged again in the use of cocaine.

If it is true that Minna was (also) affected by a relapse of a tubercular disease, it is possible that Freud thought of treating her with cocaine, because when he wrote the essay *On coca* (1884e) he had consulted literature of the time, retrieving various attestations to the positive effects of cocaine on tuberculosis.[12] I also find it plausible that Freud had "secretly" decided on this treatment with Minna, without informing the doctors from the Merano thermal institute, so as to avoid criticism. This would represent yet another "secret" of the dream connected with his sister-in-law.

Freud claims to have had this dream a few days before he went to the postal office. On Saturday 1 September, he wrote to Martha from Lavarone that he would return on "Sunday week, eight days from now" and on 5 September he wrote from Riva del Garda that he would "leave for Merano the day after tomorrow (Friday)". The same day, he sent a postcard to Fliess from Torbole, on Lake Garda, and a letter from Vienna on 14 September in which he says: "I have been in Vienna since September 10." Thus, we should conclude, with Swales (1982), that in the "Company at table d'hôte" dream, the person sitting with the dreamer at the restaurant table, while he was sojourning in Tirol and by whom he was deeply irritated because of her scarce discretion around the people sitting nearby, was not his "dear wife", but his sister-in-law.

Freud's first association to the dream involves precisely Frau E. L., with whom the dreamer has substituted his "wife-sister-in-law", and comments that it is "a person with whom I have hardly at any time been on friendly terms, nor, so far as I know, have I ever wished to have any closer relations" (S. E., 5, p. 637). Through this substitution with a person with whom the dreamer did not and would not have wanted to be on friendly terms, dream-censorship appears to suggest the unseemliness of such a close relationship with his sister-in-law.

Freud was aware of this unseemliness, because in a letter to Martha from *Riva del Garda* during this summer holiday, he mentions the presence of several professors at the Hôtel du Lac where he was staying with Minna, and says he stayed away from them not only because he did not yet possess the title of "Professor", but also because he was not in his wife's company:

> The company at the hotel comprises most pleasant people, among whom there are many famous university professors and high school teachers, such as Czermak (Vienna), Dimmer (Graz), Felsenreich, Jodl (Vienna), Sigm. Mayer from Prague (I should have become his assistant). Since I am no Professor and since I am with a woman who is not my wife, I give them a wide berth. [Tögel, 2002, p. 131]

Tögel (2002), who edited his travel letters, informs us that the last two doctors mentioned by Freud were oculists,[13] which could be a further source for this dream since numerous references to the eyes are included. After Freud's remarks on his desire to give his colleagues a wide "berth" because of his "irregular" position in terms of both his title and his female companion, the references to the eyes and to the bowl against the evil-eye would appear to acquire new significance in relation to Freud's concerns over being *looked* at askance by his colleagues, and in regards to his subsequent need to hide himself, to keep his distance.

Let us now briefly dwell on the "second association to table d'hôte":

> A few weeks ago, while we were at table in a hotel at a mountain resort in the Tyrol, I was very much annoyed because I thought my wife was not being sufficiently reserved towards some people sitting near us whose acquaintance I had no desire at all to make. I asked her to concern herself more with me than with these strangers. This was again *as though I were getting the worst of the bargain at the table d'hôte*. [S. E., 5, p. 638]

Now, let us compare this passage with the version Freud gives of it in *The Psychopathology of Everyday Life* (1901b), which is quoted below, and with the help of his travel letters we can perhaps try to picture the situation:

> We were sitting at table d'hôte opposite a gentleman from Vienna whom I knew and who no doubt remembered me too. However, I had reasons of my own for not renewing the acquaintance. My wife, who had heard no more than his distinguished name, revealed too plainly that she was listening to his conversation with his neighbours, for from time to time she turned to me with questions that took up the thread of their discussion. I became impatient and finally irritated. Some weeks later I was complaining to a relative about this behaviour on my wife's part but was unable to recall a single word of the gentleman's conversation. As I am normally rather apt to harbour grievances and can forget no detail of an incident that has annoyed me, my amnesia in the present case was probably motivated by consideration for my wife. [S. E., 6, pp. 136–137]

I would now like to exchange the wife for the sister-in-law in both passages, which will prove to be a rather useful exercise. In *The Psychopathology*, Freud does not say he is on holiday in Tirol, but mentions instead a generic summer period spent with his wife (in truth, his sister-in-law). Freud had every reason to hide this episode, leading his readers to believe he was in his wife's company. I think that this episode alludes precisely to his vacation with Minna on Lake Garda (at the time Riva del Garda was under Austrian rule), in the hotel where several colleagues of his had gathered, whom he knew and whose company he avoided at all costs.

This said, I will now attempt to reconstruct the episode on the basis of my own suppositions. Freud is sitting at a table at the Hôtel du Lac in Riva del Garda with Minna, and before him sits "a gentleman from Vienna whom I knew and who no doubt remembered me too. However, I had reasons of my own for not renewing the acquaintance." (S. E., 6, p. 136) This person might have been the colleague Anton Felsenreich, who had worked at the Gynaecological Clinic, at Vienna Hospital General, in the same period as Freud. Minna, who had grasped "his distinguished name", was eavesdropping on the conversation with another colleague, and would from time to time address "questions that took up the thread of their discussion" to Freud (ibid., p. 136). Now, if Minna was asking for elucidations from Freud about their neighbours' conversation, it is most likely that she was snooping on a dialogue between doctors, on topics that were familiar to Freud. Certainly theirs was no ordinary conversation, or Minna would not have bothered Freud with questions about what she had overheard. Freud, at this point, probably feared that, through no will of his own, Minna's curiosity about the scientific discussion would result in his own involvement in it. Once he had returned home, Freud had possibly intended to recount the episode to his wife, but he had forgotten its content out of respect for both his sister-in-law and his spouse.

A composite female figure: Martha, Minna, and Dora

The female figure of this dream, Frau E. L., seems to condense many different identities, analogously to Irma, in the "Irma's injection" dream, which Freud assumed as a specimen in *The Interpretation of Dreams* (1900a). In that dream, we can also grasp many references to cocaine.

Freud indulges in a detailed description of the dream-work that leads to the formation of these "collective and composite figures", through the process of condensation:

> The process of condensation further explains certain constituents of the content of dreams which are peculiar to them and are not found in waking ideation. What I have in mind are "collective" and "composite figures" and the strange "composite structures" […]. There are many sorts of ways in which figures of this kind can be put together. I may build up a figure by giving it the features of two people; or I may give it the *form* of one person but think of it in the dream as having the *name* of another person; or I may have a visual picture of one person, but put it in a situation which is appropriate to another. In all these cases the combination of different persons into a single representative in the content of the dream has a meaning; it is intended to indicate an "and" or "just as", or to compare the original persons with each other in some particular respect, which may even be specified in the dream itself. As a rule, however, this common element between the combined persons can only be discovered by analysis, and is only indicated in the contents of the dream by the formation of the collective figure. [*S. E.*, 5, pp. 650–651]

In the comment on the dream, Freud says that Frau E. L. "is the daughter of a man to whom I was once *in debt*" (p. 638). In his associations, Frau E. L. is the wife, in other collateral associations "a relative", "a member of my family of whom I am fond" (ibid., p. 656).

Freud's first associations refer to the

> cab with a taximeter [that] always reminds me of a table d'hôte. It makes me avaricious and selfish, because it keeps on reminding me of what I owe. My debt seems to be growing too fast, and I'm afraid of getting the worst of the bargain; and in just the same way at a table d'hôte I can't avoid feeling in a comic way that I'm getting too little, and must keep an eye on my own interests. (ibid., p. 637)

If the table d'hôte constantly reminds him of his debt it is because this reunion of friends takes place at the house of his friend, the oculist Königstein, to whom he owed money, and because of Frau E. L.'s presence, the daughter of another person to whom Freud was a debtor. If we wanted to unearth the infantile root of this fear of not receiving enough at the table d'hôte, we would probably need to refer back to Freud's greediness as a child, which just a year beforehand he had deemed to be at the origin of his "former railroad phobia":

> My phobia, then, was a fantasy of impoverishment, or rather a hunger phobia, determined by my infantile greediness and evoked by my wife's lack of a dowry (of which I am so proud). [Masson, 1985, 21 December 1899, p. 392]

The episode with Frau E. L., with her confidential approaches to the dreamer under the table, remind Freud of an anecdote from the time of his secret engagement to Martha. Also, Frau E. L.'s unfamiliarity, according to *The Interpretation of Dreams* (1900a), is now the marker of a "secret relationship". Frau E. L., Freud had previously said,

> is a person with whom I have hardly at any time been on friendly terms, nor, *so far as I know*, have I ever wished to have any closer relations with her. I have not seen her for a long time, and her name has not, I believe, been mentioned during the last few days. The dream-process was not accompanied by affects of any kind. (S. E., 5, p. 637; italics added)

It is curious that, just after he finishes telling the dream, and even before he begins with the associations, Freud immediately reveals Frau

E. L.'s presumed identity, and then communicates something which would have found a more natural place at the end of the exposition of the dream, that is, the fact that the dream "was not accompanied by affects of any kind". It seems to me that Freud wanted to cover his back. I am under the impression that the urgency with which he provides this information derives from his impellent need to specify the lack of any emotional connection with Frau E. L., even if he had just conceded that other hypotheses were indeed possible, stressing that on a conscious level ("so far as I know") he had not wanted to be on friendly terms with this person. Yet he could not be aware, before concluding the analysis of the dream, of what his unconscious wanted, just as he was unaware of the real identity of this female figure.

The people to whom Freud owed money were Breuer, Hammerschlag, Königstein, Fleischl, and Paneth. If Frau E. L. was Breuer's daughter, then Freud's reluctance to be on friendly terms with her, his creditor's daughter, would be more understandable, also because at the time his relationship with Breuer had already long deteriorated.[14] We have a few elements with which to hypothesise that the lady in the dream is Breuer's daughter, Gretel. In a letter to Fliess from 4 October 1899, Freud reports news on Gretel:

> I can tell you as a secret that Gretel Breuer really did become engaged to Arthur Schiff. I heard about it from a patient in treatment and therefore must treat it as a secret; otherwise I know of no reason to do so. [Masson, 1985, 4 October 1899, p. 377]

On 27 October, he speaks of the issue once again:

> I have every reason to assume that Arthur Schiff is engaged to Gretel Breuer (a big secret, of course). But I guess at all sorts of things. So your nasal findings may find official recognition in the not too distant future. Political marriage. [Masson, 1985, 27 October 1899, p. 381]

Freud twice underlines the absolute secrecy of this engagement, and in the dream we have reference to this when he mentions his secret engagement to Martha.[15] Breuer's presence in this dream, albeit in an indirect form, would not be completely out of place, insofar as Breuer was Fleischl's family doctor and had probably, according to Bernfeld

(1981), been consulted when Freud suggested to his friend that he should detox from morphine through the use of cocaine. Thus, Breuer was also involved in this unpleasant story, and not even as indirectly as Bernfeld would have us believe (see Hortense Koller Becker, 1963, p. 326).

Furthermore, the reference to the secret engagement of Breuer's daughter is even more important for Freud because this implied a closer bond between the Breuer and the Fliess families, since Schiff was either a relative or at least a person very close to Fliess and his wife's family. "When the engagement became known Freud called it a 'political' one and anticipated that now Fliess's theories would be fully accepted by Breuer and his circle, which apparently was actually the case" (Schur, 1972, p. 204). This bond between the two families would make Freud's relation with Fliess problematic, considering his declared hostility towards Breuer, and implied unavoidable repercussions for his honesty with and spontaneity towards his friend. In a letter to Fliess from 11 March 1900, as we have just seen, he provides us with a clear explanation of these events, and this seems to me to represent an important dream-source of the "Company at table d'hôte" dream. Freud explicitly refers to this incumbent bond (the marriage then took place on 27 May 1900), using the ironical term "Breuerization":

> [...] with the prospect of being pushed even farther from you and your family by the impending Breuerization—it would be utterly senseless to try to deny the influence of such circumstances and that of the women, at any rate, on our relationship—in short, in view of all these considerations I have resolved to reduce my claims on you. [Masson, 1985, 11 March 1900, p. 402]

Perhaps this letter could shed some light on the passages of the dream under examination here. In the dream, Freud appears to allude to this concern for the future of his relationship with Fliess, because of his imminent "Breuerization". Consequently, in Freud's associations, we have his fear of a loss at the table d'hôte, the feeling of not getting enough, and of being compelled to look after his business. After all, Freud clearly states in this letter that, because of the upcoming event, he has decided to "reduce his claims on Fliess", and thus has already lost something on a personal level, since he has spontaneously withdrawn part of his investment in his friendship with Fliess because of the latter's "Breuerization". He also implies, furthermore, that another, non-secondary, reason for this disinvestment must be attributed to women. Ida Fliess had become jealous of Freud, as a result of an inopportune comment on Breuer's part, verging on gossip: he appears to have told Fliess' wife that Freud was in the habit of ruining other people's marriages. Freud speaks of this comment in a letter to Fliess from 7 August 1901:

> What is your wife doing other than working out in a dark compulsion the notion that Breuer once planted in her mind when he told her how lucky she was that I did not live in Berlin and could not interfere with her marriage? [Masson, 1985, 7 August 1901, p. 447]

In the dream in question, we also find an ambiguous, seductive, female presence, extraneous to this merry company of friends engaged in a game of Tarock. This presence seems to disturb the party somehow, with a seductiveness consonant with neither the place nor the moment. The dreamer might have conjured up this image to represent the negative interference of women with male friendships, to which Freud had made explicit reference in the abovementioned letter to Fliess. In the same letter from 11th March 1900, towards the end, Freud explicitly mentions the Tarock game in the following terms: "On Saturday evenings I look forward to an orgy of taroc ..."

In another letter to Fliess, from 14 October 1900, he confesses to his friend that he is working on his essay on dreams unenthusiastically:

> I myself am writing the dream [essay] without real pleasure and am becoming a professor by way of absentmindedness while collecting material for the "Psychology of Everyday Life". [Masson, 1985, 14 October 1900, p. 427]

In this same letter, thoughts can be identified which become dreamsources for the "Company at table d'hôte" dream, or at least thoughts that have entered Freud's ideational associations during the drafting of his writing. We find another reference to Breuer here, formulated in metaphorical language that is fitting to the dream in question:

> Through a lucky card game, not through knowledge or ability, he won the game of life and made his fortune. Woe to the one who dares attack him! [ibid., p. 427]

No better metaphor could be found, for a keen tarock player, to describe a Breuer winning the "game of life", while he, Freud, at the *table d'hôte*, was afraid of suffering a loss, and not receiving enough. In the game of life, Freud had proven himself to be an amateur, because the cocaine card did not turn out to be the right one, and he had allowed Koller to win the game. Thus one could have righteously responded thus to this "naïve" person: "Do you suppose I'm going to do this or that for the sake of your *beaux yeux* [beautiful eyes]?" (p. 638)

Yet Breuer also had another daughter, Dora. If the woman in the dream was Dora Breuer, she could have easily reminded Freud of another Dora, the patient Ida Bauer, whom he was treating at the same time that he was working on the essay on dreams. Breuer's daughter and the patient Dora were basically coetaneous, since the latter was born on 1 November 1882, Dora Breuer on 11 March 1882. Lest one judge it incoherent that Frau E. L. could have lent her identity to the eighteen-year-old Ida Bauer, it is worth mentioning Mahony (1996, p. 52) who remarks how, in his account of the case history, Freud refers to Dora as a "female person, child, girl, woman, lady". Yet problems arise as to the dating of the dream, if we suppose that the dream's female figure, surely a composite one, represents at the same time Martha Freud, Minna Bernays, Dora Breuer, and the patient Dora.

As for the communication of 14 October, that he was working on while writing up his paper *On Dreams* (1901a), we must not take it literally as it does not provide any conclusive proof of the dream's actual date. Because Freud was a prolific dreamer, he could have begun drafting the essay by writing an introduction, waiting for a suitable dream to analyse and present to the reader's attention. Thus the dream could even date back to after 14 October 1900. Also, Freud's temporal references appear unreliable, because he could have been deliberately misleading his readers so as to hide the autobiographical references, and also because he has on many occasions given evidence of the unreliability of his temporal memory.

Kuhn (1999, p. 950) affirms with absolute certainty that Freud had the "table d'hôte dream in the early hours of Sunday morning 30 September 1900" and that this "precision dating [...] makes it possible to construct a new chronological narrative of this uncertain period in Freud's biography". Kuhn refers to the figure of Oscar Rie to justify Freud's fear of becoming poor and his feeling of being *schuldig* (of being in debt) with his colleague for the free medical treatment given to

Minna. Kuhn (1999, p. 952) believes that "parts of the table d'hôte dream analysis were written against the domestic background of Oscar Rie's subsequent free treatment of the invalid Minna Bernays". To endorse the thesis that "Rie's involvement also raised the significant problem that often troubled Freud; whether a doctor should charge a friend or colleague for his medical services" (p. 952), Kuhn mentions the dream referred to in the letter to Fliess of 3–4 October 1897, which, as Freud says, "could be summed up as 'bad treatment'" (Masson, 1985, p. 269).

At the time, Rie was an intimate friend of Freud's and had been chosen by Minna as her personal doctor, thus it was highly improbable that he would have requested payment for his visits to his friend's sister-in-law, just as it was equally unlikely that Freud could have felt in debt with his friend for these visits. It has always been a deontological norm that a doctor does not request colleagues, family, and friends to pay for his services, and I find it likely that such norm would have been in effect in Freud's *fin de siècle* Vienna. This is deducible from the letter to Fliess dated 4 October 1897, according to which one theme of the "bad treatment" dream was precisely the request that Freud give free medical treatment to the wife of a colleague of his:

> A special part was played by Mrs. Q., whose remark you reported to me: that I should not take anything from her, as she was the wife of a colleague (he of course made it a condition that I should). [Masson, 1985, 4 October 1897, pp. 269–270]

Furthermore, it does not seem to me that either the "company at table d'hôte" dream or Freud's interpretations contain any clues that would prompt us to ascribe such a prominent role to the figure of Oscar Rie; just as I cannot find clues that point, as Kuhn suggests, to Oscar Rie's being the friend who offers the cab drive to Freud. To conclude, the theme indicated by Kuhn—the "becoming increasingly indebted to Oscar Rie" (p. 952)—does not really chime with the central theme of the dream indicated by Freud: "to get some enjoyment without cost". [*S. E.*, 5, p. 650]

I am still of the opinion that Minna is the central figure of the dream, although Freud never makes any specific references in this regard. Yet as Anzieu has claimed (1986, p. 543), Minna is censored. At this point a question arises as to Freud's reliability, because in *On Dreams* (1901a) and in *The Psychopathology of Everyday Life* (1901b) he offers two different accounts of the temporal relationship between the dream "company at table d'hôte" and the "mistake in the Post Office Savings Bank". In *On Dreams* Freud affirms:

> What was the dream-instigator in the specimen that we have chosen for analysis? [...] But I can also point to the important experience which was represented by this trivial one. A few days earlier I had paid out a considerable sum of money on behalf of a member of my family of whom I am fond. [S. E., 5, p. 656]

In this account, the mistake at the postal office and the ensuing fear of growing poor is therefore the stimulus for the dream of *a few days later* that prompted the same interpretation, that is, the fear of growing poor. The account later included in *The Psychopathology of Everyday Life* would be contrasting:

> I intend to draw the sum of 300 kronen from the Post Office Savings Bank, which I wanted to send to an absent relative for purposes of medical treatment [...] There is no doubt that I regretted this expenditure. My affect on perceiving my error can be understood better as a fear of growing poor as a result of such expenditure. But both these feelings, my regret at the expenditure and my anxiety over becoming poor that was connected with it, were entirely foreign to my consciousness; I did not have a feeling of regret when I promised the sum of money, and would have found the reason for it laughable. I should probably not have believed myself in any way capable of such an impulse [...] had I not had a dream a few days before which called for the same solution. [S. E., 6, pp. 119–120]

Here the temporal sequence between the dream and the "mistake" is reversed, and the fear of growing poor as a result of the post office withdrawal is analogous to the same fear that had manifested itself in the dream *a few days earlier* relating to the visit to the Post Office Savings Bank. To which of these two accounts should we give credence? I have chosen to follow the account in *On Dreams* (1901a), according to which the dream occurred a few days after the money had been withdrawn from the postal office. Drawing on my thesis that Minna has appeared in this dream not only as dream-figure, but also as part of the central theme that Freud identifies as "for once experience love that cost me nothing" (S. E., 5, p. 672), we must make the following considerations:

a. The dream occurs a few days after the withdrawal of a considerable sum of money destined to a relative absent for purposes of medical treatment;
b. If this relative is Minna, Freud writes to Fliess on 23 October 1900 that Minna has returned home. Since he makes no mention of it in the previous letter from 14 October, we must deduce that Minna left Merano between 15 and 23 October;
c. In a letter sent to Martha from Lavarone on 1 September 1900, Freud claims that he has left Minna in Merano with enough money to pay for one or two weeks of treatment;
d. It is logical to think that Freud withdrew money to settle the bill for the treatments after Minna's return, being thus able to calculate how many days of treatment he still had to pay for by subtracting the days already paid for by Minna with the money he had left her before returning to Vienna.

Therefore, we should infer that Freud went to the postal office between 15 and 23 October 1900 at the earliest. However, knowing that Freud was not so swift in settling his debts, we could also infer that he took a few more days. Because, according to Freud, the dream occurred a few days after his visit to the postal office, we should conclude that dream did not occur before the period of 18 to 26 October.

However, is it likely Freud would have dreamt of his patient after only a month of analysis, according to the new date I have proposed for the beginning of the treatment? Yes, because she was "in the first bloom of youth—a girl of intelligent and engaging looks" (p. 23). She was certainly more attractive than the Junoesque Minna with whom he had probably just had a sexual relationship, for which he had paid dearly. Also, Dora's familial erotic intrigues would certainly have awakened memories of his own erotic vicissitudes in him. Furthermore, as Mahony claims (1996), Freud was emotionally and profoundly involved in the treatment of Dora,[16] and it is likely that the young patient became part of her analyst's dreams. We must remember here that waking up, Freud had the impression that the dream "was unemotional, disconnected and unintelligible; but while I was producing the thoughts behind the dream, I was aware of intense and well-founded affective impulses …" (*S. E.*, 5, p. 640).

If Freud saw in Dora an adolescent who had seduced a mature man, thus causing a great deal of confusion in the two families that had up until then lived an apparently quiet life, in other words, if he saw in Dora the prototype of female seductiveness,[17] then Wilhelm Meister's words could be understood by Freud, in that moment, as a sexist hymn addressing women in general:

> You lead us into life
> you make the poor creature guilty.

We must also bear in mind that if Dora's treatment began a month before he communicated it to Fliess, we have one more reason why Freud should dream of his patient, in that during his summer vacation Freud had seen the places Dora remembered during the treatment, those places where Herr K. had attempted to seduce her twice, namely, Merano and Lake Garda. On Lake Garda, Freud had stopped first in Torbole and then at Riva del Garda for five days, where he had "luxuriate[d] without regrets" with Minna. This was enough to bring him close to Herr K., Dora's seducer, and to bring her into his dream through her similarities with Dora Breuer, that is, their homonymy and age.

Furthermore, we must not forget that, in his second attempt at seduction, Herr K. had manifested his own emotional and sexual frustration to Dora, saying: "You know I get nothing out of my wife" (p. 98). Thus, again:

> you make the poor creature guilty.

Yet the same sentence had been uttered by Philip Bauer, Dora's father, when he had spoken to Freud about Dora's vicissitudes and had mentioned his "sincere friendship" with Frau K., justifying himself with the following words: "You know already that I get nothing out of my own wife" (p. 26). We are thus dealing with two sexually frustrated men, dissatisfied by their conjugal relationships. It is therefore not unlikely that Freud would have identified with them both, since he must have found himself in an analogous situation, which had probably led him to engage in a sexual relationship with his sister-in-law.[18] After all, in the letter which I have considered as a remote dream-source, Freud reveals to

Fliess his bitterness and pessimism about his current treatments, his depression after yet another patient had interrupted their treatment, and the fact that he was no longer getting any consolation from smoking, drinking, nor even from sex (Masson, 1985, 11 March 1900, p. 404).

In order to fight depression, Freud adopted this strategy:

> In my spare time I take care not to reflect on it. I give myself over to my fantasies, play chess, read English novels; everything serious is banished. [ibid., p. 404]

Yet I find it likely that a forty-four-year-old man—a man who was more or less coetaneous with Dora's father and Herr K., professionally frustrated and socially isolated, dealing on a daily basis with patients transforming their sexual frustrations into neurotic symptoms, and who had also stopped procreating—would have had fantasies that were, at least partially, of a sexual nature. Indirect evidence of Freud's sexual fantasies and instincts towards his female patients can be found in a letter to Ferenczi from 9 July 1913, at which time Freud was treating Loe Kann, Ernest Jones' partner (they lived together), who was presented by the latter as his own wife. Freud reveals the following to Ferenczi (9 July 1913):

> This Loe has become extraordinary dear to me, and I have produced with her a very warm feeling with complete sexual inhibition, as has rarely been the case before (probably owing to my age). [Brabant, Falzeder, & Giampieri-Deutsch, 1993]

At the time, Freud attributed his ability to dominate his sexual instincts to his fifty-seven years of age, but he also alludes to the fact that it had previously been difficult for him to do so. Thus, I would argue that these sexual instincts would at least have become manifest in sexual fantasies involving his female patients. We therefore have reason to believe that when he was forty-four, at which point he was treating the young, blooming Dora, he was not yet able to achieve the sexual inhibition that he thought would come with age, and he would allow himself to fantasise erotically about his young patient.

If, in the "Company at table d'hôte" dream, Dora was the one to pronounce the sentence, "You've always had such beautiful eyes", this would be a marker of an eroticised transference wherein Freud takes the place of Dora's father, who had suffered from serious sight-related problems, namely a detachment of the retina, as a result of which "his vision was permanently impaired" (p. 19). In the *Postscript* to Dora's case history, Freud admits that he was unable to "mast[er] the transference in good time" (p. 118).

> At the beginning it was clear that I was replacing her father in her imagination, which was not unlikely, in view of the difference between our ages. *She was even constantly comparing me with him consciously*, and kept anxiously trying to make sure whether I was being quite straightforward with her, for her father 'always preferred secrecy and roundabout ways'. [p. 118; italics added]

Moreover, we know that Dora, also unconsciously, frequently used to compare Freud to her own father. We can therefore suppose, and with even more justification, that Freud put those words into his patient's mouth in his dream, and just as in her fantasy Dora would substitute him for her father, so too would Freud in turn substitute himself for Herr K. Consequently, if, as Freud claims, "the transference took me unaware" (p. 119) in Dora's analysis, we must deduce that he failed to identify Frau E. L.'s real over-determination in the "Company at table d'hôte" dream and the fact that this figure might also represent his young patient, his transferential movements. As a consequence, he failed to recognise that the analyst's countertransference could also manifest itself in the dream. This intuition of Dora's transference away from Herr K. to her analyst—which, though formulated afterwards, during the drafting of the case history, must have somehow been present in Freud's unconscious during Dora's treatment—seems to receive a plastic representation in Freud's dream, in Frau E. L.'s attitude:

> Frau E. L. was sitting beside me; she was turning her whole attention to me and laid her hand on my knee in an intimate manner.

Not only does Frau E. L. make *her attention towards the dreamer* manifest through her corporeal movements, but the gesture with her hand also reveals her physical attraction. I would thus argue that the dreamer, through this dream-image, intended to stage his patient's transference, an erotic attraction engendered by some characteristic of the dreamer that captures the patient's attention. In the dream, the detail that seems to ignite Frau E. L.'s attraction is the dreamer's eyes, while in his case history Freud had argued that the trigger of Dora's transference was either jealousy towards another patient, or money. In the *Postscript* to the case history, a passage seems to indicate that, in formulating these thoughts on the transference, Freud had in mind the "Company at table d'hôte" dream. Freud seems to be retranslating the plastic images of the dream into a colloquial language, when he asks himself if he should have posed Dora the following question: "Have you been struck by anything about me or got to know anything about me which has caught your fancy?" (p. 118) Here, personal factors extraneous to the treatment are again involved, just as in those questions that Freud had asked Dora on the relationship between the governess and Herr K. Freud suspects that Dora might have come to learn something about him, that some indiscretion about his private life must have reached her, which would then have induced her to compare him to Herr K., and, therefore, to move the transference onto him. Freud thinks about what he could have told Dora:

> "Now" I ought to have said to her "it is from Herr K. that you have made a transference on to me. Have you noticed anything that leads you to suspect me of evil intentions similar (whether openly or in some sublimated form) to Herr K.'s? Or have you been struck by anything about me or got to know anything about me which has caught your fancy, as happened previously with Herr K.?" [p. 118]

This possibility was not even particularly remote, because Dora lived in the same neighbourhood as Freud, very close to his house. But what was that "anything" that Herr K. and Freud had in common, especially after the latter had come back from his vacation with Minna, "feeling outrageously merry and well"? It could only be conjugal infidelity. Allegedly, Freud feared Dora had come to know something about him, which would lead her to suspect him of being unfaithful to his wife, just like Herr K. Then, had Dora heard some indiscretion about a sexual relationship between her analyst and his sister-in-law, she might have felt in danger, just as she had in her bedroom in the lake house. She might also have suspected mischievous intentions on her analyst's part, as she had done with Herr K. when he had entered her bedroom while she was resting. Freud continues to fantasise that, after this hypothetical intervention of his, his patient's attention

> would then have been turned to some detail in our relations, or in my person or circumstances, behind which there lay concealed something analogous but immeasurably more important concerning Herr K. And when this transference had been cleared up, the analysis would have obtained access to new memories, dealing, probably, with *actual events*. [pp. 118–119; italics added]

Yet if Dora's transference indicated that she felt threatened in the consulting room—that she thought that, instead of looking after her, her analyst might have bad intentions towards her—then the real memories that could emerge from the clearing up of the transference would lead Dora back to her childhood and to her first dream. Thus, the figure of the father would have emerged, who, instead of protecting her, was standing beside her bed with bad intentions, just as bad as Herr K.'s had when he entered Dora's room and observed her while she was resting. We have seen, though, producing more than sufficient evidence in the first part of this book, that Freud could have in any case accessed these actual memories by correctly interpreting the first dream and by applying theories that he had previously formulated, and which he had intended to corroborate with this case history.

Still in the *Postscript* to the case history, Freud claims that Dora's intention to abandon the treatment could already be grasped in her first dream, as could, therefore, her perception that Freud's consulting room was inhabited by inflamed passions (see Mahony, 1996). Maybe Dora had actually guessed that there was an eroticised countertransference in her analyst, those "bad intentions" that had prompted her to formulate, according to Freud's interpretation, the idea that "men are all so detestable" (p. 120), so that she had preferred to abandon the treatment. Had Dora perceived Freud's desire for a love that would cost him nothing?

Thus, it is possible that the desire emerging from this dream is an aspect of Freud's countertransference towards Dora. In any case, I would argue that this dream and the underlying dream-thoughts are part of a range of sexual desires that, more or less surreptitiously, affected Dora's treatment. After all, it is Freud himself who reminds us that

> most of the dreams of adults are traced back by analysis to *erotic wishes*. This assertion is not aimed at dreams with an *undisguised* sexual content, which are no doubt familiar to all dreamers from their own experience and are as a rule the only ones to be described

> as "sexual dreams" [...]. A great many other dreams, however, which show no sign of being erotic in their manifest content, are revealed by the work of interpretation in analysis as sexual wish-fulfilments; and, on the other hand, analysis proves that a great many of the thoughts left over from the activity of waking life as "residues of the previous day" only find their way to representation in dreams through the assistance of repressed erotic wishes. [*S. E. 5*, p. 682; italics added][19]

Freud had also acknowledged the sexual content of this dream and that part of his desire was centred on the idea of a love without cost. He had said of Frau E. L.'s behaviour: "A woman seems to be making advances on me" (p. 655). Because Freud had elaborated marriage plans for Dora, according to which Herr K.'s repeated advances should be crowned with a wedding, it is not surprising that these thoughts should become part of Freud's dream-language, as represented in the scene that reminds him of his secret engagement with Martha, and reinforced by the by then remote event of Gretel Breuer's secret engagement. Freud had defined her wedding as a "political" one. Yet was the marriage he had suggested between Dora and her seducer not just as "political"? Were this the case, I would argue that Breuer's intuition about Freud ruining other people's marriages, which had made Ida Fliess jealous, was probably to the point. Did Freud, for "political reasons", not intend to rearrange these two families, having Dora married to Herr K. and Dora's father to Frau K.?

In his associations to the dream, soon after having declared that the more he proceeded with his reasoning, the more he felt "intense and well-founded affective impulses", Freud claims that "the contrast between 'selfish' and 'unselfish' and the elements 'being in debt' and 'without paying for it' were central ideas of this kind, not represented in the dream itself" (p. 640). Thus, the *selfish/unselfish* dilemma of the dream finds confirmation here. In the Dora treatment, he appeared all the more interested in finding a justification for his patient's illicit relationship with her seducer, possibly for personal reasons, since he had unconsciously identified with two middle-aged men to whom, as a result of his relationship with his sister-in-law Minna, he felt himself to be in close affinity.

But why would Freud think that Dora was interested in his money, or that she was jealous? Maybe these were, rather, her analyst's projections. Maybe Freud, identifying with his coetaneous Herr K., who "was still quite young and of prepossessing appearance" (p. 29, note 3), had reason to be jealous, or at least envious, of this relationship. As for Dora's interest in his money, he knew that she used to receive expensive gifts from her suitor. Furthermore, her father's relationship with Frau K. was not free of charge either, because, as Dora herself reported, "there could be no doubt that she had taken money from him, for she spent more than she could possibly have afforded if taking out of her own purse or her husband's. Dora added that her father had begun to give handsome presents to Frau K." (p. 33).

Thus, all these illicit relationships appear rather expensive in the dreamer's eyes, and very far from his desire "to get something sometimes without paying for it", "to get some enjoyment without cost" (*S. E.*, 5, p. 650) "experience love that cost me nothing" (*S. E.*, 5, p. 672). Thus, this is possibly why the dreamer, because of his fear "of getting the worst of the bargain", rejects E. L.'s advances and removes her hand from his knee. Perhaps Freud's guilt towards Martha also emerges from this dream, as well as his sense of being *schuldig* (guilty) as a result of his relationship with Minna and consequent fear that he was compromising his marriage.

There are two other moments when Freud's personal circumstances seem to have affected Dora's analysis, or to have found direct expression within it. Speaking of the jewel-case, he says to Dora:

> He [Herr K.] gave you a jewel-case; so you are to give him your jewel-case. That was why I spoke just now of a "return-present".
> [p. 70]

Here, Freud is expressing a rather sexist view, claiming that when a man gives an expensive present to a woman, he expects her to pay him back sexually, that is, to concede her "jewel-case" to him. This thought is also connected to the "Company at table d'hôte" dream, and with Freud's desire to experience a love that would cost nothing, that would imply no expense. Another moment when Freud's own vicissitudes, involving Minna, seem at play is in his interpretation of the latent thoughts in the first dream:

> This other train of thought culminated in the temptation to yield to the man, out of gratitude for the love and tenderness he had shown her during the last few years ... [p. 85]

Arguably, this was what Freud would also have expected from Minna, that she return the attention and love of her illustrious brother-in-law by yielding to him. I would argue that on several occasions during Dora's treatment, her analyst listened to her by projecting expectations, desires, fantasies, anxieties, and preoccupations that derived from his incestuous relationship with his sister-in-law.

As for cocaine, what was its connection with Dora? None, apparently, but both she and her Viennese analyst had shown curiosity, almost a morbid interest in fact, in the Italian physician Mantegazza. Dora had read his *Physiology of Love*, as had Freud, who had also read *On the Hygienic and Medicinal Properties of Coca*. The cocaine episode has demonstrated that the reading of the latter text provoked an excitation in Freud, which was no less than that attributed to Dora (by Herr K.) following the reading of *The Physiology of Love*.[20]

Furthermore, in order to deal with Dora's gastralgias, Freud had considered the use of cocaine. Fortunately, however, he never got round to suggesting this option to her, which prevented him from inflicting any further damage, besides that already being caused through his analysis. We have proof of this idea in Dora's case history, wherein Freud affirms:

> According to a personal communication made to me by Wilhelm Fliess, it is precisely gastralgias of this character which can be interrupted by an application of cocaine to the 'gastric spot' discovered by him in the nose, and which can be cured by the cauterization of the same spot. [p. 78][21]

As for the scene that took place under the table, involving the intimate gesture of laying a hand on the dreamer's knee, it reminded him not only of a secret promise between himself and his fiancée, but also of something else:

> behind this recent recollection there lay concealed an exactly similar and far more important scene from the time of our engagement, which estranged us for a whole day. The intimate laying of a hand on my knee belonged to a quite different context and was concerned with quite other people. [S. E., 5, p. 649]

Freud says no more about this issue, and it is therefore difficult to guess at the identity of the other person involved in the event. Yet, since he warns us that dream-censorship can transform an actual scene into its contrary, we could even argue that, in the actual scene, Freud himself had been the author of the intimate gesture under the table. Freud only tells us that it was a scene similar to that of his engagement with Martha, but which had taken place at a later point, when they were already engaged, estranged for one day, a gesture that was far more important than the one which sanctioned Martha's consent to marry the dreamer.

Some time after their engagement, sanctioned by the scene under the table, Martha gave her father's ring to her fiancée, as a symbol of her love. Yet, shortly after the pearl which was mounted on the ring went missing, and the superstitious Freud interpreted the incident as an omen of Martha's infidelity (see Jones, 1953, p. 119). Now that the mature Freud was reconsidering, in his associations to the dream, the period of his secret engagement—while he was also gathering material for his *The Psychopathology of Everyday Life*—his memory could also have stumbled upon the episode of the ring. In light of his new knowledge about the "parapraxes", he could have seen in this incident an omen of his own infidelity instead of his fiancée's, or, at least, an indication of his desire to temporarily interrupt the engagement, of which the ring was a symbol. Is this another allusion to his "wish for a love that cost me nothing"?[22]

After all, already after the first associations Freud tells us that the dream, which first appeared as unemotional, then revealed, through its analysis, an unsuspected affective intensity:

> The dream was unemotional, disconnected and unintelligible; but while I was producing the thoughts behind the dream, I was aware of intense and well-founded affective impulses; the thoughts themselves fell at once into logical chains, in which certain central ideas made their appearance more than once [...] At the point which I have now reached, I am led to regard the dream as a sort of *substitute* for the thought-process, full of meaning and emotion, at which I arrived after the completion of the analysis. [*On Dreams, S. E.*, 5, pp. 639–640]

CHAPTER ELEVEN

Conclusions

Was the analysis of this dream really complete? In *The Interpretation of Dreams* (1900a) Freud warns anyone novice to this field of research against judging the interpretation of a dream to be fully concluded as soon as one has attributed meaning to all its elements. "It is only with the greatest difficulty that the beginner in the business of interpreting dreams can be persuaded that his task is not at an end when he has a complete interpretation in his hands—an interpretation which makes sense, is coherent and throws light upon every element of the dream's content. For the same dream may perhaps have another interpretation as well, an 'over-interpretation', which has escaped him" (S. E., 5, p. 523). This rule, obviously, also applies to Freud's dreams, and even though, he is not exempt from making a mistake in interpreting or from omitting, even consciously, an over-interpretation of his own dreams. This is what I have hoped to demonstrate by analysing this dream.

Thus, before concluding this analysis, let us see if this dream, "which seems obscure and meaningless" (*On Dreams, S. E.*, 5, p. 636), and precisely because of this also highly over-determined, leaves room for another interpretation, beside the hypotheses I have already formulated in relation to its female figure. In a paragraph added in 1911 to *The Interpretation of Dreams* (1900a), Freud affirms: "We can assert of many dreams, if they are carefully interpreted, that they are bisexual, since they unquestionably admit of an 'over-interpretation' in which the dreamer's homosexual impulses are realized—impulses, that is, which are contrary to his normal sexual activities" (S. E., 5, p. 396). The topic of bisexuality had, after all, been a recent object of discussion and controversy with Fliess during their summer meeting, compromising their relationship. I would argue, therefore, that this recent breaking-off of their friendship had triggered Freud's homosexual and unconscious fantasies, which might thus have left a trace in the dream in question.

We know very well that the neurotic component of Freud's male friendships was not only represented by his ambivalence, by his need to have both a trusted friend and a hated one, but was also evident in the homosexual traits he himself acknowledged much later in his life. Thus, we can also assume that "a love that cost nothing" is also a reference to his friendship with Fliess, all the more so because in a letter dated 26 August 1898, Freud addresses him with the following words:

> I rejoice once again that eleven years ago I already realized that it was necessary for me to love you in order to enrich my life. [Masson, 1985, 26 August 1898, p. 323]

Already in the letter from 22 December 1896, sent to Ida Fliess the week before little Robert Fliess' first birthday, Freud had declared: "You are aware of my love for the big one", that is for Wilhelm Fliess.

In a letter that closely followed the one I took as a possible dream-source for the dream in question, Freud confesses to Fliess that

> no one can replace for me the relationship with the friend which a special—possibly feminine—side demands. [Masson, 1985, 7 May 1900, p. 412]

I have already highlighted the possible sexual references contained in the associations to the *cab drive*.

Yet what is the meaning of this dream? Was Freud's interpretation congruent with the dream theory expressed in *On Dreams* (1901a), and with the technique carefully detailed in *The Interpretation of Dreams*?

Freud affirms in *On Dreams* (1901a), that:

> Analysis has taught us something entirely analogous in the case of obscure and confused dreams: once again the dream-situation

represents a wish as fulfilled—a wish which invariably arises from the dream-thoughts, but one which is represented in an unrecognizable form and can only be explained when it has been traced back in analysis. The wish in such cases is either itself a repressed one and alien to consciousness, or it is intimately connected with repressed thoughts and is based upon them. Thus the formula for such dreams is as follows: *they are disguised fulfilments of repressed wishes.* [*On Dreams, S. E.,* 5, p. 674]

According to Freud's interpretation, which he reiterated on more than one occasion, the "Company at table d'hôte" would represent his desire for a sincere love, that would cost him nothing, and also, more generally, his desire to obtain something for free, that is, to enjoy something without having to pay for it. This is what Freud deduces from associations and from his analysis. Yet following his theory, the dream-content of this dream, which he places among the "obscure and confused ones", should represent this desire being fulfilled, and thus the dream should stage a situation in which Freud could finally enjoy a genuine love, that would cost him nothing.

Furthermore, Freud claimed on several occasions that desires that manifest themselves in dreams are of the erotic kind, and these desires are "repressed infantile sexual wishes" (*ibid.,* p. 682). However, Freud's analysis of this dream never goes so deep as to bring to light these infantile, repressed, sexual wishes. When he comes across a "nodal point", Freud becomes reticent, adducing private reasons to justify his restraint, which prevents us from fully comprehending the dream. Thus he informs us the first time that he cannot continue with the interpretation:

> I might draw closer together the threads in the material revealed by the analysis, and I might then show that they converge upon a single nodal point, but considerations of a personal and not of a scientific nature prevent my doing so in public. I should be obliged to betray many things which had better remain my secret, for on my way to discovering the solution of the dream all kinds of things were revealed which I was unwilling to admit even to myself. [*On Dreams, S. E.,* 5, p. 640]

In another moment of the analysis—when he argues that spending a certain sum of money on a relative of his had bothered him, even if he had not hesitated, even for a second, before doing so—he does not explain why this regret did not find expression in the dream.

> Yet I can honestly say that when I decided to spend this sum of money I did not hesitate for a moment. My regret at having to do so—the contrary current of feeling—did not become conscious to me. *Why* it did not, is another and a far-reaching question, the answer to which is known to me but belongs in another connection. [ibid., pp. 672–673]

According to Falzeder (2001), these repeated episodes of reticence greatly damaged the power of persuasion of *Traumdeutung* among Freud's colleagues. Freud's *The Interpretation of Dreams* (1900a), though promising to describe a replicable method of dream analysis, did not contain a single, complete, analysis of a dream. As a matter of fact, it did not demonstrate his principle thesis in any comprehensive manner at all, that is, the thesis that the dream is the fulfilment of an unconscious desire (probably an infantile one). Freud, as is well known, never revealed the nature of his desire, or the "navel" of all of his dreams. The interpretation of the "specimen dream", the dream of Irma's injection, is totally lacking in this respect (Falzeder, 2001, pp. 31–32).

Also, in interpreting the "Company at table d'hôte" dream, the specimen dream of the shorter 1900 writing on dreams, Freud remains reticent on a few fundamental points, from which he appears to actively divert the reader's attention through many associations and interpretations of other parts of the dream. Yet he does not provide us with indications as to how, in his personal case, "it is that repressed infantile sexual wishes provide the most frequent and strongest motive-forces for the construction of [his own] dreams" (*On Dreams, S. E.,* 5, p. 682).

Twenty years later, in *Psycho-Analysis and Telepathy* (1921), and then again in *Dreams and Occultism* (1933a)—the XXX lecture of *New Introductory Lectures on Psycho-Analysis* in which, as Roazen (2001) has noted, Freud returns twice to the same clinical case that was the object of his "secret essay"—he no longer seems as determined to defend the theory of dreams as wish-fulfilment. He will refer to two dreams that appear to indicate a solution to the patient's personal conflicts. The patient in question had a sexual relationship with his sister-in-law but had then decided to marry her daughter instead, that is, his own niece, who, in treatment with Helene Deutsch, had revealed a family romance wherein she herself figured as her mother's and uncle's daughter. Unfortunately, Freud withholds important information from us, as he does not disclose the content of the dreams. He says only that:

> I detected from his dreams a plan that he was forming by means of which he would escape, be able to *escape from his relation with his early love without causing her too much mortification or material damage*. [S. E., 18, p. 192; italics added][1]

Freud comes close here to the conception of dreams—which was only elaborated fifty years later, by integrating knowledge derived from cognitive theory and neuroscience—to which the majority of researchers, in the second half of the century, subscribed: the function of problem-solving (see Mertens, 2000). According to the most recent viewpoints on dreams, the dreamer would be busy with "attempts to find a solution or an optimised adaptation for these experiential, maladaptive, schemes, that have been reactivated by recent events" (Mertens, 1999, p. 34).

Yet, when he discusses dreams on a purely theoretical level, even Freud will continue to reiterate, in *New Introductory Lectures on Psycho-Analysis* (1933a), his thesis of wish-fulfilment. It almost seems that, faced with the actual clinical case, Freud feels free to abandon his own theoretical stances without having to account for them, provided he was aware of these waivers. These moments when Freud is, paradoxically, so un-Freudian in his technique, appear determined by a particular, personal involvement evoked by the patient, and by what the latter tells him, which engenders flashes of projective identification. Thus, I would claim that when this patient tells Freud of his dreams, on the one hand, the account evokes in him fragments of his own personal history and, on the other, on such occasions Freud gives an interpretation that is not only congruent with the patient's account, but also with the personal elements which are evoked by the account. Thus I would advance that, when dealing with this patient's dreams, Freud completely forgot to search for infantile wish-fulfilment and interpreted the dream instead as expressing an attempt to find a non-traumatic resolution for the relationship with the sister-in-law, which would at the same time not have compromised her marriage. Thus, in my view, he had been reminded of his "Company at table d'hôte" dream, thus attributing meaning not only to his patent's dreams, but also to his own dream about whose crucial nodes, twenty years before, he had been so reticent, thereby revealing his paradoxical resistance in the redundancy of the associations with which he impresses the reader.

In *New Introductory Lectures on Psycho-Analysis* (1933a), in the twenty-ninth lesson wherein Freud provides a revision of the dream theory, he claims: "We are certainly right in thinking that the longer and more roundabout the chain of associations the stronger the resistance" (Freud, 1933a, *S. E.*, 22, pp. 13–14). It is probable, therefore, that after many years and after having accumulated extensive practical analytic experience, Freud realised, at least unconsciously, that the interpretations of his own dreams were also affected by a fundamental resistance. In this respect, the dream I have analysed is exemplary. Since every dream is overdetermined, so too, perhaps, are its interpretations, and more than one can be plausible. I cannot but agree with Fromm's (2013, p. 112) conclusion that Freud, with his "heaping association upon association which end up in practically nothing, […] succeeds in covering up the awareness of the meaning of the dream". Freud, Fromm continues, very often hides the true meaning of the dream itself through numerous associations, doing so as to avoid acknowledging its significance. In other words, according to Fromm, Freud's method of endless associations is the mark of his resistance to understanding his dreams.

We have seen above that Freud had himself reached this conclusion in 1932, at least with respect to his patients' dreams. Yet to admit to his own resistance when interpreting his dreams would have meant affecting the entire work of self-analysis carried out in *Traumdeutung*, whilst also discrediting his dreams interpretation technique, since the dreams he takes as specimens in order to illustrate it are his own. This confirms an intuition of Freud's, however, which he had expressed to his friend Fliess, namely, that self-analysis is in truth an impossible work, an intuition which seems all the more justified when the dreamer must also become the interpreter of his own dreams.

NOTES

Foreword

1. Kohon (1984) affirms that "it is clear that Freud did not like Dora. It is also clear that Freud did perhaps feel attracted and seduced by Dora; perhaps there are reasons for thinking that they had both embarked on a game of mutual seduction, but this need not necessarily imply that he liked her" (p. 76). Gay (1988) also recognises that "Freud's inability to enter Dora's sensibilities speaks to a failure of empathy that marks his handling of the case as a whole" (p. 249).
2. Since the amount of existing literature on the case is so vast, it is possible that other authors have already exposed a few conclusions that I have reached autonomously. I have thus attempted, throughout the writing and revision of this book, to acknowledge viewpoints similar to, or coinciding with my own, even those I came across after the completion of the present work.
3. More than one author has made this mistake. Among others, see Glenn 1993.
4. It is rather appalling that, even nowadays, much criticism attempts to discredit Freud's seduction theory. I quite agree with Mary Marcel (2005, p. 88): "While other critics have happily demonstrated shortcomings in Freud's procedures, generally they have not commented on

the fact that subsequent studies in the twentieth century, both clinical and epidemiological, have confirmed Freud's initial concern, that child sexual abuse is indeed a widespread phenomenon, with a substantial number of survivors experiencing serious mental health and other sequelae". Jacqueline Lanouzière (1991, p. 18) expresses a similar opinion, claiming that the failure to appreciate this problem would prove problematic, even harmful, since younger and younger children are nowadays used to satisfying adults' perverse passions: the magnitude of this problem is disquieting. From a clinical perspective, Huopainen (2002, p. 99) has unveiled a continuity between the borderline pathology and Freud's diagnosis of hysteria: "If traumatic events accumulate, as is often the case, they result in symptoms of complex posttraumatic stress disorder, dissociative symptoms such as identity disorder and disruption of personality development and maturation such as that seen in borderline personality disorder or similar states. These symptoms correspond to the hysteria diagnosis of Freud's time". Lothane (2001, p. 713), too, refers to the clinical confirmations of the seduction theory: "The troubled and misunderstood 1897 letter of recantation is invalidated both by the weight of the historical record and the daily clinical experiences in the practice of all varieties of psychotherapy." For a brief summary of existing studies on the trauma from Freud until now, see Bohleber (2010).
5. Although Akavia (2005, p. 203) attempts to demonstrate, through the familial model, the family's responsibility in the development of Dora's condition, she is forced to acknowledge the father's preponderant role: "Entrusted as Dora was with both the responsibility for his health and his intimate secrets, she developed a special bond with her father and took him as her primary object of identification. Indeed, he was the most influential person in the development of her hysteria and in the manifestation of its specific symptoms".
6. Collins, Green, Lydon, Sachner & Skoller (1990) have also unveiled a correspondence between Freud's narration and the narration of the hysteric, although in a different context. Showalter (1993, p. 24) has claimed that: "During the past decade, the concept of 'hysterical narrative' has become one of the most popular formulations in literary criticism. It has developed at the busy crossroad where psychoanalytic theory, narratology, feminist criticism, and the history of medicine intersect, drawing both on the vogue of Freud's case studies, especially the canonical *Dora*, and the recent recognition that not just psychoanalysis, but all medical practice, depends on narrative, the 'doctor's story', which both shapes the formal case study and determines practical treatment."

7. Even Foucault (1994) believed in Freud's deceitful interpretations of Dora's dreams, despite his own critique of the Freudian method of dream interpretation.
8. Mahony (1996, p. 24) has also remarked on this overlooked aspect of psychoanalytical historiography: "Freud did not finish his first psychoanalytic case until April 1900! That initial success, the case of Mr. E., was followed by two others that terminated in May; the sexual secrets of these first three were opened by Freud's 'keys'. From the start of his systematic self-analysis in mid-1897, until the century had ended, then, he did not bring any analysis to a successful conclusion." Possibly, focusing on Freud's initial failures would, in the eye of a certain psychoanalytic historiography, compromise the image of the father of psychoanalysis, partly because he had only privately admitted to his lack of success, to Fliess. As a matter of fact, in his account of Dora's case history, Freud simply declares that he has drawn on preceding analytic treatments, somehow implying he had brought them to conclusion. We have seen, though, that rather than concluded analyses, Freud had so far accumulated only fragments of analyses.
9. If, as Israël and Schatzman claim (1993), it is true that these various failures are also the cause of the abandonment of the seduction theory, which Freud himself advances in his well-known letter from 1897, we should come to the conclusion that Freud abandoned that theory due to an error in judgement, because he sought the cause of the failures in the theory, rather than in the technique, which was back then imprecise and too direct. When Freud "thrust the explanation" (letter to Fliess of 3rd January 1897), his patients, unprepared, broke off the treatment or reinforced their resistances.
10. Freud confesses his interest in the publication of the case in its preface: "The case history itself was only committed to writing from memory after the treatment was at an end, but while my recollection of the case was still fresh and was heightened by my interest in its publication" (p. 10). For a convincing reconstruction of the tormented publication process of Dora's case history, see Kuhn (1999b).
11. The dream had already been included in *The Interpretation of Dreams* (1900a), in Chapter Seven of which Freud expresses an analogous concept, saying that "a dream might be described as *a substitute for an infantile scene modified by being transferred on to a recent experience*. The infantile scene is unable to bring about its own revival and has to be content with returning as a dream" (*S. E.*, 5, p. 546). In this regard, Lothane (2001, p. 711) claims: "The idea that dreaming is a valid historical record and a way of remembering is worth emphasizing and comparing with Freud's other, much better known law, that dreams are

wish fulfilments. The latter formula has forever obscured the former insight, as well as the understanding that the dream is a wish-fulfilling *reaction* to painful day residues, or, reality."

Chapter One

1. "The case books of late-nineteenth-century psychopathologists record harrowing accounts of early seductions, by no means all of them imaginary. Even after Sigmund Freud abandoned his sweeping theory that all neuroses are caused by the seduction of young girls by their fathers, he continued to recognize that reports of such seductions were often enough true. Certainly the incidents that left traces in the medical records represent only a modest fraction of precocious initiation into sexual activity, for most of these never came to the attention of a priest or a psychiatrist. Their victims were inhibited by shame, or had repressed the experience without suffering immediate visible consequences" (Gay, 1984, p. 333).
2. After only ten pages of narration, Freud himself draws the attention to the "father's shrewdness which I have remarked upon more than once already" (p. 24).
3. Mahony (1986, p. 18) has stressed that Freud neglects the mother figure in other important case histories, such as in those of Little Hans and of the Rat Man. In all these cases, Freud provides an asymmetrical description of the parental couple, placing much more emphasis on the father's role. The fact that Freud did nothing to meet Dora's mother contrasts with the methodology enunciated in this writing: "It follows from the nature of the facts which form the material of psycho-analysis that we are obliged to pay as much attention in our case histories to the purely human and social circumstances of our patients as to the somatic data and the symptoms of the disorder. Above all, our interest will be directed towards their family circumstances—and not only, as will be seen later, for the purpose of enquiring into their heredity." Van den Berg (1987, p. 64) also focuses on "Freud's disregard of the mother and her important role in Dora's history, Dora's dream, and his own interpretative work". A dissonant and unconvincing opinion is expressed by Juliet Mitchell (2000), who considers Dora's case to be an example of how the centrality of the father vanishes to let that of the mother emerge.

Chapter Two

1. Even though the autumn season actually begins on 23 September, in Vienna the autumnal climate was felt in advance of that date. In an

illustrated postcard sent from Spalato to Minna on 9 September 1898, Freud mentions the previous "letter from Mother, who says that over there is already deep autumn" (Tögel, 2002, p. 115). Also in a letter to Fliess on 16 September 1899, he says: "Fall has really started." Furthermore, we must not forget that Dora's family lived very close to Freud's place and thus they may have noticed his return to Vienna. Back then, the Bauers lived in *Lichtensteinstrasse*, a road that perpendicularly crossed the *Berggasse*, where the Freud family lived at number 19.

2. Through this ironic term, Freud is referring here to Artur Schiff's marriage to Breuer's daughter, Gretel Breuer, celebrated on 27 May 1900. Schiff was either related or in any case very close to the Fliess family, as Schur claims (1972). This implied a close relationship between Fliess and Breuer, with whom Freud had long since ceased to have any contact. Thus, this "Breuerization" negatively affected the relationship between Freud and Fliess, as Freud told his friend in the letter of 11 March 1900. Anzieu (1986) incorrectly affirms that it was Dora Breuer that was engaged with Schiff, but Freud mentions Gretel Breuer twice, in his letters to Fliess dated 4 and 27 October 1899.

3. The new periodisation I am suggesting here for the length of the Dora treatment is supported by a statement of Freud's. In a footnote to his *Fragment* he refers to the case of a girl, sent to him by a Viennese colleague who did not believe in the sexual aetiology of hysteria. Freud writes: "She afterwards come to me for treatment, and proved—*though not during our very first conversation, to be sure*—to have been a masturbator for many years, with a considerable leucorrhoeal discharge (which had a close bearing on her vomiting)" (p. 25, footnote 1; italics added). Since one of the locks Freud thought he had opened in Dora's case, through his "collection of picklocks", was precisely the secret of her masturbatory activity, we may also assume, as suggested by the case study reported here, that this discovery was certainly not achieved during the first encounter with Dora, as those who take the therapy to have begun when Freud announced it to Fliess would have us believe.

4. Gay (1990, p. 198) acknowledges that Freud and Minna had a very intimate relationship, but he questions the sexual nature of it, claiming that those who hypothesised this type of relationship formulated conjectures which were more ingenious than they were convincing. Eissler (1994) dedicates an entire chapter of his book *Three Instances of Injustice* to the stern confutation of Jung's allegations on Freud and Minna's relationship. Nowadays new information is available, which endorses the theory of an incestuous relationship between the two, as Anzieu (1986) has already remarked. See also Maciejewski (2007, 2008) and Rudnytsky (2003, 2011).

5. Mahony (1996) identified the place where the Bauers (Dora's family) and the Zellenkas (the K. couple) spent their holidays, and the lake in Dora's dream, as Lake Garda.
6. We can assume that Minna had herself encouraged Freud to embark on this extra-conjugal relationship, if Jones (1953) is right in claiming that, since the beginning of their relationship, when the young Freud was attempting to win over Martha, Minna interpreted his interest as being addressed to her, too. To Martha's account of her future fiancé's attentions, she "got the rather damping answer: 'It is very kind of Herr Doctor to take so much interest in *us*'" (Jones, vol. I, p. 115). In a recent article, Silverstein (2007) formulates the idea that Minna, who was described as "more aggressive than Martha", outside of the Freud household was more than a passive participant in her relationship with Freud.

Chapter Three

1. In a letter to Fliess dated 29 December 1897 Freud writes: "I have not yet found the time to have a word with my female side", and it seems that he would never find it, not even later, at least not at the time he was treating Dora.
2. He is referring here to Emmy von N., the patient we will read of again in *Studies on Hysteria* (1895d).
3. The patients' flight was probably motivated by the overly direct technique that Freud would have used back then. In *Draft J* he refers to the case of a patient with whom he managed to reconstruct two sexual scenes, and claimed the therapy was "Interrupted by the patient's flight" (Masson, 1985, p. 158).
4. "Because Freud never mentioned Baginsky's teaching in any significant way, not even in his report on his studies in Paris and Berlin (Freud, 1956a [1886]), this experience has not been considered relevant for the history of psychoanalysis" (Bonomi, 1998b, p. 32).
5. Rachel Blass observes that Freud is perplexed and disturbed by the reaction of disgust, and goes back to the matter several times, with different explanations (Blass, 1992, p. 169).
6. In a previous passage of his conference, Freud had said: "Perhaps the abnormal reaction to sexual impressions which surprises us in hysterical subjects at the age of puberty is quite generally based on sexual experiences of this sort in childhood, in which case those experiences must be of a similar nature to one another, and must be of an important kind" (*S. E.*, 3, p. 202).

7. If this memory, which I consider to be a screen memory, were testimony of an older sexual episode involving both Dora and her brother Otto, as supposed by Lopez (1967), our interpretation would in no way be affected, because in *The Aetiology of Hysteria* (1896c) Freud claimed: "Where the relation is between two children, the character of the sexual scenes is none the less of the same repulsive sort, since *every such relationship between children postulates a previous seduction of one of them by an adult*" (S. E., 3, p. 215, italics added). In this case, it is evident that Dora had plausibly been the one victim to receive the sexual attention of her father.
8. The *Standard Edition* mistakenly renders the term as "continuity" instead of "contiguity" (Cfr. the correct version in: Sigmund Freud, *Collected Papers*, translated by Alix and James Strachey, New York: Basic Books, 1959, vol. 5, p. 52).
9. It would be useful to know at what age Dora had come to know of this sexual oral practice, because such type of sexual knowledge, or behaviour, which would be inappropriate at an early age, could be a marker of sexual abuse. "Children, of all ages, cannot imagine what goes beyond their luggage of experiences. Thus, they are unable to infer sexual experiences that they have not somehow learnt of" (Malacrea & Lorenzini, 2002, p. 143). Dora was not informed of this practice by Mantegazza's *The Physiology of Love*, of which I will speak below. Later, Freud will admit that a *fellatio* fantasy can also emerge in female subjects who have not come to learn of this practice through reading (see footnote 33).
10. Freud increased or diminished Dora's age at his will, depending on the questions at stake. Because of the thorniness of the current topic, he attributed one more year to her, when at the time Dora could have only turned eighteen. In 1924, Freud added a note, wherein he attempted to lessen the extent of his falsification, adding "nearly".
11. Ten years after the writing of this case history, Freud returns to the topic in *Leonardo da Vinci and a Memory of His Childhood* (1910c), where he claims: "The inclination to take a man's sexual organ into the mouth and suck at it, which in respectable society is considered a loathsome sexual perversion, is nevertheless found with great frequency among women of to-day—and of earlier times as well, as ancient sculptures show—, and in the state of being in love it appears completely to lose its repulsive character. *Phantasies derived from this inclination are found by doctors even in women who have not become aware of the possibilities of obtaining sexual satisfaction in this way by reading* Krafft-Ebing's *Psychopathia Sexualis* or from other sources of information. Women, it

seems, find no difficulty in producing this kind of wishful phantasy spontaneously." (Freud, 1910c, *S. E.*, *11*, pp. 86–87; italics added). Freud claims that this phantasy originates in the first enjoyment of the child, namely, breastfeeding. Paolo Mantegazza mentions this sexual practice only in a footnote of his book *The Sexual Relations of Mankind* (*Gli amori degli uomini*, 1886), in Chapter Five, where he deals with "the perversions of love" and refers to ancient Greek and Roman sexual practices. "Lesbian was the term applied to [love] between two women, who employed their mouths; while the woman who prostituted her lips to please the man was known as a *fellatrix*; in the case of children and slaves, they were *fellatores*" (2001, p. 84, footnote 4).

12. With this claim, Freud seems to go back to that letter to Fliess from 27 September 1898—which I have already mentioned when speaking of Dora's enuresis—where he was asking himself whether or not the sexual excitement experienced by that enuretic child was spontaneous or the result of seduction. Freud now adds masturbation, which will only apparently lead him away from the seduction theory, because back then he had attributed the origin of masturbation to the seductive influence of an adult or of an older child.

13. "Freud clearly allows for the coexistence of seduction and infantile sexuality in his *Three Essays*, allegedly the locus classicus of the official recantation of the seduction theory [...] With this transition, a false antinomy was set up between sexual seduction and spontaneous sexual desire, outer and inner reality, perception and imagination, the dream as an adaption to trauma and the dream as wish fulfilment" (Lothane, 2001, pp. 693 and 677).

14. In the letter to Fliess in which Freud communicates that he is dealing with a new case, Freud had used a clearly sexual metaphor: "It has been a lively time and has brought a new patient, an eighteen-year-old girl, a case that as smoothly opened to the existing collection of picklocks." Many authors have drawn attention to the clearly sexual symbolism used by Freud. Makari (1997, p. 1062) says: "At that time Freud's existing collection of picklocks came from his earlier experience with hysteria and his recently published work on dream interpretation, in which he argued that dreams were disguised representations of unconscious wishes", but as I have commented in the *Foreword*, these "picklocks", up until then, had not yet opened a door, since Freud had not yet brought a single analysis to completion.

15. A child's precocious intellectual development, in some cases, could be a sign of an infantile traumatic episode. Ferenczi will later express his opinion on this, with his theory of the "wise baby", namely, a child who had reacted to a precocious sexual trauma through an acceleration

in their intellectual development, independently from their emotional development.

Chapter Four

1. By adding this detail to Dora's account, Freud does not realise that he could be satisfying the morbid curiosity expressed by Viennese doctors who had read this case history "as a *roman à clef* designed for their private delectation" (p. 9), which Freud had rigorously elected to avoid. As regards this "evidence", which did not belong to Dora's memory, we are reading Freud's last declaration, as the "archaeologist"; he recognises that his reconstruction may be arbitrary. From this moment on, he will leave the floor to the "burglar".
2. In his letter to Fliess from 21 September 1897, which is usually considered the moment when Freud abandoned the seduction theory, he summarises his doubts about this theory and about what he had defined as the paternal aetiology of hysteria, saying to his friend: "I no longer believe in my *neurotica*". Lothane (2001, p. 713) has, however, observed that: "A close rereading of Freud shows that the notion, still voiced by psychiatrists and psychoanalysts, that Freud abandoned the seduction theory, meaning external trauma, is wrong."

Chapter Five

1. In a footnote, Freud stresses by means of italics that Dora had already had this dream when in L. (the place on the lake) *for the first time*, but in *The Interpretations of Dreams* he claims: "There is another way in which it can be established with certainty without the assistance of interpretation that a dream contains elements from childhood. This is where the dream is of what has been called the 'recurrent' type: that is to say, where a dream was first dreamt in childhood and then constantly reappears from time to time during adult sleep" (S. E., 4, 190). The necessity to omit that the dream of the fire was an infantile one that re-occurred in adulthood came from the need to divert the reader's attention away from the idea that the scene on the lake with Herr K. had reactivated a childhood dream, derived from a scene of seduction with the father. The reader had to be convinced that the only "trauma" responsible for Dora's hysteria was her infantile masturbation.
2. Commenting on Robins (1991), Mahony (1996) claims, that, in recounting the first dream, when Dora refers to her father standing in front of the bed (*Er steht*), she uses an ambiguous expression which also

has a sexual meaning. In colloquial German, *Er steht* also means "his penis is erect". This second meaning would confirm my hypothesis that the dream represents an episode from Dora's childhood in which the father was involved. The fact that Dora's father was described as impotent, especially with his wife Käte, does not exclude the possibility that he could have had spontaneous erections. Continuing with the sexual metaphor, Freud had claimed that *Schmuckkästchen* (jewel-case) represented female genitals. Banks (1991, p. 259, fn. 3) observes: "The word has sexual connotations in both German and Yiddish. In Yiddish Schmuck means penis or 'prick'; the pun here is that *Schmuckkästchen* means both female genitals and penis, and therefore is a metaphor for sexual intercourse."

3. Actually, Freud never completely abandoned the seduction theory, but merely subjected it to later revisions. Even in his last writings, he reiterates the importance of the real trauma alongside neurotic fantasies (see Schimek, 1987). There are a variety of divergent opinions on this matter: among historian and critics of psychoanalysis, many claim that only the abandonment of the seduction theory could have engendered the discovery of the Oedipus complex and, with it, psychoanalysis be born, psychoanalysis which had until then been opposed because too connected with the real trauma. Blass and Simon (1994, p. 691) have observed that "it becomes apparent that Freud's theories regarding seduction and the process involved in their abandonment were considerably more intricate than is assumed by those who accuse Freud of having abandoned his early and correct views on seduction, as well as by those who defend Freud's abandonment."

4. Glenn (1986, p. 591) stresses "Freud's attraction to Dora revealed itself in his libidinal imagery of the treatment and his premature sexual interpretations, the effects of which he misjudged." According to Kohon (1984, pp. 74–75), "the development of a mutual seduction in the relationship between Dora and Freud seems fairly evident. Many of his interpretations, and the way they were made, could not be understood by Dora except as an attempt at a parental, incestuous seduction."

5. Among those "few times" when Freud had to seek "a narrow escape", we could probably include the therapy with Dora. Another potential case is that of Emma Eckstein.

6. Decker (1991, p. 64) affirms that "Freud was astonished to learn that Dora at eighteen knew that her father has syphilis; obviously he considered such an awareness highly unusual for an adolescent girl." Dora had known about her father's illness since she was twelve. However, perhaps back then she could not fully grasp its meaning. Yet Freud is not at all surprised that Dora knew what the practice of *fellatio* was,

and he seems to deem this knowledge normal for an adolescent of her time.
7. The many hygiene precautions taken by Dora's mother were not sufficient, though, to protect her from contagion. Rogow (1978, p. 345) tells us that Dora's mother "developed tuberculosis. Both Philip and Käte eventually died of the disease, Käthe in a tuberculosis sanatorium in August 1912, and Philip almost a year later."
8. In 1850 Auguste Ambrose Tardieu, Professor of Legal Medicine at the University of Paris, published a treatise titled *Étude médicale-légal sur les attentats aux moeurs*, read by Freud during his sojourn in Paris, and then reprinted many times. Tardieu claims that it was a diffused and deep-rooted, popular belief that one could cure oneself from venereal diseases by engaging in sexual intercourse with a little girl. If such a belief were so widespread, we cannot exclude the idea that more than one father might have thought of curing his own syphilis by abusing his daughter. If we connect Freud's seduction theory, in which hysteria originates from sexual abuse by the father, with his other theory, that syphilitic fathers often have a neurotic lineage, we cannot but conclude that this popular belief could have been put into practice more often than one might think, so much so that Tardieu felt the need to publicly prove it wrong. As regards this, Gay (1984, pp. 339–340) claims that in *Étude médicale-légal sur les attentats aux moeurs*, Tardieu "avoided technical language and cast his exposition in the manner of the catechism. Among the questions he asked himself was whether it is true that one can cure oneself of venereal disease by having sexual intercourse with a little girl. He found it 'sad' to have to touch on such a topic, but felt constrained to refute this disgusting superstition explicitly, since he judged it to be widespread and thoroughly engrained in the popular mind" (pp. 339–340).
9. I am here referring to Ferenczi's "Confusion of tongues between adults and the child" (1932), where he goes back to Freud's seduction theory and further develops it.
10. Although he comes to a conclusion different from my own, Lewin (1973, p. 523) also underlines that Dora's playing with her reticule entailed keeping "her finger in the phallic position of the male during intercourse, while her reticule was the passive recipient".
11. If we assume Ferenczi's standpoint, Dora's symptomatic action could have originated within her relationship with her analyst, and could have somehow represented Dora's answer to the unconscious perception of Freud's countertransference. Borgogno (2014, p. 87) has stressed that Ferenczi "traces back the symptomatic actions of his patients, dreams included, not only to the endopsychic vicissitudes illustrated by Freud,

but also to intersubjective events elicited by unconscious elements in the analyst that act as the exogenous trigger in connection with their individual histories."

12. We do not know why Freud speaks of the father's nocturnal visits to the mother, as if the spouses would sleep in separate bedrooms, unless Freud were unconsciously thinking of the father's nocturnal visits to his daughter. We will see that, in a letter to Fliess, Freud uses the expression "nocturnal visits" to refer to episodes of sexual seduction.
13. This concept of "transposition from a lower to an upper part" had already been affirmed in *The Interpretation of Dreams*: "But I should like to draw attention to the frequency with which sexual repression makes use of transposition from a lower to an upper part of the body. Thanks to them it becomes possible in hysteria for all kinds of sensations and intentions to be put into effect, if not where they properly belong—in relation to the genitals, at least in relation to other, unobjectionable parts of the body" (1900a, S. E., 5, p. 387).
14. The reader must take this metamorphosis in sexuality as a dogma, because Freud does not provide us with any explanation of the mechanism that would bring about this change, which substitutes masturbation with anguish.
15. Banks (1991, p. 253), claims: "When Dora's first dream is subjected to structural and symbolic analysis, it discloses, in my view, elements of the incest taboo, the exchange of women, and seduction."

Chapter Six

1. In a footnote, Freud observes: "There can be no doubt that sexual satisfaction is the best soporific, just as sleeplessness is almost always the consequence of lack of satisfaction. Her father could not sleep because he was debarred from sexual intercourse with the woman he loved" (p. 98, n. 1). In *Three Essays* he would say the same thing, within the context of the nurses' seduction: "sexual satisfaction is the best soporific. Most cases of nervous insomnia can be traced back to lack of sexual satisfaction. It is well known that unscrupulous nurses put crying children to sleep by stroking their genitals" (S. E., 7, p. 180, fn. 1).
2. This ambiguity is also present in the original German, because in the sentence "*du kannst kommen*", the verb *kommen*, just like the English verb *to come*, can have a sexual meaning and indicates the act of the orgasm.
3. Paolo Mantegazza has published a volume entitled *Anthropological Studies in the Sexual Relations of Mankind*, also known as *The Sexual Relations of Mankind*, which focuses on sexual aberrations, ceremonies of

sexual initiation, ritualistic sexual mutilations in ancient and modern times among "savage" "populations" and "primitive" ones, sexual perversions and prostitution. In the preface to the first edition of this volume (1855), Mantegazza himself claims: "This work with the two already published, the *Physiology of Love* [...] and the *Hygiene of Love* [...], completes the *Love Trilogy*" (2001, p. iii). Decker (1991) maintains that if the title of the first volume were intended to refer to the whole trilogy, Dora could have drawn information from it of an anatomical and functional nature.

4. It is worth observing here that before formulating his diagnosis of *"petite hystérie"* Freud had mentioned that Dora had fainted "after a slight passage of words between him [the father] and his daughter". In a footnote, he had added: "The attack was, I believe, accompanied by convulsion and delirious states" (S. E., 7, p. 23, n. 2), which would further confute the theory that Dora's was a *"petite hystérie"*.

5. Of this gossip Freud provides us with a precise testimony in the letter to Fliess from 7 August 1901: "What is your wife doing other than working out in a dark compulsion the notion that Breuer once planted in her mind when he told her how lucky she was that I did not live in Berlin and could not interfere with her marriage?"

6. On the subject of governesses in Freud's case histories, see Colombo's article (2010), where she writes: "The Dora case is written on the cusp of that [...] abandonment [of seduction theory]. But the 'real memory of the maid' continues to play a surprisingly central role [...]. Moreover, the nursemaid [...] is insistently located in the realm of hard fact rather than fantasy. Even as Freud enlarges the role of unconscious fantasy, these nursemaids, with their unquestioned real seductions, constitute a theoretical blind spot. There must be some pressure, outside of the exigencies of theory building, to collar them for the crime (pp. 836–837) [...]. Most important, these treatments of nannies have not considered how they may function as an exegesis of the difficulties Freud had in moving beyond the seduction theory, a theory linked to his own early seduction [...]. That 'real' seduction continued to be attributed so consistently to female servants, even as the roles of reality and fantasy in seduction theory shifted, suggests the curious and powerful role played by these ostensibly secondary figures for Freud. He never concluded that these reports about maids were themselves fantasies, arising at least sometimes from a projection of a child's own powerful wishes and longings" (p. 841).

7. Freud, who more than once gave proof of his superstitious nature, diffidently welcomed Dora also because she had retuned on the 1 of April, that is "a date which is not a matter of complete indifference"

(p. 120). Perhaps he also felt fooled by Dora on account of her return on such an inauspicious date, especially for a superstitious analyst such as himself.
8. Gay (1988, pp. 247 and 255) draws out the following considerations: "No doubt the case had some peculiar, vaguely uncanny meaning for Freud; when he referred to it in retrospect, he consistently pushed it back from 1900 to 1899, a symptom of some unanalysed preoccupation. Freud's reserve hints at intimate reasons why it disconcerted him and why he kept the manuscript on his desk [...]. What is astonishing about the case history of Dora is not that Freud delayed it for four years, but that he published it at all."

Chapter Seven

1. The subtitle of the paper, "The Language of Tenderness and of Passion", significantly alludes to the theme of infantile sexual seduction enforced by an adult, through the eroticisation of a language that should remain only that of "tenderness", rather than "passion".
2. One of the arguments Freud advanced in a letter to Fliess to justify his rejection of the infantile seduction theory amounted to the "continual disappointment in my efforts to bring a single analysis to a real conclusion; the running away of people who for a period of time had been most gripped [by analysis]; the absence of the complete successes on which I had counted ..." (Masson, 1985, 21 September 1897, p. 264). It is interesting to observe how, with an analogous motivation, exactly thirty-five years later, Ferenczi advanced the necessity to return to the traumatic theory of neurosis that Freud, conversely, had abandoned. At the beginning of the conference, explaining to the public the motivations that had led him to deal with the subject, Ferenczi observed that "certain bad or incomplete results with my patients" had forced him understand the need to put "more emphatic stress on the traumatic factors in the pathogenesis of the neuroses which had been unjustly neglected in recent years".

Chapter Nine

1. This is a citation from Goethe's Faust, which appears in the letter to Fliess dated 14 October 1900.
2. Decker (1982, 1991) also identifies the breaking off of the friendship with Fliess and Freud's sexual dissatisfaction, as determining elements in his countertransference during Dora's treatment. Yet she does not further expand on this point.

3. Freud returned to the theme of vengeance in *Observation on transference-love* (1914 [1915]), where he claims that rejecting *tout court* the patient's transference love would entail that "she will not fail to take her revenge for it" (S. E., 12, p. 164). If, according to Freud, in the second dream Dora wanted to take revenge against her father for exposing her to danger with Herr K., it follows that, through the transference from Herr K. to Freud, abandoning the treatment, Dora wanted to take revenge against her analyst for having exposed her to a new danger, in the intimacy of the treatment.
4. From *Preliminary Communication* (1893) to the *Studies on Hysteria* (1895d), speaking of the overreaction of the affect linked to psychic trauma, Freud ascribes a positive function to revenge: "The injured person's reaction to the trauma only exercises a completely 'cathartic' effect if it is an *adequate* reaction—as, for instance, revenge" (S. E., 2, p. 8).
5. The *Wiener Zeitung* announced Freud's appointment in mid-March, because in the Freud/Fliess letter from 8 March 1902 Freud says: "Next week the *Wiener Zeitung* will announce it to the public who, I expect, will honor such a seal of official approval."
6. For a detailed reconstruction of Emma Eckstein's case, see Schur (1966, 1972), Masson (1984), and Bonomi's (2013) brilliant analysis. To absolve his friend Fliess from the responsibility of the appalling episode, Freud, without quoting him, had retrieved an anachronistic theory of his old mentor Charcot, who claimed: "Nous avons eu souvent l'occasion de constater, même chez des hommes, des hémorragies que nous appelons hystériques parce que véritablement elles ont ce caractère" (p. 206). (We have, on several occasions, in male patients too, diagnosed hysterical bleeding because their haemorrhage presented precisely this type of characteristics). See Charcot, 1971.
7. The episode is referred to in *The Psychopathology of Everyday Life*, S. E., 6, p. 146, note 1. I find it bitterly ironic that Dora should have also died of colon cancer.
8. After all, in a note to the *Postscript* in *Fragment*, Freud acknowledges his own difficulties with homosexuality: "Before I had learnt the importance of the homosexual current of feeling in psychoneurotics, I was often brought to a standstill in the treatment of my cases or found myself in complete perplexity" (S. E., 4, p. 120, n. 1).
9. In his letter to Fliess from 1 February 1900, he says: "For I am actually not at all a man of science, not an observer, not an experimenter, not a thinker. I am by temperament nothing but a *conquistador*—an adventurer, if you want it translated—with all the curiosity, daring, and tenacity characteristic of a man of this sort."

10. Silverstein claims that Freud and Minna's trip to Maloja in August 1898 was also the subject of the "table d'hôte" dream that occurred in October 1900, and says: "If this dream concerns Freud's two 'wives', it may well reflect his state of mind during his trip with Minna in 1898" (p. 285). I find Anzieu's version to be more plausible, as I also believe that the dream refers to Freud's two-week vacation with Minna between the end of August and early September 1900. Furthermore, it is my view that, in the dream, one can trace references to Dora, whose therapy, according to my reconstruction, had started around mid-September 1900. Thus, the dream would refer to Freud's mental state during the vacation that had just ended, before embarking on Dora's therapy, but this does not mean that it could not also have contributed to the evoking of moments and mental states from the previous holiday in Maloja.

11. Glenn (1993, p. 136) claims: "Dora's self-representation included picturing herself as a maid. She looked after K's children. She became furious at Herr K. because he propositioned her the same way he had propositioned a governess, who was a mother surrogate. Similarly, picturing Freud as a seducer, she thought of giving Freud two weeks' notice, but she did not tell him about until the day she left the analysis—a maid's notice. Here, in a neat reversal, she also treated Freud as a maid by dismissing him with two weeks' notice." Actually, Dora did not behave like a governess, but Herr K. treated her as such, by addressing her with the same words he had proffered to his maid, for which Dora could not but bear resentment. Also Freud, as Glenn acknowledges, treated her like a governess, but Dora never identified with such a figure. *She* fired him just as one would have fired a maid. That Freud would then choose for his patient the name of his sister's governess, appears to me a further act of revenge on his part, confirmed by Rogow's interpretation (1978, p. 341) of Freud's thought: "You have behaved like a maidservant, very well, you will be called after one." Less apt is Decker's viewpoint (1982), as she refers to Breuer's daughter, and even more so Banks' opinion (1991), which dwells on the Pandora myth, and on the Greek meaning of Dora (Gift).

12. See the Freud/Fliess letter of 3 October 1897, and the dream added the following day.

13. In a letter to Fliess from 11 March 1900, Freud reveals to his friend: "You know how limited my pleasures are. I am not allowed to smoke anything decent; alcohol does nothing for me; I am done begetting children; and I am cut off from contact with people." This means that all sources of pleasure had dried up, and his life was marked by frustration. This was happening six months before his vacation with Minna in Trentino and on Lake Garda.

14. "In this you too have come to the limit of your perspicacity; you take sides against me and tell me that 'the reader of thoughts merely reads his own thoughts into other people', which renders all my efforts valueless" (Masson, 1985, 7 August 1901, p. 447).
15. According to Mahony (1996, p. 37), "Fliess also figured in the manifold interaction between Freud and Dora. As we know, Freud and Fliess increasingly rejected each other's theories toward the end of their relationship; Freud indicted the numerologist and Fliess the 'thoughts-reader' [...]. In reacting to Dora, Freud became a caricature, of the thoughts-reader, fulfilling Fliess's accusation with a vengeance. Like Fliess but in her own parlance, Dora accused Freud of mind reading. And he thought that she had paranoid traits, a negativity that he later saw in Fliess."

Chapter Ten

1. This section is the shortened and modified version of an article of mine, entitled "Freud e la cocaina" (Freud and cocaine), published in *Medicina delle tossicodipendenze* (2006).
2. Marsala probably represented, for Freud, a surrogate for the more famous Vin Mariani, a beverage made with Bordeaux vine and coca leaves which was very popular in the 1860s, and which Mariani himself advertised as "a tonic wine and stimulant for the tired brain" (Madge, 2001, p. 68). In the letter to Fliess from 8 July 1899, Freud claims: "I cannot manage more than two hours a day without calling on Friend Marsala for help. 'He' deludes me into thinking that things are not really so bleak as they appear to me when sober." This sentence testifies to Freud's strong addiction to stimulating substances, which he turned to in moments of depression and discouragement.
3. Although Mantegazza, whose work Freud quotes many times, had also enthusiastically described the positive effects of cocaine in his writing of 1859, *On the Hygienic and Medicinal Properties of Coca and on Nervous Nourishment in General*, and in 1887, in *The Nervous Century*, after having stigmatised morphine addiction and hypodermic injections of morphine, he claimed: "We have all sorts of addictions—to hetaerae, chloroform, chloral, and who knows what ... soon we may even end up with new rank of cocaine addicts" (Mantegazza, 1995 [1887], p. 40).
4. The construction of this sentence is somewhat puzzling: Freud seems inclined to blame his debts on his creditor.
5. If, as Swales claims (1982), the dream refers to the celebration party for Leopold Königstein's appointment as professor, the scarcity of the menu appears even more unexplainable. In the dream, though, there

are no elements that would make us think of a special gathering, different from the usual meetings dedicated to the Tarock game. After all, Freud clearly mentions a "small party" of friends, and I would think that the wealthy Königstein would have celebrated his appointment by also extending his invitations to people outside of his limited circle of friends, the Saturday night Tarock players.
6. Freud himself admits to the assonance of his friend's name with the word for meat in *The Interpretation of Dreams* (S. E., 4, p. 206).
7. According to Kuhn (1999a), this would be the friend Oscar Rie.
8. At least on one occasion, this belief should be contradicted, because speaking of his fiancée Martha, Freud always recognised that he had met a woman he did not deserve: "Can't I too once have something better than I deserve" (Freud, 1960, 27 June 1882).
9. Examining family portraits published by E. Freud, Lucie Freud, and Ilse Grubrich-Simitis (1978) this supposition appears plausible, although it is obviously solely based on subjective opinions.
10. On the theme of infantile jealousy, see Romano, 2000a.
11. Madge (2001) remembers "more significant are the testimonies of those known 'coke addicts' who often report that, although no longer users, they dream about cocaine frequently. In this respect, it may resemble nicotine" (p. 19). He also thinks that Freud had without any doubt "bec[ome] addicted to cocaine, in whatever sense we mean and even if only for a short time" (p. 57), and that Freud himself was aware of it because he "spent a lifetime after these early years eschewing any pain relief, in part brought on by remorse over Fleischl-Marxow. Possibly, though, this was the result of his much longer experience with cocaine and a continuing fear over his acknowledged addictive personality (manifest in his desire for cigars, a desire that would eventually kill him through cancer)" (p. 57).
12. "Long-term use of coca is further strongly recommended and allegedly has been tried with success—in all diseases which involve degeneration of the tissues, such as severe anaemia, phthisis, long-lasting febrile diseases, etc.; and also during recovery from such diseases." According to the studies he consulted, cocaine was said to reduce temperature and sweating in cases of tuberculosis. He dwells on Pekham, and specifically on a case of phthisis the latter diagnosed with certainty. Pekham used the fluid extract of the substance with this patient for seven months, and it appeared to have had a highly beneficial effect. The substance would have revealed itself to be useful, Freud continues, in the case not only of tuberculosis but also of other consumptive illnesses. As regards cachexia, he then writes that Mantegazza and numerous doctors attribute to coca the same, unparalleled, property:

that is, a decrease in physical decline and an increase in strength (Freud, 1975, p. 67).
13. Wilhelm Czermak, who had been an assistant in a Viennese oculist clinic, had become director of the German University of Prague oculist clinic in 1895. Friedrich Dimmer worked, during the same period as Freud (from 1 March to 31 May 1885), at the Second Clinic for Ophthalmic Diseases, at Vienna General Hospital. Anton Felsenreich worked at the Gynaecological Clinic, Vienna General Hospital in 1882 (see Tögel, 2002a, pp. 130–131, footnotes 23, 24, and 25).
14. In a letter to Fliess from 6 December 1896, Freud confesses: "I do not want to meet the Breuer clan."
15. Actually, Freud claims that the impression that works as a stimulus for the dream must be an impression from the previous day. The real dream-source, on the other hand, is not limited by this temporal prerequisite, and could thus even derive from the distant past. Thus this news of Gretel Breuer's secret engagement presents all the characteristics of the real dream-source, which establishes an associative link with the other elements of the dream. Mertens (2000, p. 19) endorses this with the following claim: "A dream can, naturally, also use contents from a precedent period of the dreamer's life, events from weeks or months before, as long as a connection exists between the day experiences (the 'recent' impressions) and the furthest ones."
16. In his ambivalence towards Dora, Freud might been expressing the hostile side of his feelings more clearly than his attraction for the young patient. Perhaps this was because the familial intrigues awoke his sense of guilt over having betrayed Martha's trust. Furthermore, I would say that his hostility, which was sometimes unaccounted for, was an expression of resistance to an unconscious, eroticised, countertransference.
17. Mahony's observation endorses my claim (1996, p. 145): "The elusive Dora was also an allegorical Every-woman, the eternal woman who engaged Freud for a lifetime in a changing configuration of desire, knowledge, and power."
18. On the controversial, alleged, relationship between Freud and Minna Bernays see the following articles, which I have previously cited: Maciejewski, 2007 and 2008; Silverstein, 2007; Lothane, 2007a and 2007b; Hirschmüller, 2007; Rudnytsky, 2003 and 2011.
19. The whole of this section was added in 1911.
20. Freud's attitude towards cocaine and his writings reveal his enthusiasm for the substance. Furthermore, evidence of his reverence for Mantegazza is provided by the fact that in the brief writing *On Coca*, which is only twenty-five pages long, he quotes him twenty-five times.

21. I believe that Freud and Fliess' tragic experience with Emma Eckstein led Freud to discard a practical application of this idea. According to Hertz (1990, p. 234), "the hyperbolic ('it is *precisely* gastralgias of this type') and a somewhat beside-the-point invocation of a colleague's expertise, with the homoerotic component that such collegial gestures usually involve here [is] considerably amplified."

22. In *The Psychopathology of Everyday Life* (1901a) Freud reports several symptomatic gestures involving rings, which are a marker of infidelity or of a repressed desire, within the context of thoughts connected to infidelity: "We shall not be surprised if an object of such rich symbolic meaning as a ring should be made to play a part in some significant parapraxes, even where it does not, in the form of a wedding ring or an engagement ring, mark an erotic tie" (*S. E.*, 6, p. 205). And as for the loss, Freud affirms: "It is consoling to reflect that there is an unsuspected extension of the human habit of 'losing things'—namely, symptomatic acts, and that this habit is consequently welcome, at least to a secret intention of the loser's. It is often only an expression of the low estimation in which the lost object is held, or of a secret antipathy towards it or towards the person that it came from; or else the inclination to lose an object has been transferred to it from other more important objects by a symbolic association of thoughts. Losing objects of value serves to express a variety of impulses; it may either be acting as a symbolic representation of a repressed thought—that is, it may be repeating a warning that one would be glad enough to ignore—, or (most commonly of all) it may be offering a sacrifice to the obscure powers of destiny to whom homage is still paid among us to-day" (*S. E.*, 6, p. 207).

Chapter Eleven

1. The censored version in the *Standard Edition* reads "early love" instead of "sister-in-law" (*S. E.*, 18, p. 192). Roazen writes that the information that the patient's lover was his sister-in-law was suppressed in the official publication, possibly as per the request of Anna Freud. The information regarding this patient's niece, and the results of her analysis, of which Deutsch kept Freud regularly informed, were not made public (see Roazen, 1975). In my view, this censorship may have served a twofold purpose: it prevented attention being drawn, on the one hand, to Freud's own ambiguous relationship with his sister-in-law, and, on the other, to a fact from his childhood to which he had explicitly referred. He had developed a family romance fantasy that featured his sister Anna the daughter of his mother Amalie and his uncle Philipp. Thus the question must be posed as to why he would

want to prevent the reader from recalling a fact he had explicitly written about in *The Psychopathology of Everyday Life*, wherein he speaks of the infantile episode of the wardrobe (*S. E.*, 6, p. 51—from the added footnote of 1924). Perhaps Anna Freud had also developed a family romance fantasy in which she pictured herself as the daughter of her father Sigmund and of her aunt, Minna? Roazen (1975) specifies that this situation was very similar to the one Freud had dealt with in the Dora case. The only element that these two situations have in common is the sexual promiscuity that characterises the two families, a family which, in Dora's case, was not, however, related by blood. The present case recalls more pertinently another situation in which Freud was involved, that is, Ferenczi's relationship with Gizella and Elma Pálos, respectively mother and daughter. What brings the two cases close together is Freud's attitude towards these "political marriages". Helene Deutsch declared that she had learnt from Freud that an analysis had to aim at teaching the patient which situations could qualify as compromises. The patient who had proposed to his niece, after he had been his sister-in-law's lover, who was also his fiancée's mother, was precisely a good example of a model that Freud (somewhat surprisingly) used to consider as a normal resolution of an analytical treatment (see Roazen, 2001). Apparently, even many years later Freud had not changed his mind with respect to the time he had been convinced that Dora's marriage to Herr K. would have been the best solution for everybody. Political marriages!

REFERENCES

Ahbel-Rappe, K. (2006). "I no longer believe": Did Freud abandon the seduction theory? *Journal of the American Psychoanalytic Association, 54*: 171–199.

Ahbel-Rappe, K. (2009). After a long pause: How to read Dora as history. *Journal of the American Psychoanalytic Association, 57*: 595–629.

Akavia, N. (2005). Hysteria, identification, and the family: A rereading of Freud's Dora case. *American Imago, 62*: 193–216.

Anzieu, D. (1959). *Freud's self-analysis*. [reprinted London: Hogarth and Institute of Psycho-Analysis, 1986].

Balmary, M. (1982). *Psychoanalyzing Psychoanalysis: Freud and the Hidden Fault of the Father*. N. Lukacher (Trans). Baltimore, MD: Johns Hopkins University Press.

Banks, C. G. (1991). A dream of incest taboo, exchange of women, and seduction: A reinterpretation of Freud's Dora. *Psychoanalysis and Contemporary Thought, 14*: 251–269.

Barale, F. (1993). Transfert: dalle origini al caso Dora. (Transference: from the origins to Dora's Case) *Rivista di psicoanalisi, 39*: 481–498.

Becker, H. K. (1963). Carl Koller and Cocaine. In: R. Byck (Ed.), *"Cocaine Papers" by Sigmund Freud* (pp. 263–319). New York, NY: Stonehill, 1974.

Begel, D. M. (1982). Three examples of countertransference in Freud's Dora case. *American Journal of Psychoanalysis, 42*: 163–169.

Behling, K. (2002). *Martha Freud. Die Frau des Genies.* (Martha Freud. A genius' wife) Berlin: Aufbau Taschenbuch.

Benvenuto, S. (2005). Dora Flees ... Is there anything left to say about hysterics? *Journal of European Psychoanalysis,* XXI, 2: 3–31.

Berger, N. F. (1975). Sigmund Freud and cocaine. In: S. Freud, *Cocaine Papers.* New York, NY: Maridian.

Bernfeld, S. (1953). Freud's studies on cocaine, 1884–1887. *Journal of the American Psychoanalytic Association,* 1: 581–613.

Bernfeld, S., & Cassirer-Bernfeld, S. (1991). *Per una biografia di Freud.* Turin: Bollati Boringhieri.

Bernheimer, C., & Kahane, C. (1990). *In Dora's Case. Freud-Hysteria-Feminism.* New York, NY: Columbia University Press.

Blass, R. B. (1992). Did Dora have an Oedipus complex? A re-examination of the theoretical context of Freud's "Fragment of an analysis". *The Psychoanalytic Study of the Child,* 47: 159–187.

Blass, R. B., & Simon, B. (1994). The value of the historical perspective to contemporary psychoanalysis: Freud's "seduction hypothesis". *International Journal of Psychoanalysis,* 75: 677–694.

Bohleber, W. (2010). *Destructiveness, Intersubjectivity and Trauma: The Identity Crisis of Modern Psychoanalysis.* London: Karnac.

Bonomi, C. (1994). Why have we ignored Freud the "Paediatrician"? The relevance of Freud's paediatric training for the origins of psychoanalysis. In: A. Haynal & E. Falzeder (Eds.), *100 Years of Psychoanalysis. Contributions to the History of Psychoanalysis. Special Issue of Cahiers Psychiatriques Genevois* (pp. 55–99). London: Karnac.

Bonomi, C. (1998a). Sigmund Freud: un neurologo tra sapere pediatrico e sapere psichiatrico del XIX secolo. *Psicoterapia e Scienze Umane,* XXXII, 1: 51–91.

Bonomi, C. (1998b). Freud and castration. A new look into the origins of psychoanalysis. *Journal of the American Academy of Psychoanalysis,* 26: 29–49.

Bonomi, C. (2007). *Sulla soglia della psicoanalisi. Freud e la follia infantile* (*At the threshold of psychoanalysis. Freud and the insanity of the child*). Turin: Bollati Boringhieri.

Bonomi, C. (2009). The relevance of castration and circumcision to the origins of psychoanalysis: 1. The medical context. *International Journal of Psychoanalysis,* 90: 551–580.

Bonomi, C. (2013). Withstanding trauma: the significance of Emma Eckstein's circumcision to Freud's Irma dream. *The Psychoanalytic Quarterly,* 83: 689–740.

Bonomi, C. (2015). *The Cut and the Building of Psychoanalysis,* Volume I, Sigmund Freud and Emma Eckstein, Routledge, London.

Borgogno, F. (2014). A "work in progress" between past, present and future: The dream in/of Sándor Ferenczi. *Psychoanalytic Inquiry*, 34: 80–97.

Bornstein, M. (2005). What Freud did not write about Dora. *Psychoanalytic Inquiry*, 25: 54–70.

Brabant, E., Falzeder, E., & Giampieri-Deutsch, P. (Eds.), Hoffer, P. T. (Trans) (1993). *The correspondence of Sigmund Freud and Sándor Ferenczi, Volume 1, 1908–1914*. Cambridge, MA: Harvard University Press.

Byck, R. (1975). Sigmund Freud and cocaine. In: R. Byck (Ed.), *"Cocaine Papers" by Sigmund Freud*. New York, NY: Stonehill.

Charcot, J. M. (1971). *L'hystérie*. Textes choisis et présentés par E. Trillat. (*Hysteria*. A selection of texts: chosen and introduced by E. Trillat) Toulouse: Privat Editeur.

Cixous, H. (1983). Portrait of Dora. S. Burd (Trans). *Diacritics*, 13 (1): 2–32.

Cixous, H., & Clément, C. (1990). The Untenable. In: C. Bernheimer & C. Kahane (Eds.), *In Dora's Case. Freud-Hysteria-Feminism* (2nd edn) (pp. 276–293). New York, NY: Columbia University Press.

Collins, J., Ray Green, J., Lydon, M., Sachner, M., & Honig Skoller, E. (1990). Questioning the unconscious: The Dora archive. In: C. Bernheimer & C. Kahane (Eds.), *In Dora's Case. Freud-Hysteria-Feminism* (2nd edn) (pp. 243–253). New York, NY: Columbia University Press.

Colombo, D. (2010). Worthless female material: Nursemaid and governesses in Freud's cases. *Journal of the American Psychoanalytic Association*, 58: 835–859.

Decker, H. S. (1982). The choice of a name: "Dora" and Freud's relationship with Breuer. *Journal of the American Psychoanalytic Association*, 30: 113–136.

Decker, H. S. (1991). *Freud, Dora, and Vienna 1900*. New York, NY: The Free Press.

Eissler, K. R. (1994). *Three Instances of Injustice*. Madison, CT: International University Press.

Ellenberger, H. F. (1970). *The Discovery of the Unconscious: The History and Evolution of Dynamic Psychiatry*. New York, NY: Basic Books.

Emminghaus, H. (1887). *Die Psychischen Störungen des Kindesalter*. Tubingen.

Falzeder, E. (2001). Relazioni traumatiche tra i primi psicoanalisti. (Traumatic relationships among the first psychoanalysts) In: C. Bonomi & F. Borgogno (Eds.), *La catastrofe e i suoi simboli. Il contributo di Sándor Ferenczi alla teoria psicoanalitica del trauma.* (*The catastrophe and its symbols. Sándor Ferenczi's contribution to the psychoanalytic theory of the trauma*) (pp. 31–45). Turin: UTET.

Ferenczi, S. (1931). On the revision of the Interpretation of Dreams. In: S. Ferenczi, M. Balint & E. Mosbacher, *Final Contributions to the Problems and Methods of Psycho-analysis* (pp. 238–243). London: Karnac, 1996.

Ferenczi, S. (1931a). Child Analysis with Adults. *International Journal of Psychoanalysis, 12*: 468–482.

Ferenczi, S. (1932). Confusion of the tongues between the adults and the child: The language of tenderness and passion. *International Journal of Psychoanalysis, 30*: 225–230, 1949.

Ferenczi, S. (1985). *The Clinical Diary of Sándor Ferenczi.* J. Dupont (Ed.), M. Balint & N. Zarday Jackson (Trans). Cambridge, MA: Harvard University Press.

Flem, L. (1986). *La vita quotidiana di Freud e dei suoi pazienti* (The everyday life of Freud and of his patients) Milan: Rizzoli, 1987.

Foucault, M. (1994). *Il sogno.* (Dream and Existence) Milan: Raffaello Cortina, 2003.

Freud, S. (1873–1939). *The Letters of Sigmund Freud.* E. Freud & L. Freud (Eds.). New York, NY: Basic Books, 1960.

Freud, S. (1893g). Über ein Symptom, das häufig die Enuresis nocturna der Kinder begleitet. *Neurologisches Zentralblatt, 12*: 735–737.

Freud, S. (1893h). On the Psychical Mechanism of Hysterical Phenomena: Preliminary Communication. *S. E., 2*: 3–17. London: Hogarth.

Freud, S. (1896a). Heredity and the Aetiology of the Neuroses. *S. E., 3*: 142–156. London: Hogarth.

Freud, S. (1896b). Further Remarks on the Neuro-Psychoses of Defence. *S. E., 3*: 159–185. London: Hogarth.

Freud, S. (1896c). The Aetiology of Hysteria. *S. E., 3*: 189–221. London: Hogarth.

Freud, S. (1899a). Screen Memories. *S. E., 3*: 301–322. London: Hogarth.

Freud, S. (1900a). *The Interpretation of Dreams. S. E., 4–5.* London: Hogarth.

Freud, S. (1901a). *On Dreams. S. E., 5*: 633–686. London: Hogarth.

Freud, S. (1901b). *The Psychopathology of Everyday Life. S. E., 6.* London: Hogarth.

Freud, S. (1905d). *Three Essays on the Theory of Sexuality. S. E., 7*: 125–245. London: Hogarth.

Freud, S. (1905e [1901]). *Fragment of an Analysis of a Case of Hysteria. S. E., 7*: 3–122. London: Hogarth.

Freud, S. (1908d). "Civilized" Sexual Morality and Modern Nervous Illness. *S. E., 9*: 179–204. London: Hogarth.

Freud, S. (1912d). On the Universal Tendency to Debasement in the Sphere of Love (Contributions to the Psychology of Love II). *S. E., 11*: 179–190. London: Hogarth.

Freud, S. (1920g). Beyond the Pleasure Principle. *S. E., 18*: 7–64. London: Hogarth.
Freud, S. (1933a). Dreams and Occultism. In: *New Introductory Lectures on Psycho-Analysis*, lecture XXX, 22: 31–56. London: Hogarth.
Freud, S. (1933a). Revision of the Theory of Dreams. In: *New Introductory Lectures on Psycho-Analysis*, lecture XXIX, *S. E.*, 22: 7–30. London: Hogarth.
Freud, S. (1941d). Psycho-Analysis and Telepathy, *S. E., 18*: 175–193. London: Hogarth.
Freud, S. (1950). A *Project for a Scientific Psychology. S. E., 1*: 283–397. London: Hogarth.
Freud, S. (1955). Letter to Marie Bonaparte. In: E. Jones, *Sigmund Freud: Life and Work. Years of Maturity, 1901–1919*, Vol. II. London: Hogarth Press.
Freud, S. (1956a). Report on my Studies in Paris and Berlin, on a Travelling Bursary Granted from the University Jubilee Fund, 1885–6. *S. E., 1*: 3–15. London: Hogarth.
Freud, S. (1959). *Collected Papers*, translated by Alix and James Strachey, vol. 5. New York, NY: Basic Books.
Freud, S. (1975). On cocaine. In: S. Freud, *Cocaine Papers*. New York, NY: New American Library.
Freud, S., & Breuer, J. (1895d). *Studies on Hysteria. S. E., 2*. London: Hogarth.
Fromm, E. (2013). *Greatness and Limitations of Freud's Thought*. London: HarperCollins.
Gay, P. (1984). *The Bourgeois Experience. Victoria to Freud. Vol. 1, Education of the Senses*. New York, NY: Oxford University Press.
Gay, P. (1988). *Freud. A Life for Our Time*. New York, NY: Norton.
Gay, P. (1990). *Reading Freud: Explorations & Entertainments*. New Haven, CT: Yale University Press.
Giglioli, D., & Violi, A. (Eds.) (2005). *Locus solus. L'immaginario dell'isteria.* (Locus solus. The hysteric's imagination.) Milan: Bruno Mondatori.
Gladwell, S. (1997). Trauma, Dora and Oedipus complex. *Psychoanalytic Psychotherapy, 11*: 197–209.
Glenn, J. (1986). Freud, Dora and the maid: a study of countertransference. *Journal of the American Psychoanalytic Association, 34*: 591–606.
Glenn, J. (1993). Dora's dynamics, diagnosis, and treatment: Old and modern views. *The Annual of Psychoanalysis, 21*: 125–138.
Goretti, G. (1997). Le menti violate. Pensieri su Dora, Schreber, Paul ed altri (The violated minds. Thoughts on Dora, Schreber, Paul, and the others). *Rivista di Psicoanalisi, 43*: 635–657.

Hengehold, L. (1993). Rape and communicative agency: Reflections in the lake at L. *Hypatia, 8,* 4: 56–71.
Herman, J. L. (1992). *Trauma and Recovery.* New York, NY: Basic Books.
Hertz, N. (1990). Dora's secret, Freud's techniques. In: C. Bernheimer & C. Kahane, *In Dora's Case. Freud-Hysteria-Feminism* (pp. 221–242). New York, NY: Columbia University Press.
Hillman, J. (1983). *Healing fiction.* New York, NY: Station Hill Press.
Hirschmüller, A. (2007). Freud and Minna Bernays. Evidence for a sexual relationship between Sigmund Freud and Minna Bernays. *American Imago, 64:* 125–128.
Holmes, J. (1983). Psychoanalysis and family therapy: Freud's Dora case reconsidered. *Journal of Family Therapy, 5:* 235–251.
Huopainen, H. (2002). Freud's view of hysteria in light of modern trauma research. *The Scandinavian Psychoanalytic Review, 25:* 92–107.
Jennings, J. L. (1986). The revival of "Dora": Advances in psychoanalytic theory and technique. *Journal of the American Psychoanalytic Association, 34:* 607–635.
Jones, E. (1953). *Sigmund Freud: Life and Work. The Young Freud, vol. I.* London: Hogarth.
Kandel, E. (2012). *The Age of Insight: The Quest to Understand the Unconscious in Art, Mind and Brain.* New York, NY: Randon House.
Khan, M. M. R. (1974). Grudge and the hysteric, in: *Hidden Selves: Between theory and practice in psychoanalysis* (pp. 51–58). London: Karnac, 1989.
Kohon, G. (1984). Reflections on Dora: the case of hysteria. *International Journal of Psychoanalysis, 65:* 73–84.
Koller Becker, H. (1963). Carl Koller and cocaine. *The Psychoanalytic Quarterly, 32:* 309–373.
Krohn, A., & Krohn, J. (1982). The nature of the Oedipus complex in the Dora case. *Journal of the American Psychoanalytic Association, 30:* 555–578.
Kuhn, P. (1999a). A professor through the looking-glass: Contending narratives of Freud's relationship with the sisters Bernays. *International Journal of Psychoanalysis, 80:* 943–959.
Kuhn, P. (1999b). "Right-sided facial neuralgia": or fragmenting the history of the "Dora" manuscript. *The Psychoanalytic Review, 86:* 771–796.
Kuriloff, E. A. (2005). What's going on with Dora? An interpersonal perspective. *Psychoanalytic Inquiry, 25:* 395–407.
Lacan, J. (1951). Presentation on Transference. In: *Écrits. The First Complete Edition in English,* translated by Bruce Fink (pp. 176–185). New York, NY: Norton; 2006.
Langs, R. (1976). The misalliance dimension in Freud's case histories: I. The case of Dora. *International Journal of Psychoanalysis, 5:* 301–317.

Lanouzière, J. (1991). *Histoire secrète de la séduction sous le règne de Freud*. (The secret history of seduction under Freud's reign) Paris: Presses Universitaires de France.
Lavagetto, M. (2005). Ça n'empêche pas d'exister. Interview with Mario Lavagetto on Hysteria and Literature. In: D. Giglioli & A. Violi (Eds.), *Locus solus. L'immaginario dell'isteria* (pp. 69–83). Bruno Mondadori, Milan.
Lewin, K. K. (1973). Dora revisited. *The Psychoanalytic Review, 4*: 519–532.
Lokoff, R. T., & Coyne, J. C. (1993). *Father Knows Best. The Use and Abuse of Power in Freud's Case of Dora*. New York, NY: Teachers College Press, Columbia University.
Lopez, D. (1967). Rileggendo Freud: il caso Dora. (Re-reading Freud: the Dora case). *Rivista di psicoanalisi, 13*: 215–262.
Lothane, Z. (2001). Freud's alleged repudiation of the seduction theory revisited. Facts and fallacies. *The Psychoanalytic Review, 88*: 673–723.
Lothane, Z. (2007a). Sigmund Freud and Minna Bernays: Primal curiosity, primal scenes, primal fantasies—and prevarication. *Psychoanalytic Psychology, 24*: 487–495.
Lothane, Z. (2007b). The Sigmund Freud/Minna Bernays romance: fact or fiction? *American Imago, 64*: 129–133.
Maciejewski, F. (2007). Freud, his wife, and his "wife". *American Imago, 63*: 497–506.
Maciejewski, F. (2008). Minna Bernays as "Mrs. Freud": What sort of relationship did Sigmund Freud have with his sister-in-law? *American Imago, 65*: 5–21.
Maddi, S. R. (1974). The victimization of Dora. *Psychology Today*, September: pp. 91–100.
Madge, T. (2001). *White Mischief: The Cultural history of Cocaine*. Edinburgh: Mainstream Publishing.
Mahony, P. J. (1986). *Freud et l'Homme aux rats (Freud and the Ratman)*. Paris: Presses Universitaires de France, 1991.
Mahony, P. J. (1996). *Freud's Dora: A Psychoanalytic, Historical, and Textual Study*. New Haven, CT: Yale University Press.
Mahony, P. J. (2005). Freud's unadorned and unadorable: a case history terminable and interminable. *Psychoanalytic Inquiry, 25*: 27–44.
Makari, G. J. (1997). Dora's hysteria and the maturation of Sigmund Freud's transference theory: a new historical interpretation. *Journal of the American Psychoanalytic Association, 45*: 1061–1096.
Makari, G. J. (1998). Between seduction and libido: Sigmund Freud's masturbation hypotheses and the realignment of his etiologic thinking. *Bulletin of the History of Medicine, 72, 4*: 638–662.
Malacrea, M., & Lorenzini, S. (2002). *Bambini abusati*. (Abused children) Milan: Raffaello Cortina Editore.

Mancia, M. (2006a). Implicit memory and early unrepressed unconscious: Their role in the therapeutic process (How the neurosciences can contribute to psychoanalysis). *International Journal of Psychoanalysis, 87*: 83–103.

Mancia, M. (2006b). The Dream in the dialogue between psychoanalysis and neurosciences. In: M. Mancia (Ed.), *Psychoanalysis and Neurosciences*, (pp. 305–326). Milan: Springer.

Mancia, M. (2007). *Feeling the Words: Neuropsychoanalytic Understanding of Memory and the Unconscious*. London: Routledge.

Mantegazza, P. (1859). On the Hygienic and Medicinal Properties of Coca Plant and on Nervous Nourishment in General. In: P. Mantegazza, *The Physiology of Love and Other Writings* (pp. 319–352). Toronto: University of Toronto Press.

Mantegazza, P. (1887). *The Physiology of Love and Other Writings*. D. Jacobson (Trans), N. Pirĕddu (Ed.). Toronto: University of Toronto Press, 2007.

Mantegazza, P. (1935). *The Sexual Relations of Mankind*, S. Putnam (Trans), V. Robinson (Ed.). Honolulu: University Press of the Pacific, 2001.

Mantegazza, P. (1995). *Il secolo nevrosico (The Nervous Century)*. Pordenone: Edizioni Studio Tesi.

Marantz Cohen, P. (1986). Freud's *Dora* and James's *Turn of the Screw*: two treatments of the female "case". *Criticism, 28*: 73–87.

Marcel, M. (2005). *Freud's Traumatic Memory. Reclaiming Seduction Theory and Revisiting Oedipus*. Pittsburgh, PA: Duquesne University Press.

Marcus, S. (1990). Freud and Dora: story, history, case history. In: Bernheimer, C., & Kahane, C (Eds.). *In Dora's Case. Freud-Hysteria-Feminism* (pp. 56–91). New York, NY: Columbia University Press.

Masson, J. M. (1984). *The Assault on Truth. Freud's suppression of the seduction theory*. New York, NY: Penguin, 1985.

Masson, J. M. (Ed. & Trans) (1985). *The Complete Letters of Sigmund Freud to Wilhelm Fliess, 1887–1904*. Cambridge, MA: The Belknap Press of Harvard University Press.

McGuire, W. (Ed.) (1974). *The Freud/Jung Letters: The Correspondence between Sigmund Freud and C. G. Jung*. R. Manheim & R. F. C. Hull (Trans.). Princeton, NJ: Princeton University Press.

Meares, R. (2013). *Intimacy and Alienation: Memory, Trauma and Personal Being (3rd edn)*. New York, NY: Routledge.

Mertens, W. (1999). L'interpretazione dei sogni, cent'anni dopo. (The interpretation of dreams, one hundred years later) In: *Traum und Traumdeutung* (pp. 5–30). Munich: C. H. Beck.

Mitchell, J. (2000). *Mad Men and Medusas. Reclaiming Hysteria*. New York, NY: Basic Books.

Moi, T. (1990). Representation of patriarchy: sexuality and epistemology in Freud's Dora. In: C. Bernheimer, & C. Kahane (Eds.), *In Dora's*

Case. Freud-Hysteria-Feminism (pp. 181–199). New York, NY: Columbia University Press.

Muslin, H., & Gill, M. (1978). Transference in the Dora case. *Journal of the American Psychoanalytic Association, 26*: 311–328.

Ogden, T. H. (2001). *Conversations at the Frontier of Dreaming.* London: Karnac.

Ornstein, P. H. (2005). When "Dora" came to see me for a second analysis: Comment. *Psychoanalytic Inquiry, 25*: 94–114.

Paskauskas, R. A. (Ed.) (1993). *The Complete Correspondence of Sigmund Freud and Ernest Jones, 1908–1939.* Cambridge, MA: Harvard University Press.

Pontalis, J. B. (1990). *La forza d'attrazione.* (The power of attraction) Bari: Laterza, 1992.

Rieger, C. (1900). *Die Kastration in rechtlicher, sozialer und vitaler Hinsicht betrachtet.* Jena: Gustav Fischer.

Roazen, P. (1975). *Freud and His Followers.* Cambridge, MA: De Capo Press.

Roazen, P. (1993). *Meeting Freud's Family.* Amherst, MA: University of Massachussets Press.

Roazen, P. (2001). Using Oral History about Freud: A Case in His "Secret Essay". *American Imago, 58,* 4: 793–812.

Rodrigué, E. (2010). *Freud. Il secolo della psicoanalisi.* Rome: Borla. (Original title: *Sigmund Freud. El siglo del psicoanálisis.* Buenos Aires: Editorial Sudamericana, 1996).

Rogow, A. A. (1978). A further footnote to Freud's "Fragment of an Analysis of a Case of Hysteria". *Journal of the American Psychoanalytic Association, 26*: 331–356.

Romano, C. (2000a). Un ricordo d'infanzia di Goethe e la rimozione di Freud. (A memory of Goethe's childhood and Freud's repression) *Psicoterapia e Scienze Umane, XXXIV,* 2: 107–122.

Romano, C. (2000b). Il piccolo Hans e la fobia del professor Freud. (Little Hans and Professor Freud's phobia). *Psicoterapia e Scienze Umane, XXXIV,* 4: 45–81.

Romano, C. (2006). Freud e la cocaina. (Freud and cocaine) *Medicina delle tossicodipendenze, 50*: 7–29.

Rudnytsky, P. L. (2003). Freud a-t-il eu une liaison avec Minna Bernays? Et alors qua? (Did Freud Have a Relationship with Minna Bernays, and So What?) *Le Coq-héron, 174*: 42–49.

Rudnytsky, P. L. (2011). *Rescuing Psychoanalysis from Freud and Other Essays in Re-Vision.* London: Karnac.

Russo, L. (2003). The analyst's subjectivity in the psychoanalytic cure: self-analysis of countertransference and transference. *Bulletin of European Psychoanalytic Federation, 57*: 113–127.

Schimek, J. G. (1987). Fact and fantasy in the seduction theory: a historical review. *Journal of the American Psychoanalytic Association, 35*: 937–965.

Schur, M. (1972). *Freud: Living and Dying*. Madison, CT: International University Press.

Showalter, E. (1993). On hysterical narrative. *Narrative, 1*: 24–35.

Silverstein, B. (2007). What happens in Maloja stays in Maloja: inference and evidence in the "Minna wars". *American Imago, 64*: 283–289.

Simon, B. (1992). "Incest—see under Oedipus complex": the history of an error in psychoanalysis. *Journal of the American Psychoanalytic Association, 40*: 955–988.

Slipp, S. (1977). Interpersonal factors in hysteria: Freud's seduction theory and the case of Dora. *Journal of the American Academy of Psychoanalysis and Dynamic Psychiatry, 5*: 359–376.

Solms, M., & Turnbull, O. (2002). *The Brain and the Inner World: An introduction to the neuroscience of subjective experience*. New York, NY: Other Press.

Spence, D. P. (1994). *The Rhetorical Voice of Psychoanalysis: Displacement of Evidence by Theory*. Cambridge, MA: Harvard University Press.

Strong, B. E. (1989). Foucault, Freud, and French feminism: theorizing hysteria as theorizing the feminine. *Literature and Psychology, 35* (4): 10–26.

Swales, P. J. (1982). Freud, Minna Bernays, and the conquest of Rome: new light on the origins of psychoanalysis. *New American Review, 1*: 1–23.

Taine, H. (1870). *De l'Intelligence*. Paris: Librairie Hachette & C.

Timpanaro, S. (1974). *The Freudian Slip: Psychoanalysis and Textual Criticism*. K. Soper (Trans). London: Verso, 1985.

Tögel, C. (Ed.) (2002a). *Sigmund Freud. Unser Herz zeigt nach dem Süden. Reisebriefe 1895–1923*. In collaboration with M. Molnar. Berlin: Aufbau-Verlag.

Tögel, C. (2002b). Gestern träumte ich wieder vom Reisen. In: C. Tögel (Ed.), *Sigmund Freud. Unser Herz zeigt nach dem Süden. Reisebriefe 1895–1923* (pp. 9–36). In collaboration with M. Molnar. Berlin: Aufbau-Verlag.

Van den Berg, S. (1987). Reading and writing Dora: Pre-oedipal conflict in Freud's "Fragment of an Analysis of a Case of Hysteria". *Psychoanalysis and Contemporary Thought, 10*: 45–67.

FURTHER READING

Berman, E. (2004). Sándor, Gizela, Elma: A biographical journey. *International Journal of Psychoanalysis, 85*: 489–520.
Bollas, C. (2000). *Hysteria*. London: Routledge.
Borch-Jacobsen, M. (2011). *Les Patients de Freud. Destins*. (Freud's patients. Destinies) Auxerre: Sciences Humaines Éditions.
Cargnelutti, E. (2004). Gli Studi sull'isteria e la nascita della psicoanalisi. (Studies on hysteria and the birth of psychoanalysis) In: C. Albarella & A. Racalbuto (Eds.), *Isteria* (pp. 74–90). Rome: Borla.
Cixous, H., & Clément, C. (1996). *The Newly Born Woman*. London: Tauris.
Cohen, E. (1999). Contemporary application of Ferenczi: Co-costructing past traumatic experiences through dream analysis. *American Journal of Psychoanalysis, 59*: 367–384.
Cohen, E. (2003). L'analisi dei sogni: co-costruzione e ri-costruzione di passate esperienze traumatiche. (Dream analysis: co-construction and re-construction of past traumatic experiences) In: F. Borgogno (Ed.), *La partecipazione affettiva dell'analista. Il contributo di Sándor Ferenczi al pensiero psicoanalitico contemporaneo* (pp. 243–258). (*The analyst's emotional participation. Sándor Ferenczi's contribution to contemporary psychoanalytic thought*) Milan: Franco Angeli.
Deutsch, F. (1957). A footnote to Freud's "Fragment of an analysis of a case of hysteria". *The Psychoanalytic Quarterly, 26*: 159–167.

Finkelhor, D. (1984). *Child Sexual Abuse: New Theory and Research*. New York, NY: Free Press.

Furniss, T. (2013). *The Multiprofessional Handbook of Child Sexual Abuse: Integrated Management, Therapy, & Legal Intervention (4th edn)*. London: Routledge.

Gaddini, E. (1967). Il controtransfert nel caso di Dora. Commento a "Rileggendo il caso di Dora" del Dottor Lopez. (Countertransference in Dora's case. A comment on "Re-reading Dora's case" by Doctor Lopez). In: E. Gaddini, *Scritti (1953–1985) (Writings)* (pp. 150–154). Milan: Raffaello Cortina, 2002.

Goretti, G. (2004). Da *La Femminilità* (Freud, 1933) alle molte teorie psicoanalitiche dell'isteria. Un percorso. (From *Femininity* (Freud, 1933) to many psychoanalytical theories on hysteria. A path) In: C. Albarella & A. Racalbuto (Eds.), *Isteria* (pp. 122–155). Rome: Borla.

Halberstadt-Freud, H. C. (1996). Studies on Hysteria, one hundred years on: A century of psychoanalysis. *International Journal of Psychoanalysis, 77*: 983–996.

Hanus, M., & Strauss, M. (1988). DORA. Traumatismes sexuels et traumatismes narcissiques (Dora, sexual traumatisms and narcissistic traumatisms). *Revue Française de Psychanayse, 6*: 1305–1319.

Krutzenbichler, H. S., & Essers, H. (1991). Dora ovvero La ragazza e lo psicoanalista innamorato (Dora: the maiden and the psychoanalyst in love). In: Krutzenbichler & Essers, *Se l'amore in sé non è peccato … (If love in itself is not a sin …)* (pp. 21–29). Milan: Raffaello Cortina, 1993.

Laplanche, J. (1970). *Vie et mort en psychanalyse*. (Life and death in psychoanalysis) Paris: Flammarion.

Lütkehaus, L. (1982). *La solitudine del piacere* (The loneliness of pleasure). Milan: Raffaello Cortina.

Major, R. (1973). Un non d'amour. *Revue Française de Psychanalyse, 3*: 299–302.

Marmor, J. (1953). Orality in the hysterical personality. *Journal of the American Psychoanalytic Association, 1*: 656–670.

Meissner, W. W. (1984–1985). Studies on hysteria: Dora. *International Journal of Psychoanalytic Psychotherapy, 10*: 567–598.

Modell, W. (1967). Mass drug catastrophes and the role of science and technology. *Science, 156*: 346–351.

Nasio, J. -D. (1998). *Hysteria from Freud to Lacan: The splendid child of psychoanalysis*. New York, NY: The Other Press.

Pancheri, P. (Ed.) (2002). *La doppia diagnosi. Disturbi psichiatrici e dipendenza da sostanze*. (The double diagnosis. Psychiatric ailments and addiction to substances) Florence: Scientific Press.

Possick, S. (1984). Termination in the Dora case. *Journal of the American Academy of Psychoanalysis, 12, 1*: 1–11.

Regazzoni-Goretti, G. (2006). Una florida ragazza dai lineamenti intelligenti e attraenti. (A girl of intelligent and engaging looks in the first bloom of youth) *Rivista di Psicoanalisi, 52*: 969–990.

Reich, W. (1933). *Character Analysis (3rd edn)*. V. R. Carfagno (Trans). New York, NY: Simon and Schuster.

Rieff, P. (1979). *Freud: The Mind of the Moralist*. London: Victor Gollancz.

Roazen, P. (1995). *How Freud Worked: first-hand accounts of patients*. Seattle, WA: Aronson.

Sabbadini, A. (1992). "The truth is, Sir, my nerves are bad." Reflections on Freud's case of Katharina. *British Journal of Psychotherapy, 9*: 157–168.

Salyard, A. (1992). Freud's narrow escape and the discovery of transference. *Psychoanalytic Psychology, 9*: 347–367.

Schorter, E. (1992). *From paralysis to fatigue: a history of psychosomatic illness in the modern era*. New York, NY: Free Press.

Shepherd, M. (1985). *Sherlock Holmes and the Case of Dr. Freud*. London: Tavistock.

Thompson, A. E. (1990). The ending to Dora's story: Deutsch's footnote as narrative. *Psychoanalysis and Contemporary Thought, 13*: 509–534.

Thornton, M. (1983). *Freud and Cocaine: The Freudian Fallacy*. London: Blond & Briggs.

Vegetti Finzi, S. (1992). Le isteriche o la parola corporea. (Hysterics or the word in the flesh) In: S. Vegetti Finzi (Ed.), *Psicoanalisi al femminile*. Bari: Laterza.

Wiseman, M. B. (1993). Renaissance Madonnas and the fantasies of Freud. *Hypatia, 8, 3*: 115–135.

Wittels, F. (1930). The hysterical character. *Medical Review of Reviews, 36*: 186–190.

INDEX

abuse
    childhood 27, 31, 43, 56, 85, 94
    infantile sexual 59, 62
    oral contacts 21
    sexual 5, 21, 27–28, 35, 40, 83
accusation
    Dora's 11, 66
    repeated 43, 66
    self 11, 66
acquired predisposition 29
active masturbation 57
adolescent's fantasies 86
Aetiology of Hysteria, The 5, 21, 23, 26, 29, 34, 36–37, 41, 45–46, 50, 81, 88, 91
aetiology of neurasthenia 30
agents provocateurs 50
Akavia, N. 6, 65, 182
anxiety-dreams 96
Anzieu, D. 9, 115, 118, 163, 185, 196
archaeological work 41, 48, 57

archaeologist 45–51
    scrupulous 41, 57
archaeology 47
    Greek 41
assimilation 71
"asthma nervosa," 70
"audience" 118
autoerotic stimulation 36, 73–74

Baginsky, Adolf 27–28, 58
Balmary, M. 104–105
Banks, C. G. 190, 192
Becker, H. K. 160
bed-wetting 3, 57, 60, 63, 67, 69, 72–73, 75
Begel, D. M. 116
Benvenuto, S. 66–67
Berger, N. F. 136
Bernard, Paul 26
Bernays, Minna 10–11, 13-18, 110–112, 114, 117-121, 123,

125–130, 144, 147, 153–157, 163–166, 171
Bernfeld, S. 133, 135, 139, 159–160
Beyond the Pleasure Principle 96
birth-giving fantasy 86
Blass, R. B. 186, 190
Bohleber, W. 192
Bonaparte, M. 117
Bonomi, C. 27–28, 58, 186, 195
Borgogno, F. 191
Bornstein, M. 191
"Botanical monograph" 133
boundary idea 25
Brabant, E. 167
Breuer, D. 162
Breuer, G. 171
Breuer, J. 30, 91
Brouardel, Paul 26–28, 59
Brücke's Institute of Physiology 141
burglar 34, 39, 41, 45–51, 57
Byck, R. 136, 138

Cahiers 97
caput Nili 71
catarrh 62, 70, 73
    vaginal 65
censoring activity 145
Charcot, Jean-Martin 28, 50
Child Analysis in the Analysis of Adults 93
child-birth fantasy 91
childhood
    Dora's 49, 53–54, 59–60, 67–68, 72, 74, 84
    hysteria 58
    hysterical diseases in 28
    masturbation 27, 58, 69
    memories 9, 36, 48, 71
    obscure episode 54–55
    scenes 22, 67
    sexual assault in 61
    sexual sensitivity 33

somatic memories 43
Civilized Sexual Morality and Modern Nervous Illness 127
clarity 130
clinical novel 101
cocaine 85, 137
Collins, J. 182
Colombo, D. 193
"Company at table d'hôte" 138–139, 141, 154, 161, 167, 179
confidential relationship 13
conscious remembering 98
constitutional predisposition 65
coughing 3, 20, 22, 39, 62, 72
countertransference 11, 64
Coyne, J. C. 110

day residues 53–54, 81, 95, 99
Decker, H. S. 11, 20, 85, 190, 193–194
deep unconsciousness 95
deferred internal disgust 35
De l'intelligence (On Intelligence) 26
Des Attentats à la Pudeur sur les petites Filles 26
disgust 31, 73
    deferred internal 35
    emergence of 30
    internal 35
    internal sensation analogous to 31
    reaction of 20–22, 33–34
disgusting kiss 19–44
Dora *passim*
Dora's alleged homosexuality 124
Dora's analysis 109, 119, 130, 172
Dora's case history 125, 168
Dora's dreams 106
Dora's therapy 109, 111
Dora's treatment 8–9, 92, 109–111, 113, 128, 171
Draft B 30
Draft K 23, 25
Dream and Hysteria 152
Dreams and Occultism 178

dream book 88
dream function 95
dreams 9, 55, 120
   allusions 81
   analysis of 9, 49, 56–57, 61, 74, 80–84
   as intention 81
   censorship 140, 155, 174
   day residue in 54, 81, 95
   elements of 61
   fire in 66
   fire of 70
   hysterical phantasies 72
   infantile desire 68
   interpretation of 9, 54, 61–62, 64, 67, 75–76, 82, 87–88, 91, 96, 99
   jewel-case and 63
   manifest content of 54
   memory 98
   neuropsychoanalytic revision of 98
   of burning house 53–77
   original version of 65
   recurrence of 53–54
   resolution of 80
   situation 83
   source of 61, 74–75
   traumatic 60–61, 81, 95–96
   traumatic sexual episode 75
   traumatolytic function of 93–101
   wish-fulfilling function of 95–96
   work 8, 54, 63, 98–99
dyspnoea 69–70, 73–74, 90

Eckstein, Emma 32–33
Eissler, K. R. 118, 185
Emminghaus, Hermann 28
enuresis 3–4, 28, 55–56, 61, 65, 67, 69–70
   and asthma 70
   Dora's 69
   infantile 3, 43, 67
   nocturnal 66
erotic siege 68
erotic stimulation 68, 74
erotic transference 9, 63
Etude médico-légale sur les attentats aux moeurs 26

Falzeder, E. 167, 178
fantasy/fantasies 20, 73, 75–76
   adolescent's 86
   birth-giving 86
   child-birth 91
   fellatio 39–40
   hysterical 34
   juvenile 86
   longing 59
   oral 39
   sexual 69, 86
   unconscious 38, 41, 63
   vengeance 91
fellatio 38–39
fellatio fantasy 39–40
Ferenczi, S. 42, 44, 93–95, 99–100, 167, 188, 191, 194
Fisiologia del piacere (The Physiology of Pleasure) 85
Fleischl, Ernst 148
Flem, L. 139
Fliess, Wilhelm 4–5, 7, 8–10, 14, 20, 22–23, 28–30, 34, 41, 56, 58–60, 71, 73–74, 76, 91–92
Foucault, M. 183
Fragment 84, 92
Fragment of an Analysis of a Case of Hysteria 50, 121, 152
Franzensbad 65
Frau, E. L. 158
   attraction 169
Freud, S. *passim*
Freud, Martha 10, 13–18, 118, 129, 133–135, 137, 140–141, 143–146, 152, 154, 157–159, 162, 165, 171–172, 174

220 INDEX

analysis 123
contradictory viewpoint 145
countertransference 109, 123
dream 145
financial position 147
homosexuality 124
interpretation 139, 170
reader of thoughts 131
reports 159–160
scientific production 135
fright hysteria 25
Fromm, E. 180
Further Remarks on Neuro-Psychoses of Defence 100

Garda Lake 11
Gay, P. 11, 115, 124
Giampieri-Deutsch, P. 167
Glenn, J. 129, 181
Goretti, G. 130
governess 11–13, 92, 94
  maidservant 79, 83
  nursemaids 11, 27
  privileged nurse 11
Greek archaeology 41
grudge 42
Grudge and the Hysteric 42
guilt
  feelings of 11, 68
  sense of 94

Hammerschlag, Samuel 159
Heller, Judith Bernays 16
hereditary predisposition 47
Herman, J. L. 43, 200
Hertz, N. 200
Hirschmüller, A. 16–18, 199
hoarseness 3, 62, 72
homosexuality 94
Honig Skoller, E. 182
Hotel du Lac 16
Hotel Schweizerhaus 17

housewife's psychosis 6
Huopainen, H. 182
hysteria
  aetiology of 21, 25, 29, 40, 42–43, 47, 68, 96
  boundary line age for 89
  conceptualisation of 43
  cure of 64
  diffusion of 58
  fright 25
  germ of 33
  masturbation and 27, 58–59, 61
  memories and 34
  Nachträglichkeit as pathogenesis of 33
  paternal 56, 63, 72
  pathogenic influence for 50
  period of longing 73–74
  perversion and 76–77
  precondition for 22–24
  predisposition to 89
  radical cure of 49
  repression in 33
  seduction and 60, 71
  seduction theory and 27
  severe 89
  sexual knowledge and 85
  sexual seduction and 24
  sexual shock 23
  traumatic aetiology of 57, 76, 101
hysterical
  fainting 77
  fantasies 34, 75
  identification 71–72
  narrative 182
  neurosis 50
  reaction 21
  symptomatology 4
  symptoms 36, 40, 45–47, 50, 62, 71–72, 76–77, 88–89
hysteric's grudge 42–43
hysteric symptom 46

incest 16, 94, 118, 126–127, 129, 173
"infantile amnesia," 97
infantile masturbation 27, 49, 57–58, 70
infantile sexual abuse 59, 62
infantile sexual seduction 60–61
infantile sexual trauma 23, 100
intellectual and professional pessimism 113
"intellectual passion" 141
intellectual pessimism 113
Interpretation of Dreams, The 48, 71, 82, 88, 96, 99, 104, 111–112, 133, 138, 148, 151, 157, 175–176, 178
interpretative approach 130

Jones, E. 7, 135, 137, 141, 143, 147
Jung, Carl Gustav 62
juvenile fantasies 86

Kassowitz, Max 28
Khan, M. 42–43
Kohon, G. 181, 190
Koller Becker, H. 160
Koller, Carl 134
Königstein, Leopold 197
Kuhn, P. 133, 162–163
Kuppelei 17
Kuriloff, E. A. 117

Lacan, J. 20, 117
Lanouzière, J. 182
Lavagetto, M. 191
Les Attentats aux Moeurs 26
leuchorrhoea 69
Lewin, K. K. 6, 92, 191
Lokoff, R. T. 110
longing 59
    hysterical 60
    infantile character and 73
    meaning of 73–74
    sense of 73
longing fantasies 59
Lopez, D. 4, 187
Lorenzini, S. 187
Lothane, Z. 182–183, 188–189
love-affair 12, 16, 38, 60, 128
Lydon, M. 182

Maciejewski, F. 14, 16, 185, 199
Madge, T. 197–198
Mahony, P. J. 3–4, 6, 20, 49, 111, 124, 162, 165
maidservant 79, 83
Makari, G. J. 188
Malacrea, M. 187
Mancia, M. 97–98
manifestation of fright 25
Mantegazza, P. 85–87, 89–90, 187, 197
Marcel, M. 181
Marcus, S. 159, 161, 163, 167, 176
Masson, J. M. 4, 8, 10, 23, 25–26, 31, 33–35, 59, 71, 75–77, 112–113, 119–120
masturbation 41, 63
    active 57
    childhood 27, 58
    consequences of 59
    Dora's 62, 96
    feigning 68
    hysteria and 27, 58–59
    inclination to 73
    infantile 27, 58, 70
    leucorrhoea to 68
    memory of 96
    neurasthenia and 30
    premature sexual enjoyment 61
    premature sexual experiences 59–62
    repression and 73–74
    sexuality acquired by 30
    sexual seduction and 69–70
"masturbatory assault," 30

McGuire, W. 64, 145, 179
Meares, R. 97
memories 96
   childhood 96, 100
   hysteria and 34
   traumatic 48, 97, 99–101
Mertens, W. 145, 179
Mitchell, J. 184
Moi, T. 39
mother, Dora's 5–6, 42, 55, 64–65

nach-tragen 67
Nachträglichkeit 21, 33, 67, 98
narration 182
narrative
   clinical- 182
   hysteric's- 182
   hysterical- 182
nausea
   feelings of 20
   violent 19, 21, 35
"neurasthenia" 138
neuroscience 97–101
Neuroses of Defence, The 23
New Introductory Lectures on Psycho-Analysis 178–180
"nocturnal visits," 69–70
nonneurotic deferred action 31
"Non vixit" dream 133
nursemaids 11, 27

oedipal complex 42
oedipal inclination 40
oedipal theory 16
oedipus complex 190
Ogden, T. H. 99
On Coca 137, 154
On Dreams 9, 123, 133, 151–152, 162, 164, 176–177
On the Hygienic and Medicinal Properties of Coca Plant and on Nervin Nourishment in General 85, 173
On the Revision of the Interpretation of Dreams 94
On the Universal Tendency to Debasement in the Sphere of Love 127
oral cavity 38
oral contact 20–21
oral fantasies 39
oral predisposition 35
oral sex 22, 35, 38, 89
oral stimulation 36
oral symptoms 72
oral zone 20, 35
Origen 122–123

Passions of Adults and Their Influence on the Sexual and Character Development of Children, The 93
paternal aetiology 21–22, 56
paternal seduction 43, 55, 66–67
period of seduction 60
perverse 77
   adult 36
   sexual 36
   sexual practices 188
perversion 30, 40, 62, 76
   adult 5
   negative of 60
   paternal 76
   repudiated 77
   sexual 39
"petite hystérie," 89
Physiology Institute 135
Physiology of Love, The 85, 89, 173
Pontalis, J. B. 61, 95
Postscript 125
precocious sexual trauma 50, 83, 100
Preliminary Communication "On the Psychical Mechanism of Hysterical Phenomena" 20

premature seduction 59, 66–67
premature sexual enjoyment 61
premature sexual stimulation 24, 62
professional pessimism 113
Project for a Scientific Psychology 29
Psycho-Analysis and Telepathy 178
Psychoanalysis, of Dora
    first encounter with 3–6
    first trauma 19–44
    second encounter with 7–18
psychoanalytic interpretations of dreams 145
psychoanalytic measurement 114
psychoanalytical insight 126
psychoanalytical investigation 41
psychoanalytical technique 57, 93
psychopathology of Everyday Life, The 111, 116, 118, 121–122, 146–147, 151–152, 155, 163, 174
"pulmonary apicitis" 120

quod erat demonstrandum 72

Ray Green, J. 182
reality 57, 72, 95
    external 188
    internal 188
repellent characteristics 20–21
reproach 11, 23
    Dora's 37–38
    self 11, 23, 32, 69
repudiated perversion 77
residues 75
    day 53–54, 81, 95, 99
    -unanalysable 124
    unanalysed 114–115, 124
revenge phantasy 83
Rieger, C. 123
Riva del Garda 13, 16
Roazen, P. 122, 136, 151, 178
Rogow, A. A. 191

Romano, C. 198
Rudnytsky, P. L. 185, 199
Russo, L. 114, 124

Sachner, M. 182
Schimek, J. G. 190
Schur, M. 115, 160
Screen Memories 36
screen memory 35–36, 100
seduction 41, 60, 62
    by adult 4, 27, 74
    faking 69
    father's 56–58, 63, 72
    genital sensations and 40
    incestuous 94
    infantile sexual 60–61, 63
    masturbation and 27, 62
    of old man 43
    paternal 43, 55, 66–67
    period of 60
    premature 59
    sexual 5, 22, 24, 27, 57, 69–70, 73, 76, 83
seduction theory 5, 22, 29, 31, 34, 58, 62, 67, 75–76
    abandonment of 47
    and hysteria 27
    confirmation of 40
    disavowal of 4
    Freud's 27, 43, 94, 100–101
    recantation of 59
    refutation of 4
    validation of 74
self-accusation 11, 66
self-reproach 11, 23, 32, 69
"severe hysteria," 89
sexual abuse 5, 21, 27–28, 35, 40, 83
    infantile 59, 62
"sexual dreams" 171
sexual episode 21, 50, 75
sexual excitement 20
sexual fantasies 69, 86

sexual inclination 42
sexual relationship 13, 16, 37, 72
sexual scenes 48
  reconstruction of 100
sexual shock 23
sexual stimulation 73
  premature 24, 62
  traumatic memory of 36
sexual trauma 4, 22–23, 27, 29–30, 45–46
  in childhood 26
  infantile 23, 100
  infantile epilepsy and 29
  notion of disgust 22–23
  paternal 57
  precocious 50, 83, 100
  premature 44, 58
Showalter, E. 182
Silverstein, B. 126–127
Simon, B. 190
sinner's emotions 151
sister-in-law 171
Slipp, S. 42, 118, 122
Solms, M. 97
Spierlein, Sabina 62
spontaneous excitation 4
Strong, B. E. 84
Studies on Hysteria 5, 64
"Superman" 126
Swales, P. J. 9, 118
syphilis 21, 65–66

Taine, H. 26
Tardieu, Ambroise 26
12th Congress of the International Psychoanalytical Association 93
theme of the eyes, the 148
"therapeutic experiment" 134
Three Essays 84
Three Essays on the Theory of Sexuality 41, 75

Three Instances of Injustice 118
thumb-sucker 35
"thumb-sucking," 39
Timpanaro, S. 123
Tögel, C. 15, 140, 147, 155, 185
transference 64, 67, 97–99
  erotic 9, 63
  interpretation of 64
trauma 21
  actual 42
  adolescence 43
  banal 67
  childhood 26, 49–50, 67
  infantile 43, 58, 61, 67, 69, 80, 82, 94
  lakeside 49
  mechanism of 32
  sexual 4, 22–23, 29–30, 44–46, 50, 57, 83, 93, 100
traumatic dream 95
traumatic effect 45
traumatic effectiveness 51
traumatic force 45–47
traumatic memories 48, 97, 99–101
traumatic scenes 9, 34, 45–47, 49, 61, 82, 96
  infantile 49, 61, 96
Traumdeutung 68, 97, 100
treatment, Dora's 8–9, 92
Turnbull, O. 97

"unanalysed residues" 114–115, 124
"unknown factor" 130
unconscious 37–38
  concept of repression and 97
  day's residues and 99
  desire 63
  Dora's 67–68
  dynamic 98
  fantasies 38–39, 41, 63
  Freud's 55
  mental processes 40

notion of 97
perception 64, 84
period of life and 74–75
process of 44
repressed 37
sources of emotion 48
unconscious fantasies 38–39, 41, 63
unconscious perception 64, 84
unrepressed unconscious 43, 67, 96–98, 100

vaginal catarrh 65
Valéry, P. 97

Van den Berg, S. 184
vengeance fantasies 91
Verbrannt 67
Verbrannt sein 66
"violent love" 128
violent nausea 19

wish 57, 101
   Dora's 60, 62, 73
   father's 68
   infantile 60
   unconscious 97